DEDICATION

This book is dedicated
to my trail partner—my wife,

Bette M. O'Hern

Noah John Rondeau

Adirondack Hermit

At Saranac Lake

Jan. 16th. 1949.

CONTENTS

Preface

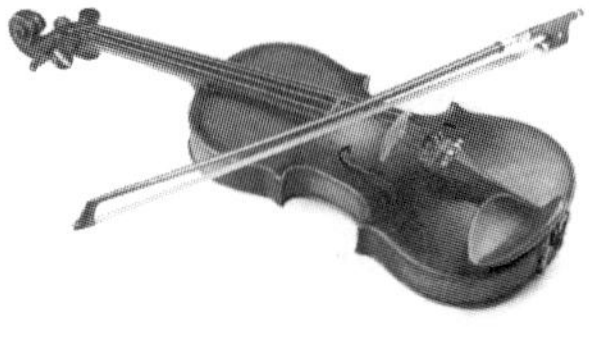

This is a True Story

I THINK THAT IS THE FIRST THING to be said about *Adirondack Wilds: Exploring the Haunts of Noah John Rondeau.* All of it really happened: the hermit's thirty-seven-year wilderness reign; the less-recognized seventeen years of his life after he left Cold River; and the public's caterwauling reception during the infancy of America's Sportsmen's shows and at other personal appearances. Add to that the ongoing celebration of Noah John's life and the "hermit magic" that continues to fascinate the public long after Rondeau's death, and you have one whale of a tale.

Noah John didn't ask to be in the public eye. The public sought him out. While it may seem that his day-to-day life in (and out of) the mountains was often tedious, the mere fact that he survived is admirable. His personal story is one of transformation. A man who once complained about his "dozen points of failure" became one who found himself and a sense of personal pride, and although he was known as a hermit, much of the improvement in his life came about because of caring friends and because of many others who crossed his path.

While Rondeau learned the ropes of the hermit profession, he also offered advice to anglers and hunters (known as "sports"), guided climbers to nearby peaks, and learned how to play congenial host to camp visitors and curious guests who appeared to pay their respects to the "town official."

Much later, as radio and television became popular, he learned how to deal with reporters and journalists (and how to promote his need for a handout). Mayor Rondeau definitely knew how to work a crowd.

As an example, when Noah was lured out of the mountains to become the hit of a Sportsmans' Show in New York City, Rondeau recounted his mountain exploits, to the awe and amazement of those attending.

Rondeau was pleased when his big-city audiences applauded the stories by tossing coins into a pack basket near where he perched, however it didn't take him long to devise a better plan.

He padded the pack basket with some newspapers, covered the padding with pine boughs, and seeded the nest with one and five-dollar bills, letting it be known he didn't want to hear the clink of coins anymore.

Early mountain climbers dubbed him "Mayor Rondeau." They always said something to the effect of "Well, you know, Rondeau was an old woodsman" —meaning he had a connection to the rough land before World War I. Some backpackers joked that it seemed as if Mother Nature had actually planted Rondeau in the thin Adirondack earth as her personal creation.

RICHARD "RED BEARD" SMITH: I met Richard Joseph Smith when I began investigating the life of Noah John Rondeau. I found Smith's stories and his adventures with Noah so fascinating I asked him to recount as much of his past as he wanted. Everything he said interested me, and I was also grateful for our growing friendship. We had much in common, but particularly a keen understanding of what a place like the Cold River country can do for (and to) a body and soul.

In his first letter, Smith notified me that I must put my questions in writing because he didn't own a telephone. "Never have," he wrote. "Such devices seem to hog tie my voice so I forget what I want to say." I thought his lifestyle was similar to Rondeau's in many ways. "Take that radio and television," Rich pointed out in his small living room. "Noah didn't care for the amount of advertising included with radio and television programming. He referred to the radio as a 'screech owl' but that didn't mean he didn't enjoy it. His favorite show was the Kate Smith program. Television was a 'screech owl with a bay window.'"

My first book, *Life With Noah*, is filled with the stories and adventures Richard Smith told me about his life with the hermit of Cold River. I admired his independent spirit, evidenced by his efforts to live as self-sufficiently as possible and to go about life in his own way without the need to feel a part of any group, organization or community. Living a portion of each of seven years there in the headwaters of the Cold River was no mean accomplishment for Smith, but he was as determined as Noah to live as he chose.

He once told me, "I've been real fortunate in being able to do exactly what I have wanted to do both in my work and my living arrangements. I am financially secure enough to where I don't depend on anybody and I hope that never changes. My years of sunup to sundown work pushed most thoughts of the carefree wilderness life I once followed before going into the Army into a recess in my memory. Now at 70, it has lessened. I've done it [lived his life] without a helping hand. All the same, I know I'm sort of out of the loop, I mean I'm in the middle, somewhere between being comfortably solitary and hermit-like."

Another time he noted, "People assume Noah could have been more successful than he was if he had only chosen to stay in school, get an education, earn a high school degree and commit himself to some line of work. Well he wasn't a big money person, and neither am I, and I'm at a point where I can just hang back and enjoy my experiences that are in the recesses of my memory. Although I am not inclined to mix with people, my River Road neighbors are a very loyal crowd. Young kids ask me for woodcraft advice. The adults are interested in my past experiences, and my next-door neighbor looks after me like I was her own grandpa. I view my life as successful in that I am contented and happy. I'm now, to borrow one of Noah's sayings, 'well as could be expected, but wearing out.' What more can I ask?"

Now, years after his death, Richard Smith's name has become recognizable to a crowd of long time readers of *Adirondack Life* magazine.

Jeff Kelly was then editor of the North Country publication. Smith said of his A Woodsman Writes column, "Jeff told me my stories were well received. Recognition that I contributed in some small way to local history as well as to the enjoyment of others was more than I expected. The stories also brought [Maitland] De Sormo back to my door. His call was twofold. [Once again] he offered to buy the Rondeau items I owned, and he told me about a man he knew whose interests in the outdoors were similar to mine; he had agreed to inquire to see if I would meet and talk with him about Noah. I told him, 'No thanks.' Nevertheless, DeSormo was persistent. He showed up on my doorstep...later to ask if I had changed my mind about selling Noah's possessions. I hadn't. He then mentioned the continued interest of a fellow down on Tug Hill who still wanted to meet me.

His continued nudging made me curious, so I relented. I said it would be fine by me if he gave him my address."

"Red Beard," as the Lake Placid kids in Smith's Boy Scout Troop 326, sponsored by the American Legion Post, called their longstanding scoutmaster, remembered more than anyone else about Noah John's personal history. In fact, Richard Smith seemed more informed (and articulate) than most anyone who spent time in Cold River country.

NOAH AND RICHARD: Smith's life became intertwined with Rondeau's when he called on the bow-hunting hermit for advice during his freshman year of high school. Later, when most high school graduates were concerned with finding a job, opening a bank account and dating, Red Beard began his wilderness life in a makeshift cabin at the base of Bear Trap Mountain north of Duck Hole, his location being one of the reasons Noah gave him the nickname "Quack." There was another reason, too. In one of Richard's letters to me, he wrote:

> *...My waddle way of walking in a pair of ever-tightening deer neck leather pants and the location of my camp upriver from the hermitage, Noah said, gave him the idea to name me Quack. He was a deep thinker, filing away little things he might use later. ...Noah, being the gentleman he was, only called me Quack when he was in a playful mood...for fear it may...offend... Of course I didn't mind, but he usually called me Richard (or at times son, when he was describing a particular deer drive...)*

Smith recalled that he and Noah developed a close father-son type bond "without [us] being conscious of it." He confided that they shared a dark secret concerning their lives as children and teens. "Something we held in common—solidified our friendship." In my book *Life With Noah*, I reported what Smith said about their close association. "During subsequent visits Noah sensed my fear of and hostility toward my father. I had been able to contain my anger until the day I left home; Noah, on the other hand, had been rebellious. Fed up with unwarranted beatings, he left home in 1898 at the age of fifteen. No wonder this kind, gentle man tried to make me so comfortable in his presence. He understood what I tolerated. He was trying to make up for the abuses I experienced."

Throughout the years I knew Richard, I never thought he looked his age at all, and he was still active, to some extent, during the early months of his final year. Slight and unassuming, he enjoyed sitting back, smoothing his thinning head of white hair, and remembering. In his salutation in one of his last letters to me, he was still reminiscing:

> *Bow Wow! Whoof Whoof! It's Jay, the Beagle from Tug Hill waiting for a letter from Duck Hole "Quack Quack" Richard...*
>
> *Sometimes...there are several things that go into a nickname. The reason I gave you The Beagle label seemed the logical one, because you are like a beagle on a rabbit's track. You won't stop until every stone is turned over, forever fishing... for facts. This I admire. When you write your books and give your lectures, it seems readers or an audience will see you have uncovered so many things... to make whatever you do a success. ...I've enjoyed helping you reach your goal. The effort you have put into the research is commendable; still in all, always keep in mind don't over scrutinize... like most things, overdone loses the flavor. Still, I understand, if you're not the lead dog, the scenery never changes...*

I laid aside Richard's July 1993 letter and reread an earlier June correspondence. It was impossible not to notice the change that had taken place. On one hand he sounded upbeat, joking that "black flies wasted no time recognizing I made a perfect blood donor as they swarmed to meet me at the hospital door." But I also noted a shift in tone as he wrote myriad details he called "threads on the loom of time." They were particular details I hadn't asked about, but which he felt I might find useful. I think Richard, knowing his time was running out, was preparing me for the inevitable. "If I could turn back the clock...," he wrote—and then the sick man would remember back to better days.

I returned to the July letter.

> *...Yesterday [July 2, 1993] I went over to the Adirondack Medical Center for a blood refill. Two units that left me with a stiff back, which was so painful I didn't get much sleep last night. A continual dull ache to match, the pain killers don't even lessen the pain. I've tried everything [non-prescription and prescription medicine] on the market it seems...My doctor gave me an anti-itch ointment for my back—a backlash from the medicine. It works! ITCH was driving me up the wall. My doctor is something else. Old Father Time keeps picking my pocket. I can't make him stop it!*
>
> *...It's up to you to tell our (Noah, and my) story. I've given you Noah's albums, scrapbooks, diaries, and artifacts that belonged to the grand old woodsman that was like a father to me...I value those last remembrances of a man I love so well...his possessions seem ever to remind me how much we meant to each other...I tried my best to follow in his footsteps but changes in the annals of time forbid to completely fulfill my goal, but never could I forget those many happy times we spent in the Cold River wilderness....*"

Richard's remembrances continued for two weeks beyond that letter, then stopped. I called his neighbor, who helped care for him. He recommended not visiting. "He's thin, weak, always in pain. He has to be carried anywhere he needs to go. He's not going to be up for company."

"My nurse (in the Lake Placid hospital) takes my mind off the pain," he wrote in his final letter. "She is truly wonderful to me—so considerate and helpful. Her actions cause me to start wishing I was 50 years younger. Dream on, as the hand on the clock of life must tick away...each passing second so minuscule it seems when one is younger...knowing that lost time is never found no matter how much we search for it." Richard was trying his best to help me learn about life to the very end of his own.

Toward the end of that 1993 summer, not too long after his last letter, I was planning a trip to visit Richard, regardless of his condition. I was also going to spend some time at a remote campsite near Noah John's old hermitage. Shortly before I was ready to leave, Richard's neighbor, Gary Schefield, phoned me from Lake Placid. Richard had died, but he had left with me written and recorded memories that told a fantastic tale of the life he and Noah lived at Cold River.

He had recited marvelous anecdotes of privation and hazards as a young man in the wilds of northern New York's High Peaks territory back in the 1930s and '40s. As the letters stood, they were not right for the biography I planned about Noah, but if I were to skim off the portions that fit my requirements and do some further research, I thought I could have a very exciting book about Richard and Noah. Having accomplished that with the publication of *Life With Noah* and *Noah John Rondeau's Adirondack Wilderness Days*, I wanted to continue my Rondeau history.

MOTIVATION, INSPIRATION, AND PERSPIRATION: I remembered something Richard told me had happened to him the year Noah died. When Smith's handwriting and hold on life began to falter in July of 1993, he wrote me simply that when he returned to Cold River "in the fall of the year Noah died" he found he had complete recall, even of events and conversations that had happened 37 years before.

How much better would my story come together if I too made another pilgrimage to what was left of the place where the lords and masters were once Richard Smith and Noah John Rondeau? I knew I wanted to go, and would, but I had a fond wish that I wouldn't be trekking alone.

So I asked my wife, Bette, if she had an interest in visiting Cold River for a first-hand look at the places I had written so much about, if she'd like to get a feel for the lives that Noah and Richard lived. She considered the possibility, and like a magic fairy granted my wish.

"I'll go, for two reasons," she told me. First, she was curious about the place that has taken up much of my research time. Second, she wanted to test her physical ability. Bette wanted a personal challenge. I understood this completely, just as Noah and Richard Smith would have.

I could hardly wait to get back to the wild country, and having Bette with me would more than double my delight. We began to make plans for our adventure immediately.

Introduction

Timeless Cold River

IN 1999, CLARENCE PETTY WROTE in a letter, "My move back to the old place is the next thing to 'camping out,' as there are so many things that have to be done to make the place more livable. Coyotes howl back of the house and wild turkeys are around—two of the species that were not here in 1911. Next month I expect the biologic part of the wolf feasibility study should be completed and the social part, which will be done by Cornell University, should be completed in December or January. Then we will hear the loudest howls of all."

Then 94, Clarence was still active in an educational campaign to win over converts to preserve the Adirondack Mountains, including the reintroduction of all its native animals. Clarence died in 2009 at age 104; his Coreys childhood home will eventually be sold to the Nature Conservancy.

I want to thank Clarence and all who allowed me to join in their Cold River remembrances. I have enjoyed leaning against trees, sitting on your front porches and in your sun rooms and living rooms, visiting at enameled, metal-topped kitchen tables on rainy afternoons, when the balmy days of September were fading and giving way once more to light snow and thin ice in the water bucket. I had not yet learned to really appreciate the importance of regional history, but I was lucky to talk to you—ace woodsmen and women—in my search for first-person hermit material. You placed a great deal of trust and confidence in me, taught me many tricks of the trade of becoming skilled in woodcraft, and that helped me better understand much of Noah John Rondeau's woodsy philosophy and his way of life at Cold River City. In the process, some of him (and you) has rubbed off on me. My time was well spent with you among our beloved Adirondack Mountains.

Noah's former safe haven was located on a hillock at the lower end of a snaking river, where its bank once dropped sharply down to the edge of an expansive basin of impounded river water—a flow then, but in 2007 a transfigured scrubby meadow of golden-brown marsh grass and pine, spruce and balsam evergreen trees in the middle of a forested valley. Lumbermen's tote teams once crossed the river on a graveled road that spanned the length of the sixty-foot-high log-and-stone sluice dam. Opposite the bluff, on the far bank, is The Finger, a small point of land choked with debris from yearly floodwater, and tough-to-navigate Bellyache Swamp. Behind and far off the South Gap or Ouluska Pass, splitting mounts Emmons, Donaldson and Seward from Seymour, are the highest peaks in the Seward Range.

This was the scene Noah first eyed from the abandoned lumber camp the summer of 1919, before the site became his permanent home for over three decades. On the eastern base of the hermit's hilltop setting was an impoundment hosting a graveyard of bleached steel-gray dead trees. Cold River Hill's other sides were ringed by an old logger's dam, a floodwater impoundment basin, mountains, swamps and glittering emerald-green ponds.

There was nothing for miles in any direction of the old, rotting-down, cracker-box-style lumber shanty in the woods but trees, streams, ponds and swamp. The Santa Clara Lumber Company's name for the place was High Dam Lumber Camp. It once consisted of a blacksmith's forge and workshop, a barn and stable and one long, horizontal log building. Typical of the day, the bunkroom was on one end, the kitchen on the other—both open rooms separated by a covered breezeway that served as both woodshed and receiver of anything that needed hanging for handy use. It was euphemistically known as the outbuilding or breezeway.

The old lumber camp site, hereafter to be referred to as Big Dam Camp, went through three metamorphoses. Today the setting is a place filled with memories. By 1930 the last remaining structure, the cooking shanty, had burned to the ground as a result of the carelessness of its caretaker. Noah had a reputation for being lackadaisical with fire.

Backpackers share this special place with black bear, raccoons, deer, pine marten, river otters, beavers, weasels and other fur bearers. Every year backpackers enjoy some of the lingering perennial flowers Noah planted. It becomes a wager by some to time their arrival to the emergence of the jack-in-the-pulpits, or the yellow and orange day lilies, or the pink and white blossoms of the sweet pea vines.

Yet there are still those who seek out the "place where the old hermit lived." They may have read about him or seen the exhibit at the Adirondack Museum. They're curious, and if they care enough to backpack to Cold River, they are already connoisseurs of steep rocky paths and clear northern air.

My best wishes go with everyone who plans a trip to this setting along Cold River. There are many spirits who ramble and ply the land trails and water routes of that region.

They—you—won't be disappointed.

With a little imagination, today's backpackers can feel the presence of Noah awaiting their arrival at his hermitage. *Courtesy of Ruth Prince*

ADIRONDACK WILDS
Exploring the Haunts of Noah John Rondeau

Section I

Return to Cold River

Chapter 1

We Hit the Trail

DURING THE YEARS I've been writing about the Adirondacks, Bette and I have met many wonderful people who share a common interest and appreciation of the places, people and rich history and heritage of the area. Many were folks who had firsthand experiences of people and places from long ago. We have both been impressed with their detailed memories of the past and the stories that were told to them by friends or relatives who lived this history. Some had kept pictures and writings and shared them. Bette believes they did so because they were so moved that someone appreciated their history and heritage enough to write about and nurture it for future generations.

While she remembers it being my idea, I recall that she asked me one day, "How about I start joining you on outings into the mountains? It's been a long time." She wasn't talking about interviewing folks in cozy living rooms. She was talking about hiking.

"I know it will involve several days and nights, a heavy pack and many miles over rough trails, crossing rocky creeks and climbing," she assured me. "I'm pretty sure if I can make it through the first mile on the trail, I'll make it the rest of the way." I could not have been more delighted.

Bette was no stranger to camping. In fact, we had spent our honeymoon at Blue Mountain Lake in September. I asked her if she remembered sleeping in our white Chevy sedan at Eighth Lake in November later that year.

"Brrr…," she said. "I remember thinking, what am I getting myself into?"

"Remember that green umbrella tent? The waxy, heavy one with no air circulation?" I quizzed.

High Peaks Wilderness Area Trailhead. Beginning and end of Bette and Jay's trek.
Photograph by William J. O'Hern

"Of course. I was frightened by every sound I heard. You kept a hatchet next to you to help me feel secure. We had no warm L.L. Bean sleeping bags back then, and I often felt cold."

"Was that the worst part?"

"Oh no. The worst was the discomfort of not wanting to get up to use the 'outhouse' in the night. I was sure there was a bear lurking around and spiders on and under the seats. Then morning arrived...ahhh...a beeline to the outhouse. You were always up with the birds and starting the fire. I think that was the most wonderful part of the day if it wasn't raining."

When our children came along, we camped at Eighth Lake Campground every summer. Bette reminded me it was then that we invested in a better tent and that I built a wooden box with drawers and shelves for our kitchen supplies. We kept that in the screenhouse.

“I’m glad we started the kids early,” mused Bette. “Remember we brought cloth diapers, a playpen and a potty chair?”

I remembered that all right. Our campsite was the “hub” of our adventures in the Adirondacks back then. We ventured out to participate in all the area had to offer within the campground as well as around it. When it rained we headed for Inlet or Old Forge.

There were campsites where bears raided our metal cooler and we spent long sleepless hours lying awake, thinking some indistinct night noise was an uninvited animal attracted to cookie crumbs that the kids had left in the tent. Hundreds of images of outdoor experiences merge in my memory—wet clothing, lumpy dinners during our go-natural days without a camp stove, a dunking when a canoe rolled over, muddy trails and grubby kids’ clothes, mud pies, stinging insects and nighttime fires, s’mores, mountain air and mountain snow. There were Adirondack “theme parks” and family hikes to fire towers when the kids’ most frequent remark was not “Oh, what an awe-inspiring view!” but rather, “How much farther to the top?”—a question usually posed just minutes from the trailhead.

Our children and grandchildren have carried on the tradition. They have hiked, climbed, biked, enjoyed the lakes and more. We often camp with them so we can enjoy seeing it through the eyes of our grandchildren. They are true Adirondack characters themselves.

Compared to camping in the old days, under pretty demanding conditions, the idea of a backpack to Cold River began to appeal to Bette more and more. She would have comfortable boots she could break in ahead of time, a warm yet lightweight sleeping bag, and no toddler paraphernalia to worry about. It would be just the two of us, a retired couple experiencing what Bette began to refer to as “Senior Citizen Survivor.”

When she told her Red Hat Society friends about the proposed backpack, they questioned her: “But aren’t you worried about black bears that might try to take your food or even attack you?” “How are you going to protect yourself from the wildlife sleeping in an open lean-to?” and, “Why would you, at your age, and with such a comfortable home life, spend time tramping around the mountains with all that weight on your back? You’ll trigger your sciatica again. You’re taking a big chance.”

Bette simply replied that slight risks could not keep her from experiencing life, that this was a personal challenge, that her spirits were high and that she looked forward to seeing the places I had long talked and written about. "This is my chance to see the Adirondacks though the eyes of my friend and my husband, a person who truly devours everything this amazing mountainous land has to offer. I'm going to enjoy it," she told them.

It was to be an adventure and a personal achievement all in one. We were committed to renewing our companionable relationship by enjoying outdoor activities as we had decades earlier.

Bette's vow hinged on her premise that there is a partnership more peaceful even than Nature's solitude, and which, truly understood, is time together made perfect. To carry on outdoors with the person you love is the most absolute and free way of living.

Climbing in the Adirondack High Peaks is a way of life instinctive to my spirit. It's a place where I've seen some of the very best times of my life, despite some broken bones (a friend's wife's mishap) and brutal winter weather. This nearly spiritual connection with the High Peaks spawned my interest in the Park's history and was an incentive to collect Adirondack stories and anecdotes from the time Bette and I went on our first backpacking trip decades ago. Without Bette's inspiration, I might have never believed I would write a series of history books centered around all the research I've done.

I remember our early climbs in the '60s. There were short ascents and time-consuming climbs with high summits and precarious descents. Bette has always been sporty, nimble, and athletic. She knew nothing at first about backpacking and mountain climbing, but because I enjoyed it she decided early on she was going to be a part of it. We did a number of high peaks—some of the Forty-Sixers'.

"Jay, does it count toward being a Forty-Sixer (a person who climbs all 46 Adirondack peaks originally thought to be above 4,000 ft.) if I scoot down on my bottom side?" Bette inquired when she reached the cable on Gothic's half-mile long pitch to the Ore Bed Trail. And then, halfway down I heard a surprised cry.

"Oh my God! I've worn big holes in my jeans from sliding on the bare rock!"

After about a half dozen high peaks, she'd joke that after all the effort required to get to the top, the view didn't look all that different from one summit to the next. What did I find so enjoyable about all this? And anyway, family obligations were tugging her back home.

Finally, between the planning and preparation, the inconvenience and hassle, the huge kitchen garden with its canning and freezing, our barnyard animals and her professional employment, Bette shelved her pioneering spirit "until the kids grow up or until I retire." While Bette backed off, she tolerated my continuing to spend countless years roaming the mountains.

In the summer of 2007, we recognized that since the children had grown up and eight grandchildren had entered our lives, there was a strange sense of something lacking in our retired lives, something we thought we might recapture on a backpacking trip together. So off we went.

Bette O'Hern skirting the shoreline of Rondeau's pond. *Photograph by William J. O'Hern*

Jaunts of three to four miles had been the limit of most of our daily walks together. Believe me, 43 years of memories fled by in the brief hour and a half of hiking, following our completion of the first miles from the trailhead parking lot off the Coreys road. I don't remember exactly what we said when we reached our first objective, the old turnoff to Cold River

By the end of the second day, Bette had adjusted to the pack's weight.
Photograph by William J. O'Hern

called the Calkins Brook Truck Trail to Shattuck Clearing, but the gist of it was that we were going to make it together.

By good luck, we enjoyed good weather during our foot trail navigation, first over the well-trodden route to Blueberry Lean-to and then along the Ward Brook Trail to its junction with the Northville-Placid Trail at Mountain Pond.

I was pretty concerned about the image I had given Bette of the Ward Brook truck trail we were hiking on. I had been there many, many years ago. The majority of my approaches to the Cold River had been from Long Lake, the Upper Works and from the old Santanoni Preserve great camp. I didn't know the Ward Brook route to Cold River had become less popular and that it was so grown in beyond the site of the old Lumber Camp 4.

My announcement as we began our trip at the High Peaks Wilderness area trailhead off the Corey's road offered assurance the worst did not have to happen. "Remember, if you find after the first mile the 35-pound pack is too heavy, we can turn around."

The weight Bette shouldered was indeed demanding, but not dispiriting. Miles from our vehicle, a passing hiker's declaration of "That's a serious sack of bagels you have strapped to the top of your pack," gave rise to Bette inventing a way to alter the chafing of her pack's shoulder straps. "Hold it a minute," she told me. "I can take off some pressure if I put a bagel in two Ziploc sandwich bags and slip them under these straps. They'll add cushioning."

I know of no more unappetizing thought than to slaughter a favorite trail food. I made more than a token protest. I found her idea interesting but overboard. My reverence for food came through loud and clear in my protest. "You don't want to do that. I'd never be able to eat it once it was squished."

Bette's voice came resoundingly back from under the strain. "Oh, so you'd rather have peanut butter smeared bagels than have me avoid tender shoulders." Fumbling for the right words, I restated my platform while at the same time endeavoring to offer sage advice. "What you feel is just part of the total backpacking experience."

I didn't need to hear all of Bette's protests as she pulled ahead of me and called back. "I might have made a senior citizen model for the L.L. Bean outdoor catalog with the padding, but if you don't want me to use *your precious* bagels, you owe me a night in comfort in Lake Placid when we get out." Her request was later stretched to two days.

There is, over to the north-northwest of Ouluska Pass Lean-to, a small body of water called Boiling Pond, because early 20th-century sports once hooked large native brook trout there in the company of Noah John Rondeau, their guide.

"I'd really like to show you Noah's pond," I told Bette. Not only did I act as her tour guide during our trip, but I wanted her to see some of the trail-less backcountry I had taken our daughter Sue through on a similar circuit through the same territory decades earlier.

"I don't like bushwhacking!" she admitted when I pointed the location out on the map, assuring her the pond was just a short scramble beyond Seward Brook and the Cold River.

She quizzed. "How short?"

"It's just over yonder." I pointed out from the rough plank footbridge where we were filtering water. (Ouluska Pass Lean-to is within sight of the bridge.)

"I wouldn't even need to use my compass," I assured her as we drank water from the stony little brook that clearly showed on our *Trails of the Adirondack High Peaks Region* map.

"I don't want to go on any wild goose chase."

I understood her objection. Ouluska Pass is filled with some of the worst slash and blowdown in the entire corner of this region. There are acres to get lost in. To her it was a place of desolation, but Bette has always been a stubborn adventurer at heart who puts up with a challenge to go the way the wind blows. We held a council of minds and decided to not only go up the mountain pass, but to make camp at the pond. A base camp would allow us to investigate the general area.

"I've been to Boiling Pond and the pass several times," I told her. "It isn't so much to see. What I'd like you to see is the area."

I fell silent, thinking of the names of places I had learned from a good friend who had traveled with Rondeau for decades. The Devil's Caldron. Summit Bridge. South Gap. High Camp. Seward Wigwam. Emmons'

Corduroy. I hoped Bette would feel there was something special and wondrously strange about these places whose names nearly sang to me.

"All right," she said. She was willing to stick her neck out if only to please me, even if she was somewhat uncertain. It was in that moment when we exchanged looks that I saw a glint of renegade in my partner's eye. It is an infection she claims I was born with. I was delighted with her decision. Bette was ready to accept a bit of arduous work just to go on a whirl around the pass with me.

It was wonderful backpacking alone with Bette for a week in the so-called wilds. The camaraderie was strong and sweet. We climbed, pitched camp, shared fatigue and heavy rain-soaked packs as we struggled toward a destination, consulted a map and dealt with all the other normal circumstances multi-day hikers accept as part of their outdoor experience. There might have been a time or two when she especially felt the hard work or looked at her way less-than-clean clothing and wondered why she was doing this, but she never said so. Bette isn't a quitter.

Retracing our route to the site of Noah John Rondeau's hermitage on our return from Boiling Pond, we stopped to rest near the commemorative metal plaque our friend George had secured to a tree years earlier atop Cold River Hill.

"You know how George managed to get Jeannie to pack in here with him?" I posed. Jeannie had played somewhat of a part in Bette's decision to begin backpacking. She frequently said, "If Jeannie was able to do it, so could I."

As she was mulling over my question, I continued. "George told me the only way he could get his wife to take the trip was if he agreed she would only carry a hair brush and toothbrush in her day pack."

George is a man who lives by his words.

"I wish I had known that ahead of time," Bette laughed. "Take a snapshot of my side view. I want Jeannie to see just how big a pack I'm carting around."

Most often we walked single file, sometimes with me in the lead, sometimes Bette, but there were times the trail was wide enough for us to walk side by side. We were generally silent as we walked together. It's typical of woodspeople. To be sure, our minds were often free of thoughts worthy of conversation, but that was most often because of weariness. To break the quiet we would say, "Beaver dam." "Slippery root." "Mossy rock." "Wet leaves." "You want to stop for a drink?" You get so you talk compendiously along the trail. But being trail buddies also leads to introspection and good talks about serious subjects later on around the campfire. And Bette is my absolutely best buddy, on the trail or anywhere else.

Bette O'Hern on Cold River Hill. *Photograph by William J. O'Hern*

Chapter 2

Wilderness Haunts

"I Could Almost Hear Noah's Hooty-Hoot."

ONE OF THE MORE COLORFUL MEMORIES of our trip for Bette was our campsite at Rondeau's Seward Pond high in Ouluska Pass. That evening Bette was sitting comfortably on a large boulder at the edge of the water looking out at the natural habitat, as if she never wanted to leave. "How long are you going to stay there?" I called to her.

"Just a little longer. I'm enjoying the scenery from this warm rock." That pleased me. I knew she was feeling the enchantment of the Adirondacks, and perhaps reflecting on the life of the Cold River hermit who had been a key figure in my story-telling during our trip.

Much of what I shared came from Rondeau's friends, and his "hieroglyphics of the Adirondacks," as Doug Gruse reported in a Glens Falls *Post-Star* newspaper column. "Noah began developing a special code to keep his personal journals private from prying eyes. The symbolic alphabet system, which evolved through the years, developed into a mysterious language that Rondeau took with him to the grave in 1967."

Gruse's column focused on Dave Greene, a native of the Adirondacks and a crackerjack cryptologist who cracked Rondeau's code. "Although Greene was able to figure out a large portion of the code, a few mysteries remained." I helped Greene clarify some information by running the translations by Rondeau's friend Richard (Smith), Greene and I determined the code had finally been broken.

Like other visitors who viewed Rondeau's display at the Adirondack Museum in Blue Mountain Lake, Bette's "interest was piqued with the hermit's 1946 diary on display with its bizarre scrawlings of scratches, circles and squiggles." In the end however, "the journal's code was far more mysterious than any of its contents," Gruse concluded.

Bob Bates has camped, explored, deer hunted and fished throughout Rondeau's territory for more than fifteen years. He's a Rondeau aficionado, and he says Noah's ghost haunts every corner in the Cold River country. Perhaps Bette felt his gentle spirit at the pond, and that promoted the calm relaxed feeling she enjoyed well into twilight atop the rock at Seward Pond's edge.

The next morning I was ready to hit the last leg of our trail, and looked forward to a stopover at some old haunts in the Lake Placid area.

We must have looked like a motley crew as we slogged for hours through wet brush and mud. A thunderstorm started about 2 a.m. and never let up all day. But backpacking even in poor weather conditions got into Bette's blood. She skillfully picked her way across swollen drainages, spotted possible

It is easy to think how Noah might have sat on the same rock. Tucked away within the recesses of his sage mind was a veritable storehouse of woodcraft and knowledge concerning the land as it was when he first came to it. *Photograph by William J. O'Hern*

trouble spots in the trail ahead of time, and adjusted and readjusted her backpack strap positions to make a smoother ride for the weight she carried.

Hermits had nothing on us as we left. Hermits generally have a reputation for being a bit off balance, but I believe Bette's sanity remained intact throughout our final miles as she continued to ask questions and I continued to tell memories of my former backpacking trips and stories of the accomplishments of some of the most interesting characters who ever shared a bowl of Rondeau's Everlasting Stew.

★ ★ ★

Richard Smith was a much bigger woodsman in the eyes of people who knew him than he ever realized. Doctor C. V. Latimer Jr. described his friend as a man who "might be quiet and reserved but when it comes to hunting, fishing, trapping and Rondeau, the sportsmen who know him consider Smith a responsible, knowledgeable woodsman."

I thought about all the questions I had fired at Rich and how straightforward, accommodating and patient he had been in his detailed answers. I had asked him about Cold River in the early days when he lived at Duck Hole, about his 32 years with Noah and how the two of them had passed the time at the hermitage. I had wanted to know about the woodcraft skills he learned from Noah.

Smith had heard people refer to Noah as an "old buck" and a "delightful hippie hermit." He said he was sure they meant no disrespect, but he thought his old friend deserved a better description. Noah, a symbol of the wilderness past, was The Hermit Mayor of Cold River City to many, but to his closest friends, he was simply a personable individual to whom they all felt very much attached. It was at that more human level that Richard spoke to me about his best friend.

Smith had told me that after Noah's funeral he had lain awake thinking about his dear friend's good heart and of the many adventures they'd shared. "There were so many incidents experienced" while at the hermitage, on hunting and fishing trips, "our 'random scoots,' the many friends of Noah's I was introduced to, and the stories he related," Smith said.

Smith's mind had safely kept so many good memories that he said it was often hard to "sort them out." He was at Rondeau's side throughout much of the early 1940s when he was a young man eager for woods knowledge.

Before *my* best partner and I hit the trail in 2007, I had given her a mini-history lesson about Noah's life, mostly things I had learned from Richard. I soon realized that I was also telling her a lot about who Richard was and about the changes he had witnessed during his lifetime. I read Bette this portion of Richard's comments:

> *Today's lifestyle is so fast paced compared to those days gone by. It was commonplace, then, to see people walking everywhere but no one appeared rushed. It seems to me that they took the time to enjoy life. Folks were neighborly—actually knew each other. There were not the modern conveniences there are today: electricity, indoor plumbing, central heating, chain saws, and whatnot. Work was more time consuming, the labor often physically demanding.*
>
> *On the other hand, neighbors took simple pleasures from a social structure that afforded more interpersonal opportunities. With televisions and computers to dominate and isolate an individual's leisure time, neighborhoods aren't the same kind of place anymore. So much for modern time-saving technology!*
>
> *Instead of people spending less time working I actually think today's age has created a situation that people do more work!*
>
> *In my youth, mountain life had adults sitting on lawn chairs with broad arms and talking, neighbors helping each other, reading, card and board games by the soft glow of a kerosene lamp, fishing a pleasant stretch of water and children playing outside in all kinds of weather. The world wasn't luxurious; it demanded. It was labor intensive. But it was a good life in spite of what people point to nowadays as being simple, modest pleasures. That was the world my parents lived in. It was not the world Noah wanted.*
>
> *When I reacquainted myself with Noah in 1934, I thought his tales were very colorful. The majority chronicled real life experiences;*

Time, weathering and erosion have destroyed the former bridges and overland tote roads that Santa Clara Lumber Company established throughout the Cold River basin. *Photograph by William J. O'Hern*

> *others had a heavy dash of his own color, flavor and brand of seasoning! Good hermit tales.*

Bette and I talked a long time that day driving home.

"Richard and Noah really had some good times," Bette commented. I told her about the day Richard surprised me with the gift of a loan. He firmly gripped his chair's arms and pushed up, motioning me to "stay put" as he stepped into the other room. He came back with a large black metal briefcase.

The initials "N.J.R." were painted in white on its side, giving away the case's original owner. Smith placed it on the floor and smiled knowingly at me as he directed me to open it.

I lifted the lid. Neatly filed inside were Noah's hand-penned poems, scrapbooks, journals recorded in English and in code, photo albums, hand-fashioned fishing lures and a few letters from their close friend Oscar

Burguiere. He also showed me other articles that once belonged to Noah. "Keep them for as long as you need them," Rich offered. He said the pieces were tangible "reminders of a truly lifelong friend."

"Their recollections are our best guide," I told Bette. "You know what Richard told me when he returned to his old 'stompin' grounds' in 1967?"

"Nope," she replied.

"Well, he claimed he could almost hear Noah's 'Hooty-Hoot' greeting as he made his way up Cold River Hill. I like to believe I'm as lucky every year I revisit Cold River Hill."

Rondeau's metal carrying case. This homemade briefcase contained lecture material he took to presentations at clubs and organzations in the late 1940s and 1950s. *Photograph by William J. O'Hern*

Chapter 3

Return to Cold River Hill

EACH TIME I RETURN to Cold River country I recall the words of my Florida friend, Mary Thomas, because her sentiments resonate with how I feel about returning to a favorite place.

"Whenever I leave for the north woods, my friends remind me, 'You can't go home again, you know.' They are trying to prepare me for the disappointment they imagine, but that's only because they haven't been there and can't conceive of a wilderness so vast and so unforgiving, especially in winter, that the small number of people who choose to live there has remained nearly unchanged for decades. I've been going 'home again' without disappointment for over half a century because my home is ice-cold lakes and rivers and waterfalls, tangles of trees and brush, huge boulders, and craggy old mountains. All I ask of my home is to let me look upon it, feel the solitude, and marvel that in this place there are long moments when there is total, utter silence. It's been that way all my life, and I think it will be that way for a long, long time."

Our trip to Cold River Hill was reminiscent of going home. Having digested so much of Noah's diary jottings, seeing hundreds of pictures from his past and learning about Noah's friends' long and exhausting days of backpacking to visit him were rewarding. The high note of 2007, however, was that I got to share the "going home" experience with Bette.

"So this is Cold River Valley," Bette said, after we had pulled off our packs at the crumbling lean-to on the north bank of Cold River and had carefully chosen a safe path down to the waterway.

I answered, "You're right. This is it."

I wanted her to see the picturesque river. I recounted that the log shelter was where Richard Smith told me he and Tony Okie found a can of sardines and some stale mice-nibbled doughnuts that had been left on a shelf when they hiked in to see Noah in 1934. It was there too that they noticed the remains of a giant trout head on the picnic table

The swift water below the lean-to is a wild river—one of the more remote drainages in the Adirondacks. Cold River country saw a buzz of activity during the early days of logging. By 1919 timber harvesting had stopped. Gradually, fruited brambles and pioneering species of vegetation began to grow, filling in slashes and lumber clearings. By the 1920s it became the preferred kingdom for trappers, fishing devotees, and deer hunters. Remote and cloaked in boulder-strewn beauty, the territory in time became alluring to a wider sporting crowd, a man who would become its only hermit, and to all sorts of seekers of less traveled trails and splashing, bubbling, churning water.

Cold River 1930. A wee bit of white water and just a few rocks makes for a spectacular view. *Photograph by Jay L. Gregory. Courtesy of C.V. Latimer Jr. M.D.*

Given its varied history, this wild river corridor is a must-see destination for backpackers who follow the Northville-Lake Placid foot trail through the granite-clad river valley carved by melting glacial water that gnawed at the earth's most ancient bedrock. Cold River Country is the heart of the Adirondacks. For Bette and me, to hike on the trail to Cold River from the High Peaks Wilderness Area Seward Mountain Trailhead was particularly poignant because we had known Richard, had heard his "Stubborn Irish Pride" story about his friend and him dragging an eight-point buck on a homemade travois over sixteen miles from their Duck Hole camp to Coreys via the Ward Brook fire road we were going to follow. Through Richard and through my other research, it seemed we had known Noah and the environs we were about to enter.

The time of year we had chosen for our fall outing was weeks before the time of year that Smith's 1939 deer hunting trip took place. Bette and I timed it to enjoy the color in the mountains soon after it peaked, dressing the forest in autumn finery.

"Two Irish jackasses" were words Richard had used to describe him and his friend dragging a hundred and fifty pounds of deer. He was convinced Phil McCalvin and he would be dragging only horns by the time they reached their destination.

Bette and I had an easier time than they did, with our internal suspension backpacks. Nevertheless, the long trail hike was Bette's initiation to backpacking. She was of the same opinion as Richard, who said he felt like "a human mule." By the time we arrived at our first night's campsite, we were both more than ready to shed the weight of our packs. Hungry as bears, we built a fire to warm pots of water for supper, and devoured the meal we had earmarked for our first dinner.

My plan was to enjoy our trip while making an effort to see the season through Noah's eyes. To help recreate the autumn mood he would have experienced, I printed out entries from Noah's diaries. Reading them provided a perspective from the long-ago days when he lived at Cold River. The hermit's words supplied an authentic feel for what was generally on his mind throughout the many Septembers and Octobers he had spent there.

In Cold River country one can get caught up in the surroundings. There are the Seward and Santanoni mountain ranges with seven major high peak summits that offer rugged views. The river offers small waterfalls, pools, chutes and shallows. The trail-less tracts of forest and marshland surrounding the river offer up challenging bushwhacking.

On Wednesday, September 1, 1943, Rondeau penned: "Shower Last Night; Quite Cloudy Today. At Mrs. Rondeau's Kitchenette. I play fiddle. 6 Mice trapped."

Later that month, as Labor Day drifted gradually into late September, the green softwood and hardwood leaves that had been growing since spring until the woodland was shadowy and dim with summer's all-out beauty began to turn to the varying shades of nature's autumn palette. This was as true for us as it had been for Noah. Reading from Noah's 1943 diary and writings, I tried to make connections with the autumn world he knew and the glorious one Bette and I saw all around us.

Noah said he sat outside peering across the river from his hilltop outlook, and was "moved" by what he witnessed. At precisely "11:17 AM" on Wednesday, September 23, 1943, he wrote, "Autumn began." The new season was the inspiration for his poem "Autumn," written over a period of days on eleven small rectangular sheets of paper. He certainly tried to paint his feelings and observations in poetic form.

September, you hop into Libra from Virgo,-
For hours you hold the Sun in two nodes;
And your balance is so perfect at zero,-
The Sun Peeks on both ends of the Globe.

September, you have eight days in Libra,
Before October claims thirty one days;
Truly it's Autumn, early, with colors gay;
And ice on last night's water pail.

Last night's frost, shrouded the fields of grass;
And modified the green as blanching white;

And crisped the foliage on Bordering Trees;
Then at Sunrise poured a shower of leaves.

Oh, that I could write, to show a reader;
The colors of the Hills...
But such reality is not in Tongue or Pen;...

...The beauty of the Mountains, Hills and Dells;
...From Donaldson Mount to Cold River Flow,
I viewed the scarlet, green and yellow.

And from the browning grass, near the Flow,
I watched the floods of colors in kaleidoscope;
As autumn sunshine, in colors played,
On Mountain Contours, like curtain waves...

...in Autumn Vallies, among superb Hills,
I have some vivid thoughts and a dormant array;
As an odor of frozen Ferns, revive a memory;
Of Sweet Grass in childhood's new mown Hay.

Ten days earlier, his journal entries had told of an advancing fall.

> ***September 13:*** *"Sunshine today, first Killing Frost last night. Cold River. First big frost last night. Perfect Sun Shine to day. At Cold River Town Hall. 184 years ago today (1759) the Battle of Quebec was fought in the forenoon on the Plains of Abraham. Joe Montcalm and Wolfe were killed. Besides them two Fools, hundreds were killed; Their names are quite unknown; They were as good as Pale Face Wolf and Catholic Joe."*

> ***September 14:*** *"A Splendid Day. At Town Hall. Ambuscade of the Devel' Hole 1763. To Hell with John Bull Big Business! White Frost last night. Perfect Sun Shine today At Cold River. 180 years*

ago today: The Ambushcade of the Devil's Hole; much the invention, and at the Hand of the Senecas; The English and others saw it as awful (as Americans see the bombing of Pearl Harbor). They wanted to hide rather than confess- The animosities they made before hand."

September 15: *"A Fair Day. At Town Hall. I take walk to Big Eddy. I see 3 Deer."*

September 16: *"Rain Last Night. Showers today. Cold River City. A Deer rattle tin Cans in Sand Pit. I walk in Tiny V. Green Maple Leaves are turning red."*

September 18: *"1st Ice on jar of Water Last Night. Perfect Sun and Calm today. At Beauty Parlor. PM I go up Paper Bag Brook. 3 PM I set Aubel Bear Trap. 5 PM I kill a doe gilp near garage. 10 PM gilp2 liver good eating."*

In this way, Noah served as a most unusual trail guide.

Throughout the day we had talked of Noah and Richard, of solitude and of how the mountains have influenced people. The sun's heat penetrated our clothing, warming our skin and adding to the perspiration that kept the backs of our shirts wet. Mile after mile we adjusted to the weight of our packs as we basked in the calming effect of the ideal mountain weather, letting our arms follow the rhythm of our steps as our trekking poles clicked on rocks, squished into muck, and supported us when we passed through streams. It was all work, but those simple pleasures enhanced the flavor of the setting much like the call of a loon does a still autumn night.

Toward the end of the first day of the High Peak hike, I had dreamed of standing at the rim of Duck Hole, the origin of Cold River, and seeing the distant mountains across the water. I felt as if I were in an ancient land of lush vegetation, providing habitat for a wide variety of birds, fish, amphibians, reptiles and small mammals. Bette didn't share the same fascination with the flora and fauna that was stirring my senses, though. As darkness began to close in, she was thinking more and more of big mammals—Mr. and Mrs. BEAR!

Ferris Meigs, owner of the Santa Clara Lumber Company, legally gave Noah permission to set up the long-term hermitage at the former Big Dam logging camp following the end of his company's logging operations in the territory.
Courtesy of Richard J. Smith from Noah's photo album

Chapter 4

Our Brief Life in the Wilds

THE NEXT MORNING'S WEATHER was as pleasant as Noah's September 20, 1943.

> *"...Autumn colors are wonderful... W. H. Burger and Samuel B. Walls called. 1321 years ago today Muhammad entered Medina, in spite of his pursuers from Mecca who were eager to kill him."*

Bette had awakened with a smile. She hadn't been bothered by a bear or any other critter the entire night. Nor had our food bag been raided. Morning showed it was still safe and sound, suspended from a rope between two trees high above the ground. I was hoping that first positive night experience would convince Bette no bear would ever try to polish her off. Yet she kept in the back of her mind the night a bear had entered the lean-to of a friend. Future nightfalls continued to work magic on her imagination.

"You know Cold River's got a reputation for harboring some of the meanest bears in the Adirondacks," Richard would say as he launched into one of his "closest shave" bear tales. He had a wonderful sense of humor, and he was an exceptionally good storyteller. You'd have to laugh at his postures of bear shoulder-hunching, foot-stomping, roaring and paw-waving. I joked that the thought of his black bear tales should sweeten her dreams.

We started hiking toward the old hermitage site by mid-morning, leaving our lean-to on a dogtrot that led from the river bank, through a low, wet area and into a small maturing meadow where once a Civilian Conservation Corps camp had stood. It wouldn't be too many more years before this spot would look like just another part of the forest beyond the river.

November 1, 1950. Ranger Lou Russell presenting Noah the hide of a 500-pound "not so friendly black bear." Russell's son, Earle, said his father "gave the meat to Reverend Ray Morgan, Pastor of the Wesleyan Chruch in Long Lake, where he was a member." *Courtesy of Earle F. Russell*

It was the same route Richard had taken so many times when he returned to the hermitage from fishing the Black Hole.

Tramping through the rustling leaves in a forest now fully in brilliant fall colors, I could hardly contain my joy and excitement, for not only was I back in the wilds of the Seward and Santanoni Mountain ranges that I loved so well; I was about to introduce Bette to the Northville-Placid foot trail along Cold River.

I found it noteworthy that the weather Rondeau documented in his September, 1943, journal mirrored what we experienced on the days we spent in Cold River country. Winter can come early in the High Peaks area, but as evidenced by Noah's jottings in his completely coded 1943 journal, the season was "Perfect Autumn Sun Shine, Autumn colors are wonderful."

> ***Tuesday, September 22, 1943:*** *I warm The Old Violin. I see a Fox catching Grasshoppers; 75 ft. from Wigwam. While I mind my own business, a Deer blows at me from his ambushment in the briars.*
>
> ***Wednesday, September 23, 1943:*** *Another Raccoon called at Wigwam again last night and tumbled the Bride's Bouquet. Alexander,- The Great ("Great" Fool and Fanatic) born 356 B.C.*
>
> ***Thursday, September 24, 1943:*** *A Raccoon is walking on Town Hall Roof. 6 – 12 PM The Sun Jump over Autumnal Equinox (so Astronomers think) it's rather the Earth –ducking under—gadding north.*
>
> ***Friday, September 25, 1943:*** *I get a few arms full of fire wood and I do much reading. Ice form snug of water buckets each night.*

Bette and I didn't anticipate flawless fall weather conditions. Our backpacks were crammed with cold weather gear. We were prepared for chilly temperatures, light ice, wind, rain and any other mix Mother Nature might toss at us. However, the Fall 2007 season turned out to be a mix of warm daytime sunshine and perfect cool sleeping nighttime temperatures and rain.

Wednesday, September 29, 1943: *Perfect weather continues At Cold River City. I cover the Town Hall with green oil cloth. Several Air Planes than usual go eastward over Cold River Valley. House flies are getting numerous in the Town Hall.*

We experienced zero insects—day and night. It was among the best fall trips I have experienced in the mountains.

The most drama we saw along the trail was mother partridges doing their broken wing danger signal act as they fluttered off through the bushes to lure the enemy away from their young. As we moved toward our second night's destination, I talked about Noah's place in the wilds.

He wanted nothing more than to live unfettered and alone in the forested mountains. While Noah's life was not without hardship, since he had to provide shelter for himself and an adequate, continuous supply of food, it seems he made the perfect decision by placing himself out of the loop. No employment. No rat race. No noise from machinery, crowds or urban hassles. He was relatively free of government and its laws, which he eyed as restrictive.

In addition Bette's introduction to Rondeau's back country, we wanted to experience a vibrant fall in the mountains and to use the opportunity to share times-gone-by stories in the environment where they took place. Our multi-day trip also provided a mind-cleansing escape from the ordinary day-to-day life two busy retired people routinely follow. The forest offered tranquility from the hustle, bustle and hubbub. Pressures were supplanted by quiet calm, and life's pace slowed to the tempo of a backpacker's footsteps. It certainly felt that way to us. We first became aware of it when we questioned what day it was.

We arrived at Noah's Handsome Hill about 2 p.m. and were relieved to slip off our heavy packs. Bette had begun to sense a "lonesome feeling." We assumed it was because she was unfamiliar with being out and about, alone except for me. Cold River country is almost absent of people during this season.

The hilltop site of the hermitage is deserted now. It is building-less. An old piece of metal chimney pipe lies near the depression where the Town Hall once stood, cold and smokeless. Instead of the sound of voices and the smell that sportsmen say wafted through the air from Rondeau's "Everlasting Stew" cooking kettle and the ringing of his double-bitted ax only the buzz of a few common flies broke the silence around the place.

The Hermitage, or "Cold River City" as Rondeau and the 1930s mountain climbing crowd came to call it, once consisted of two ramshackle huts. The Town Hall was the hermit's primary house. The Hall of Records was used for storage and visiting dignitaries. Depending on the year, four to six wigwam structures made of wooden poles stood parallel along the edge of the bank that drops to the river below. The "Flow Ground" was a vast low-lying watery area. It was a reservoir created by river water impounded by Big Dam. The extensive reservoir filled the basin up to the 2,000-foot contour interval.

The former "City" is ten and a half miles from Plumley's Landing on Long Lake and almost the same distance from the trailhead at Upper Works (Tahawus) and closer to fifteen miles from the Seward High Peak Wilderness Area Trailhead out of Coreys.

Richard's rememberences about his coming into camp created imaginary theatrical productions in my mind. I imagined Noah standing there greeting "Quack." No one hailed us from where the door of the cabin had been, looking for mail, news, a hunting license, or a sack of donations that usually consisted of Victor mouse traps and staple dry goods—coffee, sugar, flour, corn meal, dehydrated veggies, peas and beans. The forest is now closing in on the hermitage's setting. There is trampled grass in the yard around the dying black cherry trees. The remainder of the yard that is not coiled in upright, tall grass and weeds is nurturing saplings. The only sign that there was for a short while a busy little municipality here is some metal debris piled under a wooden signboard, tacked up to inform passersby that they have arrived at the homeplace of the hermit of Cold River. The "Mayor" of the "City" had long ago moved on, leaving behind items not deemed worth carrying Outside.

The late afternoon sun's rays were subdued, yellow and warm. Not a breeze stirred the tinted leaves on the forest floor and those remaining high on limbs around the brim of the hill. I peered through the foliage to catch a glimpse of the view beyond the river. The amount of forest growth reminded me of just how much time had passed since Noah had lived there. In his days he enjoyed an unobstructed view of the Santanoni Range from his rocking chair. I located the Ash Ground he had planned (but never used) for his interment. Nearby I fixed my sight on a tree with a particular marking on its bark, the location of Richard Smith's ash ground.

Turning back to the clearing that was once a hermitage, I contemplated the slight rectangular depression in the earth. "Here's the foundation of the Town Hall," I told Bette. Just beyond was the hermit's garden. It looked as if a few of Rondeau's flowers still grew. Weeds have overgrown the place where he once tended a perennial bed, yet I thought I recognized several still-surviving long-stemmed day lily stalks intertwined with dried sweet pea vines. I thought of picking a few seed pods or digging up a tuber or two to replant in my garden. In the end I chose to accept the fact that all of man's earthly accomplishments fade in time. This spot of land had been Noah's. Some of his plants might continue to multiply. It certainly isn't immortality, but it's as close as Noah would get. The land, once altered by his hand, is simply reverting to its wild state.

1926. Lean-to at Natural Dam a.k.a. Miller's Falls. Log shelters still line the Northville–Lake Placid section of Cold River Trail. *Courtesy of C.V. Latimer Jr. M.D.*

As Bette was wondering out loud how long it would take for us to reach Ouluska lean-to, I was thinking of how forlorn and forsaken the scene we were soon to move away from seemed to me compared to the scenes in the vintage snapshots I had collected. It was evident to me the clearing will eventually be fully overgrown.

The pioneering plant species of weeds, brush, brambles and softwood trees will provide the nutrients for the hardwoods that will follow. How long will it take the plant life to completely overgrow the well-known hermitage site? It has already erased the well-worn path to the river, and the hard-won garden plots where Rondeau nurtured his root and tuber crops. How long will it be before the woodpeckers hollow out a cavernous opening in the dead trees for birds or owls to move into? The mice and moles have already set up home in the grassy underbrush and porcupines have already gnawed on trees that are growing over the site of the two cabins. Long ago the rough wooden "golden stairway" that the loggers had so laboriously built to reach the pitch pool and river bed below Big Dam had deteriorated into the earth.

Under the attacks of the heaving frost and winter's ice and snow, boulders are being reduced to rocks. The small open clearing around the historical board is now a fitting sunning place for the snakes and woodchucks and humans. I know the natural process of replacement will not take long now. Already it is impossible to discern where the loggers carved this hilltop into Big Dam Camp. And "Big Dam" and the "Flow Ground" are only memories captured and seen in fading snapshots. Initially it made me sad to think that every trace of Noah's stamp on the hill would disappear. And yet the reality is the forest has always been there, waiting to settle its score with humans.

But this was only my mood. We enjoyed the wash of soft colors, Nature's brushstrokes that have repainted the scene.

As we sat relaxing on Cold River Hill, looking at it all as Noah John might have, I could only think that more of his history would have died had "Old Whiskers" not filled his journals with daily events six decades earlier.

As we pushed through the tall grass and started downhill, our boots left slight impressions in the wet black loam. I thought about how Bette and I felt about the scenery. We were born with a love of the woods and mountains.

"What do you want for supper?" I asked Bette after we had set up camp beside Ouluska lean-to.

"Maybe chicken and rice," she called back over her shoulder, "or maybe we should eat the heavy pouch of tuna. It will help lessen the weight of the food bag."

"Gee, the river valley is so beautiful," Bette reflected after she set the cooking pot and stove on the floor of the lean-to and had walked to the river to catch a view of the distant mountains. "It seems so odd to be alone back here. I can see why Noah and Richard loved the high backcountry." Bette talked on for a while about her newfound career as a backpacker/adventurer. It pleased me to hear her developing a fondness for Cold River.

Bette was listening to her own inner thoughts after several long days on the trail. She was also opening her heart to a special man. She was learning about Noah John, and this—the place so many of his friends held in their hearts.

Outdoor enthusiasts need a place to wander and to refresh spiritually. Our genetic tap roots are still soundly anchored in Nature's deep strata, where we hear her earthly voice calling.

The twenty-first century's generations will appreciate the environmentalists' dogged efforts to return the region to its natural state, yet some may also have a natural curiosity about the past, as did we.

Come. Visit. Follow the trails with Bette and me.

1943. One of Rondeau's wigwams. Only faint clues to Cold River Hill's former appearance are evident to today's visitors. *Courtesy of Dr. Adolph G. Dittmar, Jr.*

Chapter 5

Cold River's Timelessness

DAYS LATER, as we passed over Seward Brook, a stream I have always called Ouluska Pass Brook because that is the name Richard Smith always used, I recalled the "fishing cauldron" Smith and Noah had often spoken about that was upstream about a quarter mile.

The way it was described to me made me believe it had been a very large kettle hole worn into the bed rock by years of grinding rock and water rotation. Smith said it was near an old tote "trail that winds over to Boulder Brook." Had we bushwhacked closer to the brook when we came down out of the pass I might have thought of it. It would have been fun to try to find it this time if it still existed. Certainly the rain had much to do with shifting my thinking from memories to safety as we hoofed it out of the pass. By the time we returned to Ouluska Pass lean-to, Bette commented she would enjoy returning to this spot another year. We would use the log shelter as a base camp. It is easier to bushwhack with day packs than to heft full packs. But that thought was for a future trip.

Following a short rest stop, we left the shelter and continued to the intersection by Mountain Pond where the Ward Brook Trail and the Northville-Placid Trail meet.

Hours later we reached the connection, with soaking-wet packs and boots a bit heavier. I pointed out where Richard had told me an old sign was tacked to a tree in 1934. It read "To Rondeau's—Big Dam, 6 miles." Noah often called the footpath the Cold River Trail; it's the name the Santa Clara lumbermen used. The brief history lesson might have been of interest to me, but by this time Bette had three much more pressing things on her mind. First, she was weary. Second, she was eager to ford the wet drainage that flows down from the Sawtooth Mountains, and finally, she wanted to reach the Ward Brook lean-to. A change to dry clothing, a good meal and a comfortable rest were more important at that time than reliving history.

The rain had let up by the time we reached lean-tos 1 and 2 at Number 4, named for the Number 4 lumber camp that once occupied the site. A mile farther, as we pulled into Ward Brook lean-to, we were delighted to see the sun begin to peek out.

Our final evening setting at the shelter once again reminded me of Noah John's world. From places where we had sat in rustic comfort on Cold River Hill, along a pebbly shoreline, perched on top of grand boulders that ringed the western edge of Seward Pond, or at the outer edge of Ouluska Pass lean-to facing a fire ring, it seemed that the whole Cold River valley corridor was ablaze in a mad artist's penchant for color.

Long exaggerated shadows of trees were already stretching out across the leaf-strewn clearing like dark fingers creeping out of the forest beyond the open clearing where our fire pit was positioned. Autumn always augments my urge to sleep out-of-doors, and I looked forward to one last night in the greater Cold River country.

Bob "Cold River" Bates standing on the log stringer bridge that spans Seward Brook near Ouluska Lean-to. Once bridgeless, Noah would do a little jig step to keep his balance when hopping rocks to reach the opposite bank. *Photograph by William J. O'Hern*

There we were, rested, once again sharing moments of past history, looking forward to future overnight camps in the deep leaf-carpeted forest by at least one remote quiet pond, and anticipating our own private world of wonder at the very spot where Noah filled so many pages in his diaries.

Cold River is pleasant enough in summer and fall for backpackers like us, but in winter when the forest floor hibernates beneath a blanket of five or more feet of snow, life in the woods around the river calls for Spartan stamina, a time when Jack breathes frost, and cold pokes at your nose like a razor-sharp skinning knife. I thought that when winter held the Adirondack wild in its fist, Noah would have spent much more time recording in his journals, but that was not the case. Evidently the brutal stab of the sub-freezing temperatures did not move him to write longer entries.

On November 26, 1947, Noah wrote half in code followed by "It's winter like in the Big Mountains." Later that week he "look[ed] over the scenery and check[ed] the Beauty. On an afternoon "walk to Golden Ragwort" he "Saw two Deer at mouth of Seward Brook. The Trees are beautifully loaded with Snow."

This was a scene I tried hard to imagine 60 years later when Bette and I camped at the mouth of Seward Brook, the very place where Noah had seen two deer and "trees beautifully loaded with snow." It was one of his most familiar stomping grounds. In fact, as I walked the short distance from the bridge over the brook to Ouluska Pass lean-to, I also tried to picture Noah returning from his hunt at Wilson's Pill (Noah's term) past the bridge back toward Cold River Hill. It was there he wrote: "A Deer walk in my tracks to Seward Brook."

I could have so easily written the same entry in my own journal, 60 years later.

The night that we camped downriver from the old hermitage, I slipped out of my sleeping bag into the cool evening air. It was a welcome relief from the cramped confinement of the one-man tent we were using just to save pack weight. With the aid of a flashlight, I left our campsite near the base of Cold River Hill, a stone's toss from Ouluska lean-to, and picked my way carefully to the river. The velvety sound of rushing river over rocks was a pleasant sound. Above, a hazy moonlight crept from behind a cloud.

Its subdued light played on the boulders that broke the free flow of water rushing downstream toward the Raquette River. I realized there was a sound I could not identify.

I retraced my path to the campsite, rekindled the evening coals and thought about that sound and how very odd it was. The curling smoke rose over a burst of flame and simultaneously a tingling, gripping chill grasped at my shoulders. I tossed my wool buffalo shirt over my shoulders. I began to feel the presence of an approaching person—one I would never really see! I'm positive it issued out of the mist hanging over the still water. "Noah John, is it you?" I whispered with what breath I could muster.

It has been forty years since the hermit's death, but Noah, the Cold River hermit, still inhabits the now mature forest that envelops the Cold River Valley as if to say, "I am here to share my diggings with you."

The old wooden yellow-lettered marker placed by the state of New York and the new stainless steel plaque, placed in his memory by a thoughtful admirer, need not even be at the site of his hermitage. One only needs to feel a part of the surroundings to see Noah. He might be seen standing by the Town Hall with a stringer of trout hanging by his side, sitting cross-legged at his plank table or in his homemade rocking chair fiddling up a storm, pipe clenched in his mouth.

You may attribute this to a wild imagination and call it absurd fiction, but this meeting *did* transpire. Bette and I even shared the tranquility of Noah's "lost" trout pond and camped across the pond from the site where he constructed a temporary wigwam for shelter. The real test is to listen to your heart as you travel the winding pathway along the Cold River. As Bette and I allowed ourselves more and more to become part of Noah's special places, I felt we were not alone in this forest preserve of woods and waters.

A Visit With Richard: Fourteen years after Richard's death, I found myself thinking about how it had been for Richard hanging out with Noah, remembering his stories of his early years as a young man in Cold River country. His memories were happy ones—though there had been some hard times. Recalling the hermit and Cold River City, the forest, the fishing and other wonders of nature, his mountain buddies and Rondeau's friends, I

Caulkins Brook, 1938. Noah's overnight camping sites were less comfortable than Bette and Jay's. *Courtesy of Richard J. Smith from Noah's photo album*

had good feelings about Cold River. I wanted to pay another visit to Richard's grave site.

I stood on that small spot of land amidst the tall grass and had Bette take my picture by the tree under which Richard's remains were placed. As she was checking each digital snapshot, I remembered Richard saying to me once, "I want to go back [to Cold River] in the fall and see the autumn colors. It is my, and Noah's, favorite time of year. You should take Bette sometime too."

On the fall day I left Richard following a canoe jaunt on the Chubb River, a paddle he said he wanted to make "one last time before I die," he provided the answers to many of my key questions about Noah. I found it easy to ask the questions. It was an opportunity for me to come together with Richard after many years.

As I stood by his grave site, I spoke softly to my old friend.

"We're still joined by the river. You have been more than a snapshot hanging on my wall that I showed to all my friends. So, I invited Bette to come to Cold River like you suggested. She took me up on it, just like you thought. Richard, we finally followed up on your invite. You, me,

Richard Smith sharing his many memories in the fall of 1992 as he sat with the author beside his beloved upper Chubb River. *Photograph by William J. O'Hern*

Bette and time have finally gotten together. It took a while, but better late than never."

The Cold River Valley has its way of strengthening bonds between friends.

When we descended the final grade to the High Peaks Wilderness Area Trailhead, we were inebriated with the strong cocktail of success. We were in high spirits and self-satisfied. There was nothing very extraordinary about what we had accomplished—we had just set out to see some remarkable scenery and spend some time together. We were aware of that, but it didn't make any difference. In words of one syllable, we felt swell, great and high.

Past experience had taught us the bottom could drop out of our life together at any time. Twenty-one months earlier Bette had almost died of a ruptured appendix, and I would have been left to face life without my best friend.

She remained in the hospital eight days to receive intravenous antibiotics to kill bacteria that had spread to organs in her abdominal cavity—eight days without food or water.) The terrible knowledge of how close we had come to losing one another had been a shock to both of us. That experience underlined the logic that before either of us did suffer such a great loss, we were going to make the best of whatever time we had left.

Before we set out, Bette had jokingly dubbed our quest a "Senior Citizen Survivor Outing." We learned that although surviving the physical challenges was imperative, it was even more important to appreciate what each of us had gained from the experience.

Back at the trailhead, while we were changing our clothing in the car and talking about our trip to Cold River, I asked Bette what words of advice she had for anyone who wanted to try backpacking.

Her first statement, "If you sleep in a two-man tent, sleep near the door," was quickly followed with a volley of sage advice. "Forget the hair dryer and curling iron. Bagels don't *really* make good shoulder pads. Don't bother asking your partner, 'Is that your BO or mine?'" and, "You'll always walk out faster than you walked in to the woods."

I asked seriously, "What was the highlight of the trip?"

"My feelings toward you, Jay," she answered.

I was overjoyed to hear her say that because that is what I will also remember most about our first backpacking trip as senior citizens.

Singing Pines Camp, 1993. Noah continued to build pole wigwams to dry firewood during his final years at Smith's renovated chicken coop, rolled into place on logs from a farm across the road. *Photograph by William J. O'Hern*

Chapter 6

Pleasant Time Travel

VISITING NOAH'S AND RICHARD'S related places headlined Bette's and my tour of Cold River on those last days of September. We will always remember the trip, starting with our stop at Rondeau's grave site at North Elba cemetery and ending with a visit to see what had become of Singing Pines Camp, an old chicken coop Richard Smith had renovated on a chunk of wooded land he owned in Wilmington, NY. Smith told me that by the early 1960s he felt Noah's life appeared to be coming unglued. "The old fellow was about broke," he'd said. "I couldn't bear to see him continue to bounce from boarding house to any affordable shelter any longer." Smith wanted to give the ex-hermit a place to live for the remainder of his days.

I had described Singing Pines Camp to Bette years earlier as "a cleverly refurbished farm building." About twelve feet wide by twenty feet long, the inside was divided into three rooms. During the cold winter months, Noah lived in only the middle room. There wasn't any electricity, or indoor plumbing. It was rough by most folks' standards. It wasn't a real sharp-looking place either, but it was clean and tidy. The roof didn't leak, it was easy to heat with a woodstove, and it gave Noah shelter within his means. Smith said when he presented the building to Noah in 1963, the offering pleased his eighty-year-old friend greatly.

The goal of our backpack was to pass through Cold River Valley and to break off at a few major points of interest. During that same September period in the High Peaks, our plan also included an R&R in Lake Placid following the backwoods trek. During that time we took mini tours to various other points of interest. Throughout the mountain climbing and

Meetings with the hermit on Cold River Hill are now in spirit only. Circa 1930s.
Courtesy of Richard J. Smith from Noah's photo album

Lake Placid vacation, the fall foliage continued to equal the autumn so aptly described in Noah's autumn poems.

My search for a platform to share the voices of Noah's friends became clearer each day we were on the trail and as we called on familiar locations between Black Brook and the greater Lake Placid region. Perhaps getting closer to the well-known waters, the hills and mountains, the rugged valleys and miniature forest meadows was a basic ingredient for this work.

In 2007, sitting on the knoll at Cold River with Bette seemed to lend a certain continuity to all the conversations I had had with Noah's friends. I listened attentively to the cheerful language of the wilderness as we sat contentedly looking out over Cold River. There seemed to be no need to speak, yet I was again hearing the voices of those who had been part of Noah's world.

The time to take time has an uncalculated value. We sat with our thoughts, drinking in wild beauty, until the cool night air moved us into our sleeping bags. I know I was not alone on that trip in listening to the rhythms of nature's autumn season in Cold River country. Bette shared the same sunsets and the great stillness of the woodland. We heard the mountain birds just audible above the rush of the river. We hiked in the black muck that oozed between the decaying corduroy that spans soggy sections of old logging roads, and we scrambled through wet thickets of cripple brush toward what Bette felt were godforsaken stretches of the backwoods through which I was leading her to nowhere. But through it all came an innate music of the heart and spirit and history of the natural world that was once a part of Noah John's life. It was the best gift I could have given myself, and I hoped it had helped Bette better envision Noah and his friends and their wonderful memories, all set in the territory they held close to their hearts.

On Wednesday, September 29, 1943, Noah's favorite month was drawing to an end. He described his everyday life on that day.

> *Perfect weather continues At Cold River City. I cover the Town Hall Roof with green oil cloth. Several Air Planes than usual go eastward over Cold River Valley. House Flies are getting numerous in the Town Hall.*

Bette and I returned home from the mountains the last day of September. We ate breakfast in front of the window on October first. We always enjoy looking out at our garden. A border of wild apple trees is just beyond it. As we ate, we watched the deer nibble on the fallen apples. One of Bette's thoughts that morning centered on returning next year to climb the Seward Mountains. With the scene of Cold River Hill fresh in my memory, I was wondering what Noah had been doing the same October date decades before.

Morning songbirds whistled. A thin layer of frost brushed the cooler surfaces with a dusting of white; at 8 a.m. the shady areas still retained most of the nighttime coating. A great cobweb, woven between nearby shrubs, was revealed only because of the dew that clung to the fine threads of the insect's trap. I watched the maze warm in the eastern exposure. How rapidly, I noted, the sun's rays converted the heavy dew into vapor and sent it skyward. Today would be supreme, I thought. The combination of warm daytime temperatures, a deep blue, cloudless sky and browning colors of late fall, could not be better for the paddling adventure on which we were about to embark on a lake in our Tug Hill homeland.

Only one log remains of Big Dam. *Photograph by William J. O'Hern*

"So let's see what you *were* doing on the first of October, 1943, Noah," I said as I flipped to that day in my large Noah diary notebook. He noted the day was a Friday. A mixture of English and code told about the kind of day he had experienced.

> *A Nice Day—Partly Overcast. At Beauty Parlor. Leaves in Wind Beat Poet's Daffodils. Gush of Wind—Autumn Color Waves Storm Frolic. Fallen Leaves cover the Ground. Slightly overcast, never the less- a nice day. At Cold River City. A gush of wind came from the west, and for two minutes, caught yellow leaves from Black cherry Trees; and held them in a storm frolic over the River just above the Dam. They filled the air; I doubt if the show was surpassed by The Poet's Daffodil.*

I have no way of knowing if "The Poet's" October 1st nature observations gave rise to his full-of-feeling "Acrobatic Autumn Leaves" poem, but bearing in mind the sensitive feelings Richard Smith said he had, I'd bet he turned some of his routine day toward pen and paper. This was the time of year he soaked up the sights of his favorite place on Earth.

Acrobatic Autumn Leaves
by Noah John Rondeau

It was the first day of October,
And I viewed from my Wigwam;
The Autumn Setting at Cold River,
Toward Panther Peak in Libra Sunshine.
And suddenly a Gush of Wind from The West,
Snatched from Deciduous Trees, a Scope of Leaves,
And pushed them swiftly on The Air;
And left them Fluttering toward Panther Peak.

In systematic agitation tumbled the Leaves;
Like Supple Acrobats, without a Floor;

Against Autumn Sky above Panther Peak,
Elevated and deserted by The Wind that blows.

And from my Wigwam near The Old Dam,
High above The Water's Glittering Mirror;
For Two Minutes in Frolic's Dance-
I watched The Leaves Mimicked by The River.

Oh for a Reader so Prudent and so Wise,
As to seek Little Shows that gladden The Heart;
And take recognition of Natural Art,
And see Autumn Leaves as Acrobats.

For Autumn Colors in Autumn Leaves,
Even when Frost and Wind cast to The Ground.
The only excuse for not feeling appeal,
Is for The Dead and for The Blind.

Autumn Leaves make a Sublime Show,
Then Blanket The Earth under The Snow;
And Cuddle Seeds awaiting Spring to Grow,
With Woven Designs evolved long ago.

Autumn Leaves are not done when dead,
Under Rocks, in crevices and Hollow Trees,
They make many a Soft Winter Bed,
Into which many a Denizen Sleep.
Summer Flowers are always seem as life;
Autumn Leaves seldom seen as they are;
The Waving Daffodils cannot surpass,
Aquatic Reflected Acrobatic Leaves in The Sky.

The fellow hikers who passed Bette and me during our fall Cold River trip might have thought we didn't fit the image of two die-hard backpackers.

There *were* those two large plastic sacks of bagels dangling off the backs of our packs. But thinking of how we might have looked to someone else gave rise to a similar thought about Noah John.

When he lived back in the mountains, Rondeau appeared to be a hermit. When he emerged from the mountains to appear at New York City's National Sportsmen's Show in 1947, however, he didn't quite fit the image of an entertainer—either in appearance, behavior, or verbal style. Some people might have even considered him a little weird. He tended to be unkempt, one of the reasons people thought he had a "woodsy" odor, and his theatrical presence contrasted greatly with his private behavior.

"Well, it went over with the majority of the crowd, and until the curiosity stops, I'm gonna keep on doing it," he might have said. Noah was right, and the unenthusiastic onlookers were wrong. Noah didn't turn out to be a fad. His many public appearances seemed to generate more and more attention in the print and photographic media. And to this day, his Cold River hermit exhibit in the Woods and Water building at the museum in Blue Mountain, New York is one of the most popular displays.

The Cold River hermit wrote on Saturday, October 2, 1943.

> *Somber — A Sprinkle of Hydro. At Hall of Records. Overcast all day; a sprinkle of rain, - just enough to relax crispy fresh fallen Leaves at Cold River Metropolis.*

Backpacking itself is a simple pleasure. But sharing the experience with someone else who enjoyed it made it more fulfilling. As the season advances and colder weather replaces the fleeting beauty autumn brings each year, I know we will adjust to a winter routine of snowshoeing. I will also pick up my large book of notes and remembrances and reread about all the contacts people I've known and interviewed have had with Noah John Rondeau. Television news and newspapers will probably report of man's failings and jealousies. Townspeople will talk of petty irritations. There's so much that hampers and thwarts our brief lives. I am thankful for the opportunities to look at what is really meaningful in life. To me it is and always has been spending time in the outdoors.

"Adirondack Wilds" is the story of how Noah John Rondeau answered when the Adirondack Mountains called to him.

1938. Mary Dittmar, Bert Irwin, and Madeline Dodge visit with the hermit-mayor of Cold River City posed beside piles of firewood. For weeks upon weeks there was little else to do but lug, chop, saw and stack poles wigwam-style to dry. Stove and fire wood was something one just could not have too much of when the thermometer glared at a reading of forty below. *Courtesy of Dr. Adolph G. Dittmar, Jr.*

Adirondack Wilds
Exploring the Haunts of Noah John Rondeau

Section II

Legend in the Making

Chapter 7

Noah John Rondeau, Hermit of Cold River

Paths of many early Forty-Sixers often crossed with those of Noah John Rondeau as they set out for the "Point in the Wilderness," the Indian translation for Couchsachraga, according to him. Rondeau was a friend and many times host to Forty-Sixers, who called him "the most unforgettable character I ever met." My files are packed with his letters, news clippings about him and notes taken on the spot during some fifteen visits to Cold River "City" and the "Mayor of Cold River." Here is an account, in part, that I wrote thirty years ago. It contains things that had even slipped my memory.

— A. G. Dittmar

★ ★ ★

NOAH JOHN RONDEAU lives deep in the wilderness. One either hikes thirteen miles from Coreys or canoes and hikes from Long Lake village or hikes the Northville-Placid trail from Lake Placid. His hermitage is about four miles beyond Mountain Pond at the site of the Big Dam on Cold River, used in yesteryear's logging operations. Canoeing in from Long Lake, one enters the Raquette River, proceeds on down to the mouth of Cold River and turns upstream past Calkins Creek lean-to, caches the canoe and follows an old heavily overgrown trail along the river for three miles to Shattuck's Clearing and the ranger's station. Here the Northville-Placid trail intersects and is followed upstream past Natural Dam or Miller's Falls (three miles), and on to the Big Dam (another three miles) and Rondeau's "Gate to the City."

Noah is an honorary member both of the Adirondack Mountain Club and the Adirondack Forty-Sixers. On either side of his gate sign he displays large ADK and 46R emblems painted on canvas with the word "Welcome." The "City" consists of two small log huts and three log wigwams plus flower and vegetable gardens situated on a large bluff overlooking the Big Dam of Cold River, with a view of Panther and Couchsachraga. The single inhabitant, the "Mayor" himself, has lived here for twenty-five years [since then the figure has expanded to over forty years]. A pen-written note in flowery handwriting is tacked to the door for all to read. It explains that he has had trouble with the game protectors and that is the reason he is here.

At one time, Noah John hoped to become a Presbyterian minister, but this is no longer the case. His religious beliefs have made radical changes. Once he was a barber, but he failed to obtain enough customers. A devastating fire which took all of his worldly possessions was the climax. His camera and typewriter were lost, thus shattering his hopes of writing books on woodcraft. Then came the trouble with the Conservation Department in 1928, and he went to live in the woods for good. Until then he had lived in the woods only during the winters when he could not do guiding; but

Cold River City is what the hermit called his colletion of huts and wigwams nestled among the tall trees of the Adirondack wilds miles from the nearest highway.
Courtesy of CV Latimer Jr. M.D.

1938. Noah's hut framed between two wigwams. *Courtesy of Dr. Adolph G. Dittmar, Jr.*

now with the guide license revoked he felt he must remain in the woods all the year 'round.

For food there are deer, an occasional bear and a "patridge." "Civilization has spoiled the Adirondacks for me," he claims, "no longer have I the full run of the forests to meet my needs; there are the game laws which don't allow enough for food. The forest is gone too. Many years ago the virgin timber was taken and with it most of the wildlife: Seldom do I see a rabbit. There are some muskrats, a few beaver and some porcupine. Deer are the only thing in excess."

Rondeau has no trouble with the State concerning his living in the woods because his "diggings" are not on State property. They belong to the St. Regis Lumber Company and he is there with its permission. Rondeau's garden serves him carrots, onions, turnips and potatoes along with certain greens which he gathers in the woods. However, these items are not sufficient because he has been used to such civilized foods as milk, eggs, sugar, flour, etc. These he buys once a year on his annual trip out. For money, he uses the fifty to a hundred dollars income derived from a few private parties he guides. But he makes out very well. On several occasions I was very amused when we packed a small lunch and set out for a tramp up the old lumber roads to his favorite fishing spots. Occasionally he would stop along the way, go over and reach down into a hollow stump and pull out a quart jar of sugar. “I stored this here eight years ago when I would stay overnight covering my trap line,” he explained. We’d go a mile farther and he would check a hollow tree and, sure enough, pull out a jar of coffee. And so it went. He had caches all over the countryside.

Bad years are scarcely noticed at Cold River, and when visitors might remark to him about the poor financial conditions of the previous season it would be news to Rondeau, but his dry humor would play along and he would respond, “Yas, it sure wuz a bad year.” Or, “Hard times, hard times, a slump in the depression” (followed by a hearty “hah, hah, hah, hah!” then a long sigh and a stroking of the beard). He’d murder words too: “I fired my first catridge and hit a big patridge.” Or this one when he discussed the reproductive rate of rabbits: “They’re so profilic.”

Christmas time is truly a joyous season for our hermit friend. It is his one annual invasion of civilization. Early in December he packs light, gets out his snowshoes, and heads for Coreys by his favorite Ouluska Pass route. He stays overnight with his friend, the caretaker at Ampersand Park, and then on to Coreys to be met by another friend who lives at the Bartlett Carry Club. There he spends the holidays and plays Santa Claus for the two youngsters. At the post office much mail has accumulated from his summer friends. Then comes the task of answering; last year he wrote forty-seven letters while out on vacation. With Christmas over it’s back into the hermitage for another year.

Noah John has two ambitions; one is to become a writer, the other to pack up and go to Canada to live “where nature has not been destroyed by civilization.” Rondeau has a keen mind, lots of wit, is self-educated and really has learned a great deal on a wide variety of subjects, and he might do well writing on some of these. He mentioned such proposed titles to me as “My First Fifty Years in the Adirondacks,” “Cold River,” “The Forty-Six Major Peaks of the Adirondacks,” and “Astronomy” (so as to be understood by the average person). During one of our evening chats, which always lasted way past midnight, he said he would write on the forty-six after he had spent at least one night on each summit.

It was he who first told me about the forty-six and the 46'ers of Troy, of the Hudowalskis, Howard Nash, of the Marshalls and all the other pioneers. He sparked my interest in climbing. He also taught me in the way of the woods, and he taught me how to make a pack basket. Together we spent a week cutting a brown ash, soaking it, pounding out strips for weaving and finally the construction of the pack basket. But to go back to his second ambition to move to Canada, the idea seems too remote to him. He fears that he is too old now to make such a change, but if he gets the chance he will take it. There he expects real freedom in untouched nature; much less contact with the rest of the world and he would not have to depend entirely upon nature for survival.

His dislikes? He has no time for kings, queens, presidents, game protectors, Englishmen and Americans. Does he like to read? Yes, he does, and his favorite subjects are history, biology, astronomy and evolution. He likes to tell of a fellow who scoffed at his theories about evolution and Noah quoted him as saying, "You can't make a monkey out of me." This same fellow was said to remark concerning astronomy, "The only star I know is the moon." And so goes N.J.'s humor.

And now, more about the "City of Cold River." The main log hut is called the "Town Hall." Here Rondeau spends his winters and keeps many of his provisions. It is heated with his self-made oven built of an old fifty-gallon oil drum. He stokes the fire by taking one of the long notched poles from the outside of a wigwam, strikes it against the chopping block and it breaks into firewood lengths (the poles are about twenty feet in length and notched at two-foot intervals). The other hut is the "Hall of Records." The two wigwams provide firewood in the winter; in the summer they are rebuilt. He lives and cooks in one during the warmer weather and calls it his "Wife's Kitchenette." The second wigwam is the "Pyramid." Here he stores the snowshoes, and in winter a deer or a bear.

He also has one other smaller wigwam which we must not forget — the "Beauty Parlor," complete with "wet sink" (signs displayed so state). This is his joke and all female visitors pose here in the old bearskin rocking chair while the charred stick "eye pencil" is being applied by the Mayor himself. When we finally do take leave of the "City" we usually receive an invitation to return as he makes reference to the way he stores his provisions in metal cans underground for safekeeping, with this remark: "If you get tired of home cooking, come back and see Rondeau and he'll give you something good out of the garbage can."

"How do you keep track of the calendar, N.J.?" is a common question put to him. "Yas, it's easy to confuse the calendar since all days are alike unless I run around the wigwam one day and then around a log hut on the next." About Indians he states that the greatest crime in history was the way the white man robbed the Indian of his land. "The Indian has degenerated with the civilization to which he has been subjected. The Indian was a true woodsman and now he has become tired and lost his craft. He was happy then, made use of nature as it was, and survived. Today the Indian could not get along if he was sent to the wilderness; no man could, he doesn't know how. Civilization has been the curse upon the red man."

1934. Ruins of bridge and dam. 1930s mountain climbers and young men making up the workforce at the Civilian Conservation Corps Cold River tent camp near Mountain Pond would have seen remains of Big Dam and the roadway that once spanned the river. *Courtesy of Gay Prue*

"A Face Lifter." —NJR circa 1930s. Noah beautifies trail weary Mrs. Roger Jones, who will emerge from his Beauty Parlor wigwam far more feminine, with a fresh make over following her thirteen-mile trek to Cold River Hill. *Courtesy of Richard J. Smith from Noah's photo album*

★ ★ ★

That was the flavor of the Cold River we enjoyed thirty years ago and things were very much the same as that for some years later. Have you ever sat at his campfire after dark and listened to him playing his violin, and after a few minutes heard a faint snort in the shadows behind the wigwam, and seen the faint outline of a deer's face peering in at the shimmering light of the fire? We did. This was a favorite performance Rondeau loved to present to his lingering guests. Noah John loved to spin yarns for us far into the wee hours of the morning. This is a typical example of one he would tell if you were a new visitor:

> *Through the winter months my cabin lies buried so deeply in snow it sometimes shows only as a mound from which a smoking chimney juts up. Spring arrives about March 21st by the calendar, but the calendar doesn't mean much in Cold River country. The last of April generally sweeps the snow away and I start planting my garden. The ground is poor; the altitude high and the season is so short that the 4th of July doesn't come 'til the 15th of August sometimes. But I manage to cultivate a few flowers, and more important, to raise the potatoes, turnips and carrots which go with the fall venison to carry me through the winter. About mid-May the first trout fishermen find their way to Cold River. Between anglers, hikers and mountain climbers, more than a hundred hardy sportsmen visited my cabin and signed my register [1941].*

In support of all this let me quote a friend who just returned from his first visit with the "Mayor of Cold River:"

> *A pippin of a man with a face as smiley as the full moon. He gave a new twist to my idea of hermits. He talked like a whirlwind and what he said was real smart and interesting. When he was speaking*

it seemed as if he was vocalizing the mystic spirit of the woods. Never have I seen a man so chuck-full of nature. I suppose his pep was due to breathing that fresh balsamic air so long. He certainly has developed a charm city folks might envy. His vein of humor was as big as an elephant and quite as tricky. His laugh was as contagious as the measles. I could plainly see that beneath his frolicking humor there lurked a soul of rare sincerity and worth. I once heard that nature is our oldest and best teacher, and after spending those few hours with Rondeau I believe it is true. Never did I suspect that living a secluded life in a pine forest could result in such deep learning, and I began to realize that there is real and solid wisdom to be found in the pathless woods and that Noah John had graduated from this unique school with a Magna cum Laude degree.

"I don't need a radio for entertainment when I can bathe my soul any time with such heavenly music as the booming of the partridge; the pathos of the wood dove's cry; the spirit rapping of the prospecting woodpecker; the purling brook as it rambles on chattering within its banks; the cry of the hungry nestlings in the tree tops; the sweet bird songs and the moaning of the wind among the pines. All other music is imitative. And I don't lack for company in my daily contact with deer, bear, foxes, squirrels, rabbits and winged creatures galore. My table is loaded with brook trout, venison and other woodland foods which make my mouth water. I'm surrounded by lordly mountain peaks, peaceful valleys, grassy marshes, long cathedral aisles of mossy loveliness leading through the forest, deep pools of sparkling water amid overreaching foliage where water spiders swim and blue dragon flies poise in the leafy shade, flanked with dim temples of cedar and pine palaces. Who would not luxuriate and grow wise and feel real content in such a haven?"

Once after we had become well acquainted, Noah John allowed me to see his diary. Now I've heard of people keeping a diary but this one is just out of this world. No one but he could possibly read it. It is comprised of page after page of symbols and looks very much like a series of Indian signs as seen on their beaded belts. While N.J. never confided much to me about his system, he did say that it consisted not only of symbols but also a combination of English and French intermixed and was based on circles, squares and compass points. He boasted that it was indecipherable "even by experts."

Noah's handwriting was sprawly, but most distinctive and artistic. He wrote with the old-time split steel pen and very ably produced shaded script. Here is how it looked:

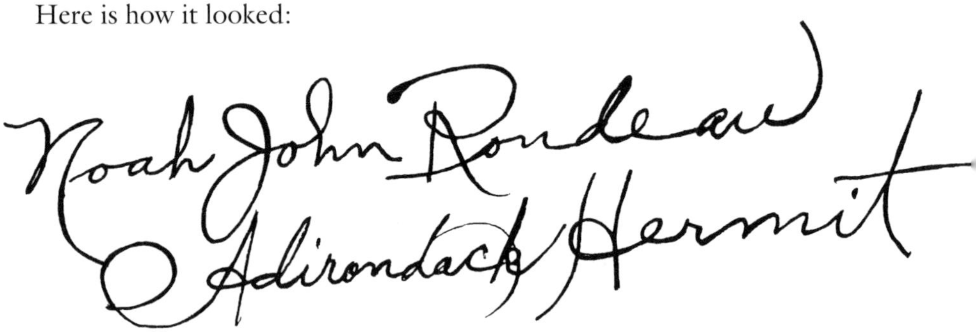

After viewing this sample of Noah's penmanship, I will share portions (unedited) of the contents of other letters received over the years. They will permit this writer to transmit the flavor of the conversations held with our hermit. Rondeau had a special way of telling things, and he had his favorite sayings, his own brand of humor.

> *January 19, 1945*
> *Addressing Dr. Ditt and our Mary that he stoled.*
> *Dear Old People-Now, Hmmmm! I was away from Cold River from June 1st to 12th the first time in 376 days. I saw no one from November 22 to March 14. And I had one woodfire that burned 138 days without relighting. That sounds like the Irishman on the subject of the clock that runs 8 days without winding, he said, "How long would it r-r-run if it was wound?" I got all the letters, cards and photographs. When I opened the Christmas cards (June 2nd) the snow-clad trees on the card did not know what to make of the Buttercups and Robins and the old farmer across the fence-planting potatoes. I just got the May June issue of The Cloud*

Splitter and I note with interest your article on canoeing and observation of the trimmed cedar borders of lakes and ponds-that in itself is closer observations than most city guys. Of course-you're semi-citified. This six-foot trim is due 100% to Deer Brousing. An old Buck comes along to breakfast and he trims a cedar; but only as far as he can reach. Then he goes to another cedar and without knife and fork, napkin or prayer – he trims it likewise. And during the winter without spirit-level or measuring tape the deer establish a line. Further you'll observe such a border until you find a spruce. You'll find the spruce like a woman of the gay nineties-wearing its skirts to the ground just because Deer don't eat Spruce... So in the meantime Saint Peter might find out what a fine Harper I am and snatch me by the seat of the breeches over the renounced Pearly Gates.

Sincerely,
Noah John Rondeau

May 11th, 1944
Dear Old People-To start away back-Sept. 6th, 1943 I launched you for Calkin Creek from the Balsams and Spruces at High Bank Cold River. I took my Pack to Town Hall; on the way I watched a doe and a fawn slowly cross the River. The Bride flowers stayed on the table in Mrs. Rondeau's Kitchenette for a week. About Oct. 20th Dr. Latimer and Attorney Gregory came to High Bank for ten days hunt. They brought in my supplies for winter and after many back loads I got the supplies to the Town Hall. In November I got a Raccoon and a 10-Point Buck and a 200.Pound Bear. And two days after I got the Bear I could have had another Bear; But you understand the law says "one bear." Now if anything makes me mad-it's to see a Bear and can't shoot. In fact I was so mad I bit the top off from a little Spruce. November 21st there was 6 inches of snow. By Christmas it was 4 feet. 1944 came along. I had no Almanac but I watched the stars and planets and kept tabs on the moon. By the time the Calendar said "Spring," at

Cold River nights below zero still felt like Winter and hard packed snow was still 4 feet deep. It took all April to sweep the snow out of the Valley. Brooks are high and the swamps wet. Pussy Willows have Kittens an inch long. They look as if they might turn into Bumble Bees if they could grow wings. The leaves have peeked out just enough to speckle the borders with green. May 9th I left Cold River and I came through Ouluska Pass. The last mile of climb to Ouluska had snow all the way-up to 4 feet. I reached the main road in Ampersand Park and went to the Pond but found no one there except a Wild Rabbit on the Lawn. So I went back to the Guide's Camp and rocked myself in Avery Rockerfeller's Rocking Chair.

By the way I think you have a nice sweet young wife especially since She got her Eye Brows lifted at the Beauty Parlor in Cold River City. Now I don't mean that Mary was not good looking before that. But every little bit helps and I tell you it pays to employ an Artist who has the equipment. My last stay at Town Hall was 374 days; the furtherest I got from Beauty Parlor was when I went to launch Newly Weds to Calkin Creek. On my last debut at Cold River I wrote four poems and a manuscript (119 pages) of prose-my recollections of 54 years ago, "A French Wedding in a Log House." It's an outstanding Scream. I will close.

Very Truly,
Noah John Rondeau

March 10th, 1943
Dear Doctor-I came out from Cold River Dec. 19th. The snow was 3 feet deep. I walked 18 miles mostly on snowshoes; reached Coreys at 9 o'clock-it was 36 below zero. And I had 5 miles more to go so called for a car. And it done me more good to ride the last 5 miles than it would have to walk another 18 miles. Then I took 2 days to rest and 2 days to wash away the Bear-Grease and the smell of the Wigwam Smoke. . . . .

Here is page one of the first letter I ever received from NJ.R.:

> *Jan. 12th, 1939*
> *Dear Dr. Dittmar-Blow your Nose and Brace up Quick! And look your Best. The Mayor of Cold River is arriving in his Full Leather Dress. He smells Wig Wam Smoke And His Whiskers are full of Deer Hair. Well, How Da Do? .....*
>
> *In 1947 a big change came to our hermit, for he suddenly became a hermit no more. He was "discovered" by the New York Sportsmen's Show people (even though in reality the 46'ers of Troy had discovered him many years before). The Show wrote him a letter which he received in six months. They sent in a reporter and a representative of a radio station asking him to come out to talk to the public. He wouldn't leave. Finally they sent in a helicopter and took him, along with some of his relics, to New York City to appear there at the Sportsmen's Show. That was the end of hermiting.*

Now he was a big name and he loved it! He went on radio and television; he was written up in all the leading newspapers and magazines; he spoke at clubs all over the state. However, it was to be short-lived. Once the public had seen him and heard him speak, he was no longer news. Noah John tried to hang on and find new audiences but they became fewer and farther between. He did appear at a few more Sportsmen's Shows in smaller cities but that was about it. In less than three years it was all over and somewhat discouraged he went back to Cold River to stay; at least this was the plan.

Then came another event that was to terminate his hermiting at Cold River forever: November 25, 1950, the day always to be remembered by hikers as the day of the big hurricane that was to close the Adirondacks for years to come. Strangely enough, it was this very day that Rondeau chose to hike through Ouluska Pass for his annual visit to civilization. No doubt the weather appeared normal for that time of year so he did not postpone his trip. Fortunately for him, he did not wait. As the day grew older the storm increased its intensity, but before it had reached its height, Rondeau managed somehow to reach Ampersand Camps where he traditionally stayed overnight. During the night, so many trees came down that he was made captive at that spot for several days before sufficient clearing could be done to open the way on to Coreys. Then the Conservation Department closed the woods and he couldn't go back.

As the years went on, Noah John began to appreciate and enjoy the comforts of civilization, and too he no doubt was feeling his age. He moved about from time to time, living in Ausable Forks, Cadyville and Jay, then in Wilmington. He spent some time at the North Pole (Santa's Workshop) on Whiteface Mountain playing Santa Claus.

At another time he set up a replica of Cold River City at the junction of the road to Coreys and Route 3, about half way between Saranac Lake and Tupper Lake—a sort of tourist attraction. Finally in the most recent years he must have longed, at least to a degree, for his old Cold River City, so he found a small cabin just south of Wilmington on the Upper Jay road and, using this as a start, he rebuilt Cold River City complete with "Gate to the City," "Wigwam," "Beauty Parlor" and garden. And here he lived for the remainder of his life until he became ill. We visited him in his new "City" once in awhile and so did others who had spent time with him back at Cold River and we all agreed that it was just like "old times." The room was just as smoky, the junk was piled everywhere just like way back when.

Noah John is gone now. He spent his last months in the Lake Placid Hospital and died there on August 24, 1967, at the age of 85. There has been no memorial built for him except what he left at Cold River. We have returned there and found the ruins of the "City," the flowers still growing in his garden. The Conservation Department has placed a sign, "Rondeau's," marking the spot. The wigwam has tipped over and the roof of the "Town Hall" has caved in. His old chains hang here and there and the old kerosene lantern hangs trapped in a tree as its branches have grown through the years. Another wigwam, the "Beauty Parlor" and the "Hall of Records" were removed and restored for the Adirondack Museum at Blue Mountain Lake. There one can also see his rocking chair, bearskin rug, his bow, his leather jacket and his fish pouch made of a beaver skin. The inside of the wigwam is decorated with photographs. The old logging chain hangs down over the fire and from it dangles the old coffee pot which at Cold

River never ran dry. (Rondeau just kept adding coffee or water, whichever was needed.)

The next time you arrive at "Cold River City" you will be greeted by the friendly Hermit of Cold River—if not in person, then by his spirit. Stop for a few moments and reconstruct in your mind how this place was years ago, as it has been described to you in this chapter. Then you too will experience the thrill many Adirondack Forty-Sixers had on this hallowed spot in the Adirondack wilderness!

Rt. to Lt. Mary and Helen Colyer. Shortly after the gals arrived at the hermit's digs, a muskrat clambered up the riverbank and waddled slowly toward the group as the sisters listened to Noah confab. *Courtesy of Helen C. Menz*

Chapter 8

The Rondeau Connection

ADOLPH G. "DITT" DITTMAR had a way with words, both descriptive and passionate. His friendship with Noah John Rondeau existed in part because both he and his wife Mary shared Rondeau's interest in the outdoors, nature studies and reading. "My wife's father knew Rondeau in the '20s. That's how Mary got to know him. Mary introduced me to Noah John about 1939. Mary, her sister Helen, and their friends climbed to the summits of the mountains surrounding Rondeau's Cold River cabins. Mary and I spent part of our honeymoon at the hermitage in 1943. We went back [to Cold River] many times to see our old friend," Ditt says, recalling his connection with the personable Adirondack hermit.

Dr. Dittmar was a college student working as an Adirondack camp counselor in the summer of 1938 when he led a group of boys on a ten-day paddle. As the canoe flotilla reached the head of Long Lake, Ditt passed on the news he had heard about a hermit who lived somewhere along the river. All agreed the hermit's camp would make an exciting side trip. The squad paddled up Cold River as far as possible, then by foot paralleled the river over a rough trail that eventually brought them to Cold River City. To the disappointment of the group, Rondeau was not in camp. All pledged they would return the following year.

Dittmar was a lifetime Adirondack Forty-Sixers club officer. Noah described him as "the best dentist a hermit could ever have." Ditt also deserves credit for taking the most snapshots of Noah and his little city. "The Mayor" was proud of his "City" and it's clear he enjoyed posing for the camera.

Ditt, who Noah John simply called "Doctor," and another close friend of Rondeau's, Grace Hudowalski, shared the same opinions about Noah when Sharp Swan asked them to describe the hermit. They both agreed he had "piercing brown eyes, sharp features and a full beard that almost hid his large smile whenever he welcomed guests to his humble abode. For a hermit, he was rather sociable; he loved to have visitors and many friends walked miles just to see him each year. Even though he scorned such civilized things as calendars, radios, and clocks (the ticking kept him awake) and had no time for government officials, when friends prepared to leave his hermitage, it was next to impossible to get away."

By the 1950s, Rondeau had given up living at Cold River. Public records bear out he was relying on Social Security and public assistance to get by. And long after the hermit's high popularity with the public had gone its fickle way, and bookings for hermit appearances had dropped precipitously, the Dittmars, Helen Coyler Menz and husband Bill, Richard Smith, Doctor Latimer, Oscar Burguiere, the Billy Burgers, the Martins, the Pettys, and other close, personal friends—the people who were tightest with Noah John—were still standing by his side as he struggled to survive outside the woods. All were full of praise for Noah's talents and personality, inviting him to their homes, introducing him to their children and grandchildren, trying to help. They still loved Noah to pieces. Everyone hoped he would not be forgotten in Adirondack lore.

Noah John's friends have retained fond memories of the hermit. Cold River Flow and its once year-round dweller remained an important part of their lives. "Noah John was a wonderful human being," they all said. Bette and my Cold River outing offered an opportunity for me to renew my connection with that High Peak territory as well as to share what Rondeau's close associates knew about the man they credited with being a Cold River "magnet."

Now, where does all the hoopla Ditt wrote about Noah John leave people who care enough to make a pilgrimage to Rondeau's former home? Part devotee and a bit nostalgic for the past perhaps, some inquisitive and a lot interested in hermit history probably, and attracted to the mountains definitely. Maybe they're just die-hard backpackers. Undeniably, the hermit connection wanders through their minds as they poke around the old place.

Young trippers from the Boy Scouts dropped in to see the Cold River hermit.
Courtesy of Richard J. Smith from Noah's photo album

Just like Rondeau and his friends, Bette and I love the river valley. It's a place of peace, where one can refuel on nature's honest truths and beauties. It's no wonder Noah John especially loved fall at the hermitage. Its splendor returns each year to bedazzle everyone who travels into the region.

Noah John Rondeau surely met a lot of people who were burned out from work. Coming into his Adirondack camp in the High Peaks of Essex County, New York—a beautiful place in a beautiful state. And once they had met Mayor Rondeau, the connection continued to echo in their minds through the years.

That winding Cold River trail is always going to draw newcomers to Cold River Hill.

Beauty above Cold River Hill. Bette and Jay gazed up the valley from where Noah poled his fishing raft. Now those unmarked trails that lead to the river are grown in with tight-grown shrubbery, and only the animals move easily up and down the bank. *Photograph by William J. O'Hern*

ADIRONDACK WILDS
Exploring the Haunts of Noah John Rondeau

Section III

Life's Whirling, Turning, Unceasing Rotations

Chapter 9

Changes in the Wind

IF ONE HAD ASKED RICHARD SMITH to speak of things of which he was most proud, one of the subjects in his top three would have been his appreciation for his nickname, "Red Beard the Woodsman," bestowed upon him by fellow Lake Placiders because of his blazing hair color, his passion for back county roaming, and because they valued his individuality. What started as a joke turned into a blessing as his name led him to be more adventurous in choosing priorities. Of course, his association with the Adirondack hermit of Cold River would have been at the very top of his "proud" list too.

On a fall day in 1992, when Richard and I were lounging around in the sun at his Singing Pines Camp in Wilmington, Smith told me about his earliest memories of Noah.

When I was a little boy—about 5 or 6 I suppose— I met this man named Noah John Rondeau. My dad used to go to his little barber shop down on Greenwood Street in Lake Placid and get his hair cut. I used to tag along, and I remember he was a curious man. He had a look about him that was truly different from anyone I had ever met. Rondeau was "an outdoors man," always talking with his customers about trapping, fishing, and hunting. He'd come to our house, and he and my father would do things together.

My family lived on a rock-bound farm in the township of North Elba, outside the village of Lake Placid. The winters get mighty cold in the high peaks of the Adirondack Mountains, and one very bad winter my father had me and my brothers hook up the heifer and pull

1992. Richard J. Smith at Singing Pines Camp. "We sat in the shade of tall evergreens, dark bottle green shrubbery and an old wigwam—two tranquil adults—one more nostalgic and a much-fascinated younger man, relaxed on a comfortable August afternoon and engaged in a soft-voiced dialogue about Rich's life-long association with Noah. The conversation was deeply rewarding. Smith said that sharing his life's memory warmed his heart." —Jay O'Hern. *Photograph by William J. O'Hern*

a load of firewood down to Rondeau's home. The snow was up to the yearling's stomach. It was so cold that without the extra wood Rondeau might have frozen. We were poor—most everybody else was too.

Well, like I was telling you, Rondeau was a strange man in many ways. He liked my mother's cooking. He'd scoop peas off his dinner plate onto a knife and eat them off the flat surface. I used to try to copy that, but I could never balance them to stay put for very long. Anyway, for entertainment, you know after a noon meal or whatever, he and my father would go out back and target shoot at bottles and such. Both were expert shots. My brothers and I would climb up on the rail fence to watch and listen to the men deep in conversation. Father would say afterwards that Rondeau was a storehouse of knowledge regarding woods lore.

Richard, the youngest of all the Smith boys, was active. He said not a day passed that he didn't make some kind of an escape and mosey across the back pasture toward the Chubb River, which ran behind their house.

One day, when Smith was a young teenager, he and his friend Tony Okie went up to Cold River looking for a man who "lived like an Indian." The boys had an interest in this Indian-like man's way of life because they'd heard he hunted with a bow and arrow. Richard and Tony Okie were into archery at the time. Smith recalled, "We wanted to know the technical side of bow making. We'd become interested in it after reading about medieval battle in history books."

We were getting our hair cut at a barber shop near school when I mentioned my interest in archery. The barber said we ought to talk to the Indian who lived somewhere back in the Cold River. He hunted with his homemade bow. That really interested me and Tony. Well, later that summer we took off into the woods. It was a real adventure. We'd never gone that far from home before.

He and Tony took a few chocolate bars, raisins, oatmeal, sandwiches and blankets and struck out on foot toward Four Corners—a short distance beyond Lake Placid's railroad station and their homes. From the corners, "We turned onto the Averyville Road and went until we reached a farmhouse close to the Northville-Placid Trail." From there the boys followed a footpath to Mountain Pond and turned onto an old lumber company road known locally as Cold River Trail.

I tell the complete story of the boys' backwoods journey in the "Road to Yesterday" section in *Life With Noah.* In short, Smith said the reception they received was an unexpected but wonderful surprise.

> *When we found the Indian's shack he was friendly enough—you know, cool but polite. It'd be natural to be a little hesitant. I suspect very few visitors came into camp. We'd been told to expect hesitancy because the Indian wasn't a lover of strangers and any authority-type class of people. What astonished me was what he said when we drew closer to the fire where the brighter light offered a better view of us in the fading light of day. In a high tone the woodsman questioned, "You must be George Smith's boy and if you're going to deny it, then explain why you have his old chicken hawk Marlin?"*

By the time introductions had been completed, Richard recalled that this so-called Indian was the same person who used to stop by his home and shoot with his father. He was "overjoyed" to find an old family friend way back in the mountains.

Smith had heard his parents talk about this man long after he'd moved out of town. He was taught that you're supposed to judge a man by the content of his character, and in this backwoodsman's case that was the truth. "I'll just tell you he was very nice and he was very interesting, and he certainly knew what he was doing back there."

Smith went on.

> *He lived in a tiny hut made out of logs and boards. You had to bend over and step down to get in. Everything inside was homemade—all the furniture and stuff. The shelter didn't have a wooden floor in it, just dirt. You could tell he'd lived there for quite a while.*

The dirt was all packed down, you know, all smoothed out. It had a look of a rough trapper's shanty. In one corner we saw his long bow. It was as tall as he was and wrapped in leather. He said the bow had a seventy-five pound pull and that the homemade arrow points were razor sharp.

When Richard and Tony returned to North Elba, Richard set about planning when next he could return to Cold River country and Rondeau's camp. Smith said that after only a few hours with the hermit, he was "hooked." To live off the land, to survive by fishing, hunting, and trapping, to be totally among the mountains with forest creatures as his only neighbors—it all appealed to him. "I remember reaching Moose Pond," Richard said as he again recounted his first hours and the day he departed Rondeau's Handsome Hill cabins. "It was clear to me in spirit as well as name, Cold River country would be *his* true home no matter where else he lived. The pond signified the end of our trip was near. My feet would carry me the remaining miles home, but my thoughts wandered back to Noah...As I covered the final miles toward home, I knew part of my heart remained back at Cold River."

Richard also recalled he was "restless" following his bow hunting woodsman trip. "My spirit of exploration was whetted and I longed to be somewhere else other than where I was—which was home on the farm."

So Richard Smith was left with his dreams for a while. The Chubb River offered his best hope of escape—along with reading trapping stories in magazines, and the occasional letters that passed between him and Rondeau. After his high school graduation in June of 1939, he had the opportunity to choose the less-traveled path. While other classmates made practical decisions regarding their futures, Richard, who recognized himself as "a dreamer," said, "I made my mind up that I was going to be a hunter and professional trapper." He favored the thought of all the freedom that style of life would offer.

Living frugally, I knew I could survive on the basics a limited income would provide. Market prices for fur were still firm. Working part-time, all I needed to do was earn enough shekels for a grub-stake. Trapping would provide the rest. And for a few years the idea worked.

However, even in mid-1940, after Richard had built an outlying trapper shanty on the Upper Chubb, and after he had established an outdoor life routine that fulfilled the spirit of his dream, things still weren't going as well as he would have liked. True, he wasn't close to starvation, as he'd been told a year before to expect, but he was thinking of leaving the Chubb watershed and trying another part of the mountainous country. The true wilderness life was still eluding him, but his friendship with Rondeau continued to evolve, and Noah offered calm, practical encouragement.

A year before Smith constructed his Chubb River camp, two older friends had "built a crude cabin at the base of a mountain they called Bear Trap Mountain," Smith remembered. "I had occasionally stayed there during the beaver trapping season; I had also deer hunted with Phil McCalvin from his camp to Duck Hole."

"Wigwam University," August 1935. Richard Smith and Tony Okie thought the hermit's wigwams looked like Indian-style tepees. *Courtesy of Gay Prue*

Life at Duck Hole Camp, as it was called, was an adventure for all the young men. For example, Phil had served at the 3-C's (Civilian Conservation Corps) Cold River side camp. He and his co-partner in the cabin, Vince (last name unknown), knew Rondeau. They'd been at his camp many times. All three fellows gathered off and on back at the hermitage. Rondeau knew a lot about cooking. Once he gave the young men his recipe for Slam Bang Stew. It was not fancy fare. Cooking in the mountains without a wood-burning kitchen range required the chef to devise simple meals because there was no refrigeration and there were few other ways to store or preserve food. So meals were modest—actually frugal—in keeping with a simple way of life.

Toward the end of 1940, a dream came true for Richard. Vince drifted away from Lake Placid, and Phil, who joined the Air Force, turned the cabin over to Richard. Once he had shifted his wilderness base from the upper Chubb River to Duck Hole, Richard began spending many more days with Noah. He said, "We roamed the wilderness, he teaching me about the network of old logging roads...I soon got caught up in my new lifestyle. Here I was, Richard Smith, with a true wilderness camp only eight miles from Rondeau and near Headquarters Camp, the old Santa Clara Lumber Company logging shanty Dick Wood and E. J. Dailey once used as their center of trapping operations." Those men were two of Smith's sporting magazine heroes, writers and trappers he had read about during his youth.

By May of 1940, Smith and a friend had finished moving all the Chubb camp possessions in advance of the turnover. Richard Smith remembered well the long hauls. On the final carry, he received help from his friend Don, who wanted to meet Noah.

Smith had memorized details of the relocation because it was meaningful to him, and I asked him to write them down for me.

> *The loads I moved had become routine by the time Don offered to help. To shorten the trip, I had carried everything upstream in my boat to The Landing, which is a popular overnight destination for canoeists [on the Chubb River] today. A short bushwhack along the outlet of Wanika Falls brought me close to the Northville-*

> *Placid Trail where I set up a cache under a waterproof canvas.*
>
> *Don was thrilled at the thought of meeting Noah. He asked many questions as we carted my supplies over the remaining miles of trail. After an overnight stay at Phil and Vince's site, which by the way was what we called a "green-timber" camp, meaning it was an illegal building on state land built from trees cut in the vicinity, we struck out downstream, arriving at Rondeau's "City" just before noon. Noah wasn't in but he'd left a wood fire smoldering inside the cooking wigwam. I figured he wasn't off too far. I mixed up some batter and baked a couple dozen biscuits in a reflector oven. Don's mother, Mrs. Beebe, had known Noah when he lived in Lake Placid. She'd sent him a couple jars of her strawberry preserves.*
>
> *Noah arrived shortly after the biscuits were cooked, noting the plate piled high on the table. He spotted the jar of jam next to the plate, and after he read her note on the label, his eyes seemed to light up as wide as a motorcar's headlamps. He didn't need an invitation to dive into her gift; he just sat down and began eating. The next morning we finished the jar using Rondeau's time-honored method of eating sourdough pancakes. First jam was spread over the flat surface; then we rolled the cakes into a cigar-shape, being careful as we bit into them not to lose a drop of the sweet juice. Don got a big kick out of Noah's saying, "Pass Mrs. Beebe's preserves this-a-way."*

Smith spent almost half a dozen years living in the Cold River wilds until eventually the draft caught up with him in 1946. By this time, his friend Noah had developed quite a following.

The next year, 1947, after decades of trapping, hunting, writing, painting, fiddling and nearly starving, it began to look as though life at Cold River was coming to an end for Rondeau. When Richard returned from military service that year, he declared "it was all downhill" for Noah and his Cold River life. While the hermit was by no means rich and famous, his life had taken a turn.

In a May 8, 1992, letter, Smith told me about the changes he'd observed:

> *...when I finally bid Uncle Sam goodbye in 1947 my first thoughts were to pack up and head into the wilds of Cold River for a long-delayed reunion with Noah John...When I gave forth my approaching camp call "Who Who Whoo!!" I heard Noah answer "Who. Who. Whooo. Me." I think now how long I had been away from my old friend and how much joy I saw in Noah's sparkling eyes. It seemed you could see his smile from a mile away. He did a little jig step to celebrate our long-awaited reunion before we sat down to confab and relate to each other our adventures in different worlds other than what we both had known.*

The army had taken Smith outside the Adirondacks for the first time in his life. It's unclear what role Richard Smith served during his army stint. All he ever chose to say about his military service was, "I'm never going to leave the Adirondacks again."

Smith continued.

> *I recall we didn't get much sleep that night. Noah had a sense of pride in the way he had found his place among the multitude of strangers during his Sportsmen's Show appearances. I was somewhat surprised to see him so comfortable with the different way of life his exhibit exposed him to—actually it was almost unbelievable to me that an old woodsman...could attract the kind of attention he was getting. Maybe he represented what they privately wished they could be. For sure Noah was not a backward, uncouth hermit. He had intelligence. He was philosophical in his thoughts and he certainly had wisdom. I guess those things, his solitary hermit background and woodlore knowledge set him well apart from their own life accomplishments.*
>
> *Oh yes! We had some good talks that day. They are ever vivid in my memory. True, Noah had changed in a way I never saw coming. He mentioned with pride and a bit of self-importance that his*

set-ups at Sportsmen's Shows were exceptional and would be hard to duplicate by anyone, hermits of other eras included. I detected a bit of an urge to brag some at that point, but a few notes from his own horn I thought were well earned, well founded, and I could do no less than cheer and compliment him.

Buoyed by Smith's safe return, Noah became fatherly when Richard shared that he had never been sadder than when he was in the army, and he followed up with his desire to pick up the shoestring living he had experienced before the draft picked him up.

Noah knew Richard saw all the magic of being up there in that wonderful make-believe Cold River City. He also knew Richard's dream wasn't realistic. Smith had told him that throughout his time in the army he had harbored a dream to live the same kind of life as Noah. "He saw the stars in my eyes," he recalled. "I did imagine making a living by trapping, but Noah told me I was 'only seeing stars.'" He discouraged Richard from aspiring to live like a rough woodsman. Rondeau pointed out the terribly small percentage of success—that "the odds are against you from the start." And if he was lucky enough to make it for a short while, he would have to work doubly hard to make a buck stretch. "I was surprised," Smith admitted. "I reminded him he'd done all right. Noah countered that he was not that sure he had, but even if he had pulled it off, times were now different."

"So what did you do?" I invited Smith to tell me.

"Well, I took his advice. Noah was one of the smartest men I ever knew."

Chapter 10

Friendship, One of Life's Riches

I REMEMBER dropping my last six dollars down at the bookstore in 1969 and purchasing the biography *Noah John Rondeau, Adirondack Hermit.* Back then the only Cold River history on the market was Maitland C. De Sormo's book. It has been part of my Adirondack library for more than 38 years.

I was excited and elated when I contacted the author and he agreed to meet with me in 1988. This first meeting turned into a dozen or so get-togethers in the following four years before he died. Mait loved anything "Adirondackana." He enjoyed learning about the historical material I had collected. "You seem to have access to much first-hand information," he said during our first meeting, adding that when I had any of my proposed manuscripts "in good shape, I'll do what I can to help even though I'm admittedly anything but sharp these days. A stroke and heart attack four years ago really took their toll mentally as well as physically."

De Sormo was a teacher, businessman, a prolific writer and editor, and a lecturer, and was active in the Adirondack Mountain Club, the Adirondack 46'ers, and the Wilderness Society. He was historian for the town of Harrietstown, and was past president of the Lake Placid-North Elba Historical Society. The Rondeau biography was the second of his nine books, and he thought the hermit story was the most successful one in terms of sales.

During one gab fest I asked him why he hadn't used many of the recollections about Noah that a long list of people he had acknowledged in the preface of his book had offered. (I was aware he hadn't because when I interviewed them, almost everyone lamented the loss of their stories.)

"Who cares what it was like to follow an old hermit around on his trap line?" he began. "Who really wants to read about hiking with him or fishing, hunting or whatever went on back in the mountains?" While Mait reported he was indebted to everyone who had offered contributions, he said the hard part of planning the manuscript was deciding what to do with the expansive amount of data he had amassed. In the end he decided to build a straight-forward biography around Rondeau's writing, leaving out most of the personal reminiscences.

I acknowledged that his "opus," as he referred to his work, had inspired me to try and write at least one if not more than one book about the hermit. Mait was very interested in my plan but ended on a down note. "You can try, but I still don't think anyone would be interested in reading a story about being back at the river with [Rondeau]."

Contrary to Mait's advice, I went on to write *Life With Noah*; *Noah John Rondeau's Adirondack Wilderness Days: A Year with the Hermit of Cold River Flow*, and this book, *Adirondack Wilds*, and I have developed the unpublished manuscripts I call *The Hermit and Us* and *Remembering Noah.* I never considered a single writing endeavor a gamble. I was pretty sure people would be interested in the more human side of the hermit and in how he related to the many people whose lives crossed his path in both large and small ways.

In a letter, Mait De Sormo told me, "About twenty years ago I contacted Dick Smith, who lived on the River Road outside Lake Placid. I mentioned him in my book on N.J.R. as a hunting pal of the hermit. At the time, I saw Smith had a large metal box with Rondeau's name on it. 'N. J. Rondeau, Adirondack Hermit,' it read.

"As I recall there were...photo albums and at least several other items inside. I tried to buy the object and container but Smith wasn't interested in selling them. Several times later on I repeated my offer but got nowhere.

"This p.m. I drove over to Smith's place but found it unoccupied..."

Mait went on about leaving Smith a note about my interest in his friend Noah and how he felt Smith and I would "hit it off." He felt we shared similar outdoor interests.

In time I received a letter from Richard Smith. The first paragraph gave me the impression there might be a feud of some sort between De Sormo and him. He wrote:

> *...De Sormo's book on Rondeau left a lot to be desired. With Rondeau's manuscript in possession and the help I gave him I think what could have been a masterpiece, in my opinion, fell a long way short of the mark!*
>
> *...I am mostly retired from caretaking work. I only have one small camp where I worked for 45 years. During the time before lake-freeze up I am usually home on River Road. If you like, let me know when you would be able to come up, and I'll try to be home...Weekends are better...*
>
> *Sure, I'd be glad to help you out.*
>
> *Best regards,*
>
> *R. Smith*

I remember showing Richard my vintage collection of Cold River photos taken by Richard Wood in the second and third decades of the 1900s. He thought they were very interesting. I told him what I knew of Wood and of his partner, Elric Jack "E.J." Dailey. In turn, he shared a few tales Rondeau had told him about the two "interlopers." I don't know if that was his word or one Rondeau used when referring to the fur trapping partners who wrote trapline experiences for national publications. What I do know is that Donald Jack Anderson, a contemporary outdoor writer and friend of E.J., included in his 1969 article, "The Last of Boone's Breed," that Dailey and his writer-photographer partner Dick Wood did come in contact with Rondeau in 1919.

In the March 1969 *Field & Stream* magazine Anderson noted...

> *...Then, they [Wood and Dailey] lived in a forsaken cabin of the Santa Clara Lumber Company on Cold Creek [sic-River] and trapped over the contiguous Santanoni, Seward, Saw Tooth, and Ampersand Mountains for marten and fisher. The only neighbor, Noah Rondeau, had carried the shack he lived in for 40 miles,*

board by board. Rondeau...scraped like a madman on a broken fiddle and once killed a bear with a homemade longbow, and sometimes fired any weapon that was handy at the folks who approached the place.

Smith followed with a remembrance that Noah John felt E. J. "was a big wind bag." As with most of Noah's remarks, there was a reason. Noah had been working at Big Dam on a winter night, doing camp chores. Dailey dropped in to the lumber camp looking for evening shelter. That evening, over a foot of snow fell. The next morning, Dailey left the camp to retrieve a sack of traps he had cached along the trail. According to Noah, Dailey returned to the camp and took Noah into his confidence, asking him to help find the traps. Noah obliged, but remarked about the man later, "If Dailey couldn't find the traps when they were all together, how could he find them after he had set them over a mile or two?"

Rev. Ryder and party. Noah's aim was legendary and accurate with a homemade bow and arrow. Gay Prue vividly recalled the bulls-eye was most often a drawing of a ranger's hat on a piece of canvas. "If the arrow missed the hat on his ranger man outline target—striking the body instead, Noah would cry out, 'Oh, Oh. Poor shot. Too bad.' Then he'd dance a little jig in the clearing." *Photo by Ed Hudowalski. Courtesy of Grace Hudowalski*

Smith's memories of Noah John's life stories were of interest to me even though biographer De Sormo had not been interested enough in his reminiscences to use them for publication.

Smith said he never thought he liked the sound of his voice when I asked him if he would allow me to record our conversations, but he was a great storyteller—and he said his high school English teachers always thought he was a great student. I was thrilled to learn he was willing to write his memories whenever we were not able to meet and talk, and he showed me some magazine articles he had written a few years earlier to, perhaps, confirm that he could write interesting non-fiction. He had published six stories in *Adirondack Life* magazine from 1985–86. After Smith's and my first two meetings, which included a sightseeing drive around Lake Placid and North Elba, Richard began inviting me to stay the weekend whenever I wanted. I had outlined my interest in writing a book that would set down the unique life Rondeau lived.

On my weekend visits, Richard would stay up late thinking about his high school "escapades" into Cold River, and speaking about his adventures with Noah. We would talk, listen to voice recordings I had found of Noah, and travel to places he enjoyed until some later hour when we would get tired and finally be ready to go to bed. One night, as we were on our way back to his River Road cabin after a wonderful afternoon at Singing Pines Camp, he told me he had gone into the hospital earlier that week for "a thorough evaluation" of his prostate problem.

I had planned to include Smith's recollections as well as those of other people who knew Rondeau and who had shared their memories in generous detail. However, after many sessions with Richard, I decided to set that idea on a back burner and to begin with preserving just the memories of Smith and his association with Rondeau during the mid-1930s through the 1940s. I knew Richard was beginning to have some medical problems and I understood longevity isn't a guarantee for anyone. It seemed best to concentrate on what I thought of as the "Richard Smith-Noah epoch."

One Saturday afternoon I met Richard at his home to pick him up for a canoe ride he had long wanted to take, he said, "one last time." He started telling me about a dream he had had a couple of nights before.

He had dreamed that he was rowing down the Chubb River with a young man who had the same interests as his own at that age. They were sharing a wilderness adventure. They had both read about the mountain men of the Old West, and both would have liked to follow in those frontiersmen's footsteps.

It gave me goose bumps all over. I told him I had had a similar dream, and that I was going to jot some notes down before I forgot it, because it would probably make a good story sometime. I too had dreamed of rowing down the Chubb, but with an older man.

At the end of our Chubb River canoe trip, after we had landed at the take-out along the Averyville Road, I studied Richard, who stood at the river's edge leaning on a paddle. He was quiet as he reflected on the river flowing by with what I was sure was nostalgia. In the main stream, white streamers of bubbles whizzed around a boulder, while lily pads with yellow flowers decorated a protective cove. Sun danced off the surface of the water.

The winding waterway of the tranquil Chubb River is full of beaver dams which we had pulled the canoe over, and we had enjoyed myriad scenes of water and picturesque mountains. They were no longer mere memories for Richard. He was back on the river of his boyhood.

The day's paddle had been a down-to-earth pleasure for both of us, but sharing the experience with Richard made it extra special for me. "There's so much that hampers and thwarts our brief lives," Richard told me as he turned and headed toward my truck. I guessed he was thinking of the many petty things people often allow themselves to get caught up in. I have one particular snapshot of him sitting in the bow of the canoe. His paddle rests across his lap. Drops of water are falling onto the nearly mirror-flat surface of the river. A panoramic mountain vista fills the horizon. At the take-out as well as during the day's paddle I know he had been thinking of all the opportunities he had had in his life and of the things that had been most meaningful to him. Suddenly our similar dreams made sense. I was that young man in Richard's dream, he the older man in mine. I knew how much the trip had meant to him, and I hoped we would be able to go again soon.

Let's say I gave Richard comfort and company in his quest to return to his childhood and his teenage wilderness world. My paddling was not always reassuring to him as he urged insistently that I pull the canoe carefully over each beaver dam to "keep his cat's paws dry," but to my credit I cautiously transported him upriver and returned him safely to the landing where we had begun that morning.

He wrote me the following week to thank me again for the outing, and said he was going to pick up his memories. I learned just what that meant. His letter was twelve pages long! Instead of 3–6 pages of correspondence a week, Richard began mailing me long letters, often three times a week. The subjects ranged from personal talk about his current situation and his fondest memories—the Rondeau decade between 1940 and 1950 and his close contact with Noah between 1960 and 1967. He had made his mind up that he wanted me to learn as much as he could share before he "went to heaven." Richard knew all Noah's "grand ole Cold River buddies," and he described what they had done back there with the hermit, and what they looked like. His letters told about Noah's nickname for him, about seeing Rondeau walk up past his parents' house in the summer on his way to pick wild berries that grew in an old clearing, about why he bought property in Wilmington for Rondeau in the '60s, and about why he frequently used the phrase "like my father" in his descriptions of Noah John.

I believe he wanted to see my dream of writing a book about their life in Cold River come true. I had exchanged letters with Richard only a short while before he stopped communicating with people and told me "Jay, this is a tough one this time, but I've really enjoyed knowing and talking to you and I'm proud to call you a friend." I will miss Richard very much. He was a very good friend of mine.

I was about 35 years younger than Richard, but the age difference didn't matter. De Sormo had been right. Smith and I enjoyed the backwoods; we shared similar ideas, wanted to rescue and preserve Rondeau's legacy, and enjoyed the thought that what we were doing might indeed recreate his and Noah's way of life in generous detail. While De Sormo had found Noah's day-by-day activities of little interest, Smith, other sportspeople, friends, and relatives of Noah's were very interested in my historical focus. Once I gained their confidence and respect, they offered me much information they hadn't made available to De Sormo. Their loyalties were solidified;

Winter, 1921. Richard Wood and E. J. Dailey snowshoeing to "Headquarters Camp" in the Cold River Country. *Photograph by Richard K. Wood. Courtesy of Inez Wood Buis*

everyone seemed eager to celebrate the great moments in their lives with the hermit. I thanked them all and promised to do my best. I'm sure none of them knew the feeling their confidence gave me—their certitude that I could do right by Noah and Richard, portray their lives as they really were, was invaluable. The gradual demise of all the people who have helped me in my research is not only a great loss for their families, but for the world and for Adirondack history.

Smith was my first "big break" into the truly personal kind of research I wanted to do. I feel blessed for the time I had with him, a friend I was really just getting to know but who had already begun to seem like family. He encouraged and inspired me and helped me to fulfill my dreams.

Richard felt he was a part of Cold River just like his backwoods partner, Noah John Rondeau, did. He said he was grateful knowing that his ashes would be interred on Cold River Hill where he had spent so many hours with the man who launched his outdoor career.

I'll always remember him, and it is some solace that part of him will always live through me and my writing.

Panther Peak from the hermitage's site. Years flow and bring changes but Cold River Hill continues to welcome visitors to the sounds and sights Noah enjoyed.
Photograph by William J. O'Hern

Chapter 11

The Gang at Cold River

"YOU KNOW, JAY, some people I know seem to take for granted that being a doctor makes them immune to illness," Richard told me one day as he remembered the regulars who frequented Noah's hermitage. "Being a physician …and having all the medical knowledge in the world doesn't protect doctors 100% from illness…" Smith was referring to Clarence Vinette "C.V." Latimer Jr., whose father, also a doctor, had also gone by his initials, C.V. The senior Dr. Latimer had built his first Adirondack sporting camp early in the second decade of the twentieth century. In fact, he arrived in Cold River country about the time Noah moved from Lake Placid to the remote hamlet of Coreys.

C.V. Jr. was slightly older than Richard. Even though both men regularly visited Noah's land, and knew of each other, they had never connected during the early days. It took Richard's March/April 1985 *Adirondack Life* magazine story, "Roaming and Trapping," to draw them together eighteen years after Noah's death.

Smith told, "C.V. read my first magazine story, called Jeffery Kelly, the editor, described who he was and asked how he could reach me."

Learning Smith lived a reticent life and did not even have a telephone, C.V. wrote him a letter that, according to Richard, was "filled with nostalgia. I recognized the Latimer name immediately" on the return address on the envelope, he said. The letter told who he was (a family physician practicing in North Hudson) and included recollections of Noah's squawky fiddle playing, interesting fragments about his father's many camps and his family's backwoods sporting glamour, his brother, Greer's bear hunt with Noah when he was seventeen, and numerous unique images founded

C.V. Latimer Jr. with Noah in October 1948 at Camp Seward. *Courtesy C.V. Latimer Jr. M.D.*

on true-life experiences. C.V. and his family knew the Seward Mountain Range well. Smith recalled, "I just love letters like that. I was on a first name basis with his brother Don but had never met C.V. I knew from Don [and talking with Noah] that the younger Doc would make his yearly fishing and hunting rounds back at the river. He got the biggest kick out of telling about his adventures back there."

I added into the picture my own wonderment about C.V. As I thumbed through his Cold River photo album I couldn't help questioning why he had a cigarette hanging out of his mouth in many of the snapshots. It's hard to believe now, but back in the '40s there was a strong tie between the AMA and the tobacco industry. R. J. Reynolds was running full-page ads in national magazines picturing a doctor wearing a white coat with a reflector around his head, the caption reading, "More Doctors Smoke Camels Than Any Other Cigarette." Incredible now, he said, but "Yes, I was one of those doctors." It was an era when not so much was made of a connection between smoking and heart and lung disease.

Richard said, as he read C.V.'s post, "My mind began to swirl about my desire to get back to Cold River one last time." The letter arrived during

Mud Season—early spring of 1985. C.V. wrote about Noah's "Lord" sobriquet for Oscar Burguiere, and asked whether it fit Smith's image of him. Oscar was a long-time friend of both C.V. Latimer Sr. and Noah. The man was a truly unique wanna-be hillbilly-type fellow whose backwoods actions spawned all sorts of camp stories. Oscar was such a regular at Rondeau's Cold River municipality that the hermit staked up Burguiere's canvas wall tent each spring and left it up through white-tail deer hunting season every fall for decades.

The senior Doc Latimer had three sons. Don was an insurance salesman; Greer was a machinist, and C.V. followed in his father's medical footsteps. For over 40 years father and sons had gathered for a minimum two-week stint each spring to fish and each fall to hunt the mountainous territory, except for the boys' absences during World War II. Smith had been to Camp Seward many times. It was discreetly concealed deep in the green timber near the southern edge of Barking Buck Swamp, a great wet area Noah named between High Banks and Miller Falls. Richard and Oscar often worked together to carry supplies the Latimer party brought into Cold River for Noah. Smith had even helped Noah look after the camp's well-being, especially following strong wind storms.

"...C.V. is a nice man," Smith wrote. "We hit it off grand the first day he and his wife arrived at my home...and though we have only been acquainted now for a few short years, our being part of the Gang at Cold River makes it seem we have been friends for a lifetime. Noah spoke of the Latimers often, so it seemed as if I knew them well, even before I met C.V. and his brother Don."

Smith went on about his newfound friend. "C.V. mentioned he had a bypass, and though he looked kind of peaked the last time I saw him (thin and pale looking) I thought it more of an aftershock and that it would take a while to adjust and recuperate. I'm sure C.V. took good care of his health as he did for others in his family and his medical practice, and certainly his good wife Henrietta made sure he followed a healthy program..."

Richard's impressions about the man were right on the money. I knew well because every time C.V. and I got together, his first questions were about my recent blood test results and my family's well-being.

Richard continued to remember Doc Latimer Sr. Noah and he "…were great friends. Noah always went downriver to his camp to spend a few days fishing, hunting, or just being in his company. A strict Republican, as was Dr. Latimer, they had a lot of things in common politically. I remember Noah speaking of election day, when Franklin Roosevelt was the presidential candidate. Dr. Latimer had a battery radio and Noah made the trip down to get in on the returns even though he despised radios, labeling them as 'screech owls.' As the returns came in over the air, Dr. Latimer, when it seemed sure of Roosevelt's victory, said to Noah, 'If Roosevelt gets to be our next president, I might just as well pack up and go home, ending what would otherwise have been a wonderful hunting season. All the pleasure would be gone.'" Richard recalled that Noah sympathized, but told the doctor "it was his own fault."

"Why?" the doctor asked.

Noah replied, "Because you had to bring a Democrat radio into Cold River."

As Richard Smith thought about his life and Cold River connection, he wondered if he should hang it up as a camp caretaker. He had worked that "sunup to sundown work schedule" since his return from military service in 1947. He had a small income from Social Security and a retirement pension, and had a paid-up roof over his head. He had an old truck, and people were always asking him if he'd do odd jobs for them, so there was no pressure to work full time in order to buy the groceries. He knew his best years had long passed him by; his younger-generation neighbors often asked him questions about things that he had always considered commonplace: "Tell us about the early days in Lake Placid." "You knew Noah John Rondeau. What was he like?" "What's happened to all the fur-bearing animals since your days of trapping?" "Why did you create Singing Pines for the hermit Rondeau?"

Each time he was asked to share early experiences, he gradually realized that as an old-timer, his lifetime perspective offered an interesting backward glance to past history. "My neighbors are genuinely interested in my woodcraft skills as well as my past experiences," he told me.

C.V. also spent a considerable part of his few retirement years thinking about his time at Cold River. He remembered his father's good-hearted ways, the many adult friends who shared time with him, and of course he remembered Noah. Both Richard and C.V. said their contact with the hermit had broadened their knowledge. Noah accepted them fondly when they were growing up. In his own way, each said that Noah "was never too busy taking care of himself to consider a young man's interest in the outdoors."

Listening to C.V. and Richard tell of their many years at the river with Old Whiskers, it was easy for me to see why each man wanted to share his memories. They never wanted their Cold River history to be forgotten.

As much as both men shared with me, there were always more stories to tell, snapshot images to talk about, chronicles to preserve. C.V. and Richard could not shake their desire to document what they loved—remembering and talking: Cold River, the mountains, their hermit connection were as much a part of them as breathing. Something deep inside of them wouldn't let it go, couldn't let it go, so they kept on talking and penning anecdotes. C.V. arranged a Camp Seward scrapbook and recorded what he knew about his father, his father's partners, and their early sporting life in Cold River. When C.V.'s son, Chris Latimer, learned Bette and I were going to go back to Cold River, he offered us the use of his father's archives. I accepted with great interest. The photos were an immense help. Every time I passed a particular point of interest pictured in C.V.s' album I thought of it and told Bette the story associated with it.

No matter how successful a man becomes, the real reason he is interested in sharing the foundations of his life is the drive to preserve history. C.V. and Richard Smith never lost that drive. No man ever forgets his first love, and they both loved the same thing: the wild Cold River.

Chapter 12

Guide and Pal

JUST AS NOAH had been Richard Smith's guide and pal, Richard quickly became mine. As I've said, he was most generous in sharing information about the famous hermit. Best of all, Smith was willing to bring me along on the many paths he had followed in the Cold River country. He even offered to take me to visit Singing Pines, Noah's last home.

When Smith and I arrived at Singing Pines, I learned it hadn't changed much since Noah lived there. "What did you and Noah do up here?" I asked Richard. Smith responded, "He enjoyed puttering around the place, hammering things and building pole wigwams. He also cooked outside and gardened like he did back at Cold River. He loved to do the backwoods hermitage cooking stuff. And he'd bake great cornbread." Rondeau planted flowers and, with Smith, started fruit trees and a garden. When his green beans sprouted, Smith told Noah he didn't see them standing a chance against the rabbits without fencing. Noah came back with, "Well, Quack, they're gonna grow because I plan to eat the rabbits."

I wondered if Noah had many friends living nearby. Richard confirmed that indeed, he did. He had relatives in Black Brook and Ausable Forks, and then there was Madeline Dodge in the Village of Wilmington. He would arrive at her kitchen door in the morning and sometimes stay all day. Dodge said that Noah told her he enjoyed the safety of her home. "It protected him from the highway carnage on Fox Farm and Springhill roads."

"How lucky I was to have known Noah and to have him take me under his wing," Smith shared. "And how lucky I am," I ended that conversation with Richard, "that you've chosen to take me into your confidence."

"My familiarity with Noah's life," he said, as we walked around the acre-and-a-half property, "spans decades. Over the years, reporters and collectors have knocked on my door for this and that about Noah, but I have avoided talking and sharing my hermit collection until now. I've been watching you. It took time, but gradually I realized you were genuinely interested in my past experiences and how lucky I was to have known Noah. Noah was as honest a man as I ever met, and if a person was honest with him he was a friend for life. So you can readily see that on more than one occasion I have thought

Noah pointing out his code's finer technicalities to Richard Smith.

Courtesy of Richard J. Smith from Noah's photo album

of him while working, hunting or fishing, remembering his wisdom and great sense of humor."

Like Noah, Smith felt he had been taken advantage of at times and was not completely trusting. "I live in my small world, and I'm careful with whom I share my thoughts and possessions," said Richard.

I knew this wasn't a time for many words. I had heard Smith was holding some Rondeau artifacts, but until he had made up his mind about me, I was not going to bring the subject up. I was going try to emulate Madeline Dodge's description of Noah as a "gentleman of the first order" who could "hold his own with anyone—king, queen, or president." I would wait politely and hope fervently.

Later in the day Richard invited me back to the River Road cabin he called Handsome Hill. "I want to show you Noah's guns, albums, journals, and scrapbooks," he explained. Handsome Hill was named after the rivertop hill Noah once lived on that overlooked Cold River.

Later on, over a dinner of Big Macs, we fell into a comfortable silence from time to time and I knew I was no longer on audition. Richard had found me suitable. He said that although he was "not inclined to mix with people," he had immediately liked me. I was proud that he felt he could share memories he had sheltered for many years. "Come up and stay with me whenever you get a chance. I think you are honest and sincere. I can tell you want to portray Noah's life accurately. That is most important to me…I don't want Noah to turn into some mythical folk hero."

The door was now open, the barrier broken by Smith's invitation to come to Lake Placid and stay with him, an invitation I took him up on as often as I could. For three and a half years Smith and I corresponded—sometimes as often as three times a week.

In a letter shortly after our groundbreaking meetings, Smith wrote about his life with Noah:

> *I am a native Adirondacker; I am thankful I decided to live my entire life in the shadows of the High Peaks of Essex County. There I discovered my greatest joys. The forest is quiet, I have heard some say. True, noise from civilization is not often heard deep in the wild*

but there is no such thing as a "silent woods." Prior to a storm when ominous clouds bring an unnatural stillness, I have witnessed a weakened limb from an aged tree [that was] standing leafless, loosen and plunge earthward. Winds can lazily rustle leaves or send great gusts in a rage. Forest creatures, whether bird, beast or insect, are also going about their travels all hours of the day and night.

I made Duck Hole my woodland home. Downriver lived the hermit, Noah John Rondeau. Noah, or the "Mayor of Cold River" was an extraordinary man and a lifelong friend.

Richard and I met at Handsome Hill and at Singing Pines. We took field trips around the greater Lake Placid area by car and met at Saranac Lake Hospital. We pored over the vast collection of Rondeau memorabilia Smith brought out—poems, hand-tied fishing lures, scrapbooks Noah had filled with articles about himself, correspondence and cards, yearly journals. Smith would shuffle through a pile of papers and say, "Oh, here is this," handing me a draft of a poem Noah had penned on the back of sheets of paper he had recycled, like the poem "Aerobatic Autumn Leaves" or a letter he received from "Friend Oscar" in Las Vegas, or from Dr. C.V. Latimer at 75 Front Street in Deposit, New York. There was a letter about his Social Security application, some correspondence about talks he had arranged to present for various local organizations, recognition patches from when he was made an honorary member of the 46'ers of Troy and the Adirondack Mountain Club, and books of snapshots of him with various people in and out of the mountains.

There were letters from friends who caught Noah up on their lives, and from acquaintances telling him how much they enjoyed listening to his Cold River days remembrances. There were his long guns, which he had used for hunting, and a newer rifle that got him in trouble with the Essex County Department of Social Services. Richard handed me the Remington Automatic .30-.06 rifle Noah had bought early in 1951. "Some people thought he had made a small fortune from his [Sportsmen's] show days and lectures." Welfare seemed indifferent to his plight too. "When he took the job as a substitute Santa Claus at the North Pole in Wilmington they [the welfare

March 6, 1948, Mirror Lake. Mereda and Carol Ann Barnes. Noah enjoyed an abundance of friends of all ages. His home in Wilmington made him more accessible to a variety of visitors. *Courtesy of Richard J. Smith from Noah's photo album*

department in Elizabethtown] made him pay back the value of the rifle." In the division's mind, if Rondeau had enough money to buy a new rifle, then he had been awarded too much welfare. "Noah was put out. He claimed they made him 'pay double for the rifle.'"

Smith had been using one of Noah's personal articles himself. He often felt unsteady after he received blood transfusions for his illness, and used Noah's old wooden cane to steady himself. From time to time he would say, "I would give my eye teeth to return once more to Cold River," but in his heart he knew his faltering health would never allow such a strenuous trip.

Even so, I wanted him to believe he would revisit his beloved Chubb River. "I want you to hold on to the goal that you will paddle the Chubb one last time," I told him, promising "I'll help you make the paddle when you feel you are strong enough."

While he never did feel he was equal to another trip, we enjoyed reminiscing about the one day we had spent together on the river. Together we somehow harmonized, I adjusting to his tune as he did to mine. My talents were minor, his major, but our lives together revealed new chords, new and unexpected figures in our lifetime duet.

Bette O'Hern negotiating through a wet section of trail. Richard realized his physical condition made it impossible to attempt a return to his old stomping grounds.
Photograph by William J. O'Hern

Chapter 13

Snippets of Past Wilderness Years

FEBRUARY 28, 1993, marked Richard Smith's 74th birthday. To prop up the year (and his mental health) I told him we should plan on making a trip by horseback or wagon back to his Duck Hole wilds. Cold River Ranch in Coreys was operating at the time. The wrangler gave me a price and said he would definitely get Richard in. Everything depended on Rich's stamina come autumn. There he could once again lay his eyes on sweet favorite sights and I could photograph him in the headwaters of the Cold River. He hadn't been back to the river since the fall of 1967, the year Noah died.

Richard liked the idea. Perhaps deep down, he knew he'd never do it, although he never told me so. For months he enthusiastically talked of our planned adventure. His words were as energized as Chris Latimer's were in 2007 when he learned that Bette's and my bushwhacking plans included skirting Barking Buck Swamp to see if any pieces of his family's Camp Seward remained.

"Tell me what you find. Take plenty of digital pictures," Chris urged. "Boy, I'd love to go back there with you. Maybe I can talk my wife and son into backpacking with me next year. I look at Dad's scrapbook and dream about Grandpa and his days back in there. Don guided us in back to the site in 1963. I was twelve years old then. Just to see a portion of the building still standing excited me. I doubt anything exists today, but I'm curious."

By May 1993, Richard's once-long letters dropped away. His frequent hospitalizations were for longer periods and once home he was very weak and unstable. I had begun to organize some of his "threads on the loom of time" remembrances from my notes and his letters. I planned to use them as springboards. My thinking was that I'd read them to Richard as we rode to the river on our planned trip. The words in combination with long-familiar sights might revive other memories I could capture on tape.

Unfortunately, time didn't advance Richard the days to follow through on our plan. Richard made that clear to me in a July correspondence: "...Jay, my dear friend. I hate to disappoint you. If I was one year younger, you would have to run to catch up with me. As it is, Father Time has slowed me down. The enthusiasm is with me still; all that's lacking is the physical will...Now, I'll end my scribble as the old washerwoman said and hang my 'close' on this line." I understood the intended meaning: Richard's health had worsened.

It was not a letter I wanted to read. I still wanted more of Rich! And I don't blame myself for feeling that way. The man had something indefinable, something that made me crave more, but after Richard's July 11 letter, he became silent.

Richard said that toward the end of his own life, Noah had told him, "Quack, there isn't anybody in the world I'd rather have alongside me on a Cold River bear hunt with a rifle in his hand than you." Smith said it was shared as though it was nothing out of the ordinary at all, but to him it meant everything. Noah was one of the few people Smith could trust implicitly. They had some great times together, and they also had some serious moments when Noah would open up and be uncharacteristically revealing. He gave Richard his hand-carved cane during one of those moments.

Through Smith's stories of being lost in blizzards, fishing Black Hole, rafting on Cold River and across the quiet surface of Boiling Pond, tramping through Ouluska Pass, and other personal details, Noah's image emerged, a clearly delightful man. He was actually one of the rarest characters Smith ever knew, a down-to-earth grass-roots barber-turned-mayor of his own little city who really loved people and knew how to mix with them. He had a wry sense of humor and was intensely independent, much like Smith. Both were marvelous storytellers, and both loved to talk about their Cold River adventures. Noah might have played his celebrity limelight card for his financial benefit, but he was always close to his circle of friends, and they were very fond of him

Richard and C.V. felt privileged that they were around during Noah John's happy times and saw more of that side than they did the other. They never saw Noah take more than the deer meat and fish he needed, nor did they ever see him overindulge on more than a limit of trout or on Doc Latimer Sr.'s original alcoholic concoction, the Cold River Sling. Noah would have found it amusing that he has been immortalized and is now considered a legend in the Adirondacks. He was just a regular ole boy raised in the North Country, as down to earth as dirt. But he had that awesome personality. "We'll never seen another like him," Richard and C.V. both shared, and I agree. They grieved when "Old Whiskers" died. The Adirondack Mountains lost a great champion.

I love to remember the trip Richard and I had planned to take. I like to recall it all, even though it never came about: the easy access by hoof, the old familiar sights that had changed since Richard's backpack in '67, hiring

1945. Doc Latimer Sr. at Camp Seward. Try as they may, Bette and Jay never saw the remains of Camp Seward until the fall of 2010, following the discovery by Bob Bates and George Dickover. *Courtesy of C.V. Latimer Jr. M.D.*

a wrangler to handle the wagon, pitch a tent and deck it out with comfortable bedding, prepare all the meals and clean up. It would have had all the old wild west charm anyone might expect from a Rocky Mountain outfitter. Sharing the sights and smells of Cold River country with Richard would have been wonderful. I like to think about how we might have acted on the way in and out, riding high and talking and remembering. To borrow another phrase from Richard, "I might not get over it myself. It's a good thing incidents crop up now and then to remind me of my place or I might have had to start buying a larger size hat."

Bette O'Hern at Ward Brook lean-to. Returning to the Cold River Country was a dream Richard Smith savored. *Photograph by William J. O'Hern*

Chapter 14

Cold River's Tug

ONE DAY RICHARD SMITH asked me, "Have you ever been to a place—a building in a particular setting, a forest clearing, a twist in a river, or mountain meadow—and experienced a sense that completely and beyond question, 'That's where I belong'?"

I knew what he was suggesting. The spot did not need to be anything dazzling. It might even have been only a quick look from a car window. It could be a place you knew you'd never lay eyes on again, or a vision of a place that had once been part of your life. What is important is the gripping impression it makes on the heart and mind because you feel a part of yourself is actually there. Call it a spiritual ownership. The spot is special to your secret life. Whether you are there or not, *it is yours* forever.

That's the way Smith felt about Rondeau's camp at Cold River the first time he saw it in 1934, and that's the way he continued to feel about it long after Rondeau's passing and until his own death.

I feel a similar tug for Singing Pines. Each time I climb Whiteface and Esther mountains I make it a point to drive by the corner setting. Nothing looks the same since Smith sold it. New owners have changed the property. Yet I still see it as Noah's last home—the way I saw it years ago when Richard and I spent many hours walking the property and lounging there as he told me about his life with Noah.

After Noah's death in 1967, when Smith wanted to feel closer to his old friend, he would drive up to the small piece of woodland bounded by roads that lead to Wilmington, Upper Jay, and Lake Placid. The autumn day we hung out at the camp, I recall him saying, "I wanted to reminisce a bit, and what better place to do it in? You could also say I had a longing for my old wilderness days."

He was referring to the years when he and Noah had been the only two woodsmen living alone in their tiny cabins in the remote backcountry. It's true they were exposed to any one of a number of misfortunes— lopping off a foot with a double bitted axe, breaking a leg, getting frostbite, developing an illness, or even accidentally burning their cabins down around them. These were inherent risks neither was troubled about, for they each had a heart that wouldn't settle for whatever security civilization offered.

Besides, they wanted the company of the animals and the rocks, the trees and the water. The wilds offered a sense of freedom they could find nowhere else. As Smith, the younger of the duo, put it, "Noah and I often thought if The Maker had given us only one cast upon the water of life (so to speak) that we would have wanted our line to splash into an Adirondack trout pool. Anywhere else would have been less meaningful, so you can see the mountains were a great help to me and Noah for many years."

Smith spoke wistfully of the life-long bond the two men had with the Adirondack High Peaks. Smith went back to Cold River in 1967, after Noah's death. He said he "...just emptied the refrigerator and screened off the chimney, tossed what foodstuff there was in the cupboard into my pack basket, asked the neighbor to look after Joe Dobbin [his horse], piled the camping gear into the pick-up truck, closed the door, and headed for the trailhead."

Smith continued. "Two years earlier, I tried talking Noah into going back to revisit the old hermitage with me. But each time I brought the outing up he was very matter-of-fact, telling me 'If I was only a year younger you'd have to run to catch up with me. I always thought I'd go back to fish Cold River in June one last time, but as it stands now you'll have to go back for both of us.'"

He said he thought the whole time about Noah's last wilderness ramble from the place he had called home for so many years. He knew how much Noah must have longed to return to his Cold River retreat, especially in the first few years of the 1950s. Now, as Noah had often suggested, Richard was doing it for him. He purposely duplicated the final route he had taken as he tagged after Noah on the day he helped move Rondeau's last personal effects. The only difference was that he hiked the entire distance.

Noah and Richard Smith, May 17, 1939. "I'd leave this minute [to Cold River] if my butt could leave this chair and my feet could find my boots." Cold River memories burned strong in Richard's heart and mind. *Photograph by Phil McCalvin. Courtesy of Helen McCalvin Sawatzki*

Ironically, in that same summer of 1967, seventeen years after the Big Blow, I made my own random scoot in quest of Rondeau's Lost Pond, located in the South Gap beyond Ouluska Pass Brook, and to search for other familiar hermit stompin' grounds. I didn't find the pond right off. It took ten hours of hiking and bushwhacking. In some places, in fact in most of the area, small balsams and spruces had grown up through the old 1950 blowdown. These were thickly spaced, about six feet high. In places I had to go through using the breaststroke!

It would be twelve years before I would meet Richard Smith, and it's unlikely that we were even in the woods at the same time, but during that summer we both struggled through the overgrown old blowdown, inhaled the fresh balsam air, and thought about the same person—Noah John Rondeau. Richard was missing his old friend, the one whose feelings about all things wild and free matched his own so well. It is no stretch at all for me to know how Richard felt when Noah's life ended.

My last trip from Smith's home back to my own is forever locked in my memory. My Easter vacation was drawing to a close. Richard had been staying for longer periods of time in the hospital. "Come up anytime you find the urge, the time, the means. I don't imagine I will be far away from Handsome Hill for some time, unless to see my doctor, go to see the expert from Albany or have a short outing or drive with my neighbor Gary," he said. "Certainly, you will be welcome as the song birds and flowers of spring."

I talked about his deteriorating health with Bette that night. Gary told me that the next three months were very hard on Rich, and I was glad I had visited him. I stayed in touch with him after that last visit through letters since he had never had a telephone. In his infrequent letters, he said he had made up his mind he was going to go back to Cold River. He also enjoyed telling me further details about Noah and Singing Pines. For example:

> *The inside of Singing Pines does not look the same…[as when Bette and I saw it.] When Noah was living there it had three rooms with doors between the two end rooms. Noah kept his treasures and lived only in the middle room, hardly larger than his Town Hall in area with the idea that the small room was easier to heat with a box stove, which he could also cook on. Nothing modern for an old hermit to change his way of life at that stage. I just let him do as he wished with no other stipulation but to use the building like it was his own, and he was happy there.*

At the end of May, Rich sent me a "Hooty-Hoot." That was his expression for mail. Actually the turn of phrase originated as a welcome greeting that Noah and he would holler back and forth as Smith approached the hermitage. Richard explained:

> *As you can perhaps imagine, anyone living or working alone has a natural tendency to talk to themselves when they get lonely. Noah did that a lot and for good reason. So, whenever I approached the hermitage—I was usually coming from the Duck Hole—I would call out loud, 'Who. Who. Who' or 'Quack, Quack, Quack.' I used*

to kid him it was because I wanted to warn him I was coming into camp so I didn't catch him talking to himself.

Within his May 31st letter, I read a line that surprised me. "I got a great deal on the selling of Singing Pines..." He said he had made up his mind to sell the treasured place because he saw the handwriting on the wall. "My weight seems to have dropped overnight from 174 pounds to 114. Bone cancer at work...thus the constant transfusions since February 3rd. It means longer hospital stays...but has to be done to deaden the pain in the large body bones...Pain killers seem to keep...tolerable control."

In his letter, my friend tried to keep an upbeat voice. He laughed and said, "I'll be a monkey's uncle if that card you and Bette sent didn't pull on the old heart strings—the one with the fish basket full of pansies. One of my first trips to the hermitage Noah had an old basket full of pansies on a stump in back of the Hall of Records hut." He closed with, "So back to bed for a short nap and to let pills work in the meantime."

The last time I *spoke* to Richard was to say hello after his death. His final wish to return to Cold River during the October deer-hunting season had been arranged. His ashes were laid to rest near Rondeau's favorite "handsome lookout" on Cold River hilltop.

Chapter 15

Notes to the Past

SINCE COLD RIVER was so much a part of Richard and C.V.'s life, before Bette and I headed into the territory, I wanted to give her some "homework" to do. I gave her my notes for the jettisoned 1993 Cold River trip. I felt reading snippets of Smith's and Latimer's wilderness years would give her a sense of the world they had known. She agreed that having a sense of historical perspective would heighten her awareness and understanding of the personal histories that permeate the wild region.

Those notes appear below.

> *During the 1940s I witnessed an increased volume of hiker traffic. It seemed to grow by leaps and bounds following the end of World War II. Noah liked his space, but he always had his welcome mat out. He even made signs where the dogtrot leading to his hermitage branched off from the public trail. He built a pole arch over each end of the u-shaped footpath so no one would miss it. The south entrance was called The Garage; the northern entrance was The Gate to the City. After a few years the public trail which had bypassed the hermitage was almost unused because most hikers coming up or down Cold River on the Northville-Placid Trail stopped at the hermitage. "Everyone was welcome," Noah told me, "except game protectors. The officers zealous enough to walk fifteen miles and more to try to catch a wise old hermit breaking the laws of the State of New York should get a feather for their Big Hats." Noah was forever joking like that.*

Noah willed some of his yearly diaries to Smith, and Rondeau's 1944 diary was not one Richard made available to Noah's biographer, De Sormo. These notes are built from that diary.

Smith noted and often repeated himself:

> *I can still picture Noah snuggled under his bearskin quilt as he lay on a spongy insulating base of dried sweet grass and balsam tips. His bunk was at the rear of the Town Hall cabin. Beside him, a candle burned, providing illumination to read and write by. Beside him was his yearly diary and a pile of unlined paper several inches thick. Across the top sheet he had written, "I Write a Book.* Recollections of 60 Years.*" He'd originally had "53 Years" but that was lined out. Evidently he'd been at the project a good long time. I've been allowed to pick up the stack written a decade earlier and thumb through the sheets by the light of the Town Hall candle. I wasn't there at the time he wrote his first-hand reports.*

Noah draped his wigwams and roofed the huts with cast off canvas tents he scavenged from a dump site when the Civilian Conservation Corps side camp completed work on the Ward Brook fire control road and Duck Hole dam and moved out. *Photo by Ed Hudowalski. Courtesy of Grace Hudowalski*

De Sormo liked them enough to lead his biography of the hermit with the collection of personal stories.

I felt that De Sormo didn't spend the time to dig deep enough into Rondeau's life. I would have liked to have seen a more in-depth biography. If he had delved beneath Rondeau's reserved composure he would have learned a great deal more about why he had a guardedness, would have been able to offer examples of his woodsman philosophy, and in general would have learned a wealth of Rondeau information from his friends who stayed at the hermitage.

Once I read to Richard Louise Dickinson Rich's statement that "a lack of civilization was not half so hard to cope with as a civilization which has broken down, leaving you with nothing to take its place." He said that viewpoint helped influence him to seek a life in the mountains at the close of the Great Depression. In the same way, twenty years earlier, in 1913, Noah had lost faith in civilization. It was his opinion that his life was rather dull and unrewarding. He didn't see himself fitting into society because of his lack of an adequate education.

When I asked Richard to describe what living at the hermitage with Noah was like, he replied:

We often shared the camp, but it was perfectly normal for Noah and me to have a lull in conversation for days; the only words we spoke were of necessity. If you didn't know him well, you might think he was angry or batty; sometimes Noah simply talked himself out. I've since come to realize that if you like someone, you don't have to always make conversation. This was certainly true of Noah.

Smith's reaction when I asked what more he might know about Rondeau's attempt to write his autobiography was to pull out Noah's metal box. In it was the hermit's 1944 diary. He flipped to March 26 and handed it to me before saying, "I remember coming into camp that day. Noah told me he hadn't seen a single soul in months. It was the day he began writing his recollections that he jokingly called '53 Years after 53 Years.'"

I skimmed the journal. Sure enough, it shows Rondeau wrote on a daily basis. In the last twenty days the journal documents that he'd written the following chapters: "Dewyer House," "Transition 1889–1890," "Jackson Hill," "Home Pets," "Billy Peckhum's Shot Gun," "New Year Day in 1890," "Cats and Pussy Willows," "Streamlined Snow," "Cow Bell Carols," "Gram's Quiz," "Pondering on a Wedding Cake," and "Bixby's Boot Black."

The diary entries also confirm that more chapters were added as the year continued. While Smith was in camp he was witness, during their "quiet times," to the early stages of two poems Rondeau began to pen. They were titled "Autumn Leaves" and "Allen's Bear Lies."

"The poems came from Rondeau's life," Smith said. He didn't think they would be considered good poetry, but "they amused Noah. They collected a whole store of catch words, most of which would probably mean nothing outside of Noah's experience."

Those poems, diaries and other Rondeau memorabilia formed the basis for my own manuscript that remembers Noah.

Here are several firsts the 1944 diary recorded beyond "Quack's arrival from Lake Placid," written on March 26.

April 10, 1944 Monday Cold River City
...The Christmas tree tumbled the snow bank.
First noticeable raise of the River.

April 19, 1944 Wednesday
...Perfect Sun Shine...First Robins. 24 years ago,
Earl A. Vosburg stold [sic] a Musk Rat.

April 20, 1944 Thursday
...A junco arrive to celebrate Hitler's 55th.
April 23, 1944 Sunday
...Ice well worked out of (Cold River) Floe.
I write verses "Allen's Bear Lies."

If you hiked in to Cold River Hill most any time during a warm summer afternoon, you'd be most likely to find Noah resting contently, puffing on his pipe and checking his fishing gear as a glorious sun filtered through a mixed green canopy of evergreens and softwoods. *Photograph by E.A. Harnes. From the library of John M. Harnes*

Smith had seen and read Rondeau's manuscripts. He had lived in the Town Hall cabin with Noah. Having known the hermit on a close personal basis, he was definitely a reliable source when he stated, "Noah wrote the best story of his life there, sitting at a table that had seen better days, scratching out in longhand with a steel-tipped pen that needed to be dipped into a bottle of ink every so often." Noah, having escaped the rat race to live a lifetime in the woods, learned to recognize his own restrictions and he had even pushed the limits of most men's transgressions.

It's true the black-bearded hermit lived in a country-bumpkin shack. He tossed his wash water out the front door. He had no choice but to fish and hunt for meat if he wanted a decent meal. Otherwise, he'd have to settle for a starvation diet of a handful of cornmeal gruel. There was no daily newspaper or telephone link to the Outside. But none of this put Noah out. I doubt that he felt hopelessly handicapped because he had to take summer baths in rainstorms or winter ones from a heated kettle, or because he read by candle and kerosene light, and slept in a box of hay and sweet-smelling boughs, covered from winter's frigid breath with a bearskin quilt. There are other matters that comprise one's prosperity besides a sleeping system, a balanced diet, natty clothing and communication with the world. There are the paddles up the river to enjoy its daytime beauty and the sun's glow on the water before it sets behind Seward Mountain, the delicious speckled trout just caught in Cold River, the smell of fresh-cut grass, the fragrance of wild flowers that permeates the mountain air. Sunlight. Tall trees. Vast woods. The quiet. The peace of dusk. The lack of nervous tension.

Clearly, Noah had found a most pleasing life in Cold River country. For 37 years he had lived freely in a territory where no one else resided full-time. To all who knew him, he was the old dog who had learned all the tricks. No wonder his traveling exhibit in the outside world was so popular.

Section IV

Way Back in the Hermit's Territory

Chapter 16

Cold River Partners

THAT WAS ABOUT IT FOR RONDEAU'S duration in the wilds. His long existence as a hermit was the very thing that jet-propelled him into an instantaneous attraction in 1947 at New York City's Sportsmen's Show.

However, eighty-eight years before Bette's and my Cold River adventure (twenty-eight years before Rondeau resided full-time in the Dam Camp), two other interesting woodsmen had called the Cold River country their temporary mountain home.

Before Bette and I set our boots down on the narrow footpath that evaporated into the Adirondack forest from the Seward Mountain trailhead, I had acquainted her with the almost 100-year-old collection of photos Inez Wood Buis had given me—prints her father, Richard (Dick) Wood, had taken during his Adirondack trapping days in the early part of the 20th century. Wood's pictures were predominantly of the cold and desolate mountainous country he had wandered through. Wood lived in Tennessee, but came to the Adirondacks in 1919 where, over thousands of years, the Cold River had eaten through the mountains and formed a narrow valley. This section, "Cold River Fur Prospectors," traces many of the circuits Noah, Wood and his partner trekked—sections Rondeau claimed as his territory and locations Bette and I explored on our backpack trip.

Richard "Dick" Wood was a young, talented professional photographer and outdoor/nature writer. Wood's partner was Elric J. Dailey, a New York state guide, a noted professional trapper and writer whose articles appeared in sporting magazines.

By 1919, the Cold River Valley was seeing fewer and fewer people. The Santa Clara timber operations were drawing to a close. The lumber company's tote roads snaked through the woods throughout the surrounding area. Some roadways trailed to abandoned logging shanties, and one main haul road passed over Big Dam—reminders that this was one of many Adirondack locations in the entire Forest Preserve where lumbermen were once active. Luckily for Dick Wood and Noah, they were the right kind of people for these remote trapping grounds. In the teens and '20s, trappers and determined anglers and a few deer and black bear hunters from the cities ventured into the mountains, and they were invariably thrilled at what they found: Perfectly habitable shelters and a variety of discarded paraphernalia were common. Long Lake trappers ran lines in from the south, but didn't establish long trap lines as far as Big Dam. Other trappers entered from the north—Tupper Lake, Coreys, Lake Placid. Dick Wood described it as a trapper's paradise, "A veritable wilderness in the backyard of a civilized country."

Because of my desire to learn about Wood's Cold River history and his connection with Noah, I was grateful that Inez Buis had saved a great deal of information regarding her father, Dick Wood.

Wood documented his introduction to the mountain country. "This Cold River basin was new to me, but I had studied the topographic maps until I had more of it in mind than one pair of legs would cover [from my Duck Hole camp at the headwaters of the Cold River in a general western course toward the Raquette River]."

> *This Cold River country was cracked up to me by a guide who had been in there [as a river driver] twenty years previously. [Bill Randall and I met him when we were trout fishing on the Boreas River.] I expected an old cut-over country, hard to travel through, and perhaps with no way in after the water freeze-up. And although this Cold River country was less than a hundred miles away [from the Boreas River the old man claimed] it was a veritable wilderness in the backyard of a civilized country, as it were. I could find no one else among the many trappers, guides, hunters and natives of the Boreas River country who had been to Cold River since the lumbering days of twenty years in the rear. Apparently the country had gone back to its original wild state, so…the*

breed guide…insinuated and I was inclined to assume, [the] vast region [saw] no trappers and [had] many fur-bearers. A land of more or less mystery, far back from human habitation, seemed an ideal place to me.

The story that follows tells of the trapping entrepreneurship of partners Wood and Dailey.

One afternoon in the late fall of 1919, two men crossed the railroad tracks in Lake Placid and started down the faint "government trail," fighting their heavy pack baskets and the black muck of an almost-untracked bog.

The partners' expedition to the wilds of the high Adirondacks was their first official trip into unknown fur country, as well as a first glimpse into their future business partnership. The men would return to face fearsome blizzards,

Natural Dam, identified as the Nymph's Bathtub in the 1920s. The sky had begun to lighten. The clouds were leaving. The air had a slight chill and the water level in the river was low. Before Jay could pull the camera from the backpack, Bette had begun to hop around this perfectly idyllic rest stop. *Photograph by William J. O'Hern*

snow as deep as ten feet, and dead-calm temperatures that at times registered fifty below zero.

★ ★ ★

The men met a number of years earlier, when Wood was trapping in Dailey's home territory, St. Lawrence County. Encroaching settlement had left both men feeling restless.

Testy and idiosyncratic Dailey took substantial pride in snorting that he'd never "work for another man" nor "live in any damn town." He seemed destined for the title "Dean of America's trappers." He was an inventive bait-maker. His green-shingled Trapper Supply House in Flackville, several miles south of Ogdensburg, N.Y., was celebrated for producing the world's largest supply of vocational cologne, trapping lure, and animal urine. His one-man operation produced three to four million bottles a year, at a dollar or more per bottle.

From today's perspective, it might seem that Dailey's Trapper Supply House attracted an odd breed of individuals. Its patrons did not gag at the lively odor of animal organs and capped jars of scent sacs, kept for eventual compounding into glandular mixes for trapping lures. They probably found the aromas clean and natural, a far sight better than the stench of a modern chemical or pulp mill.

By 1919, at the age of twenty-seven, Dailey had revolutionized the trapping industry with what he marketed during the pre-World War I days as a breakthrough "Triple-Call" Animal Gland Lure, made from animal glands and secretions. The scented decoy appealed to an animal's chemistry, drawing it closer to the steel trap waiting nearby. Dailey began to bottle the stuff and sell it to other trappers on both sides of the Atlantic Ocean. As a result, a trapper could end the season with more catches.

That winter the young inventor-trapper declared not only that his trapping concoction was a success, but that he had mixed another potion that had saved a human life. A drunken lumberjack, near death from an overdose of moonshine, had stumbled into a lumber camp shanty way up in Ouluska Pass. Rummaging through his canvas first-aid bag, Dailey scanned the little

Winter 1922. "Long-legged camp fixture with decided culinary gifts" at No. 1 Camp at the head of the Cold River Flow." The time was late winter; the place, the heart of the Adirondacks, as far back as it was possible to get in the woods. And late winter in a deep snow country is a caution to trappers.

Self-portrait by Richard K. Wood. Courtesy of Inez Wood Buis

Elric John "E.J." Dailey, Dean of American trappers. His experience of nearly 70 years involved pursuing fur pockets deep in the Adirondack wilderness. He introduced the famous dirt-hole set for foxes, was a prolific writer of outdoor articles and books, owned a trapper-supply house and edited *Fur-Fish-Game* magazine's question and answer department for many years. "One of, if not the foremost, experienced fur trappers of all time."—Rev. Roy C. Johnson.

Photograph by Richard K. Wood. Courtesy of Inez Wood Buis

paper packages of medicine a doctor had given him. With a chuckle, Dailey explained that the doctor had "...noted dosages, not purposes, on the envelopes. It looked like life or death, so I put the prescribed dosages of each into a tin cup and made it into a tea. That lumberjack couldn't keep his pants up for three days. But he lived."

Dick Wood was managing editor of *Fur News*, a field tester for the Triumph Trap Company, and a competent photographer. He longed for the wild and colorful life of the bearded trappers of old who lived on intelligence, industry, and innovation. Years earlier, growing up in Tennessee, he had read the Reverend Samuel Parker's *Journal*. Parker had written about beaver trapping and the lives of 200 American Fur Company trappers. The 1837 history portrayed trapping as the typical way to make a living in those days, and Wood was determined to carry it well into the 20th century.

A talented but frugal businessman, Wood preferred to carry his corporate assets on his back in a woven black ash 'briefcase.' To him, gracious living was a pack basket full of steel traps, salt pork, and coffee. The other necessities could be found in the woods: a lean-to built of inch-thick saplings, a bed of balsam boughs, and red cedar and birch for heat against the long cold nights. His music was the telltale clink of a trap chain set off by a fox, pine marten or fisher. Their pelts would be fashioned into mufflers, scarves and neckpieces that looked as luxurious and expensive as if made from the Romanoffs' Crown Sables.

Having sought Dailey out to discuss a common interest in trapping marten, fisher, otter, fox, mink and bobcats, Wood was taken with the success of Dailey's Triple-Call on a trap line that wormed its way over Seymour Mountain. Stirred by 'wilderness fever' and a passion for running long fur lines in remote territory during every hardship Mother Nature could dish out, Wood and Dailey made plans to join ranks and trap in the Adirondacks. For a number of deer hunting and trapping seasons, they returned to the Sawtooth-Seward-Santanoni ranges. When the weather permitted, they trapped almost continuously, sleeping and resting as little as possible and relying on cooperation and teamwork.

The everyday scenes of their lives repeated themselves as the winter days wore by: waking to a cold wind that beat hard against the side walls of their cabin at Duck Hole, sitting in the predawn yellow light of a winking wick burning in a tin can filled with animal fat, tightening the harnesses of their rawhide-laced snowshoes to once again move over the snow at first light to follow the fur trail.

Their staples were dried fruits, rice, beans, dried vegetables, sugar, and flour. Sourdough batter was held in a pail in a warm spot behind the wood stove. Bread or biscuits could be made with the addition of flour. In their moments of greatest need, long strings of jerked venison satisfied their gnawing hunger.

Time and time again, they rescued themselves from cutting winds and plummeting temperatures by quickly constructing temporary encampments from materials they could find in the woods—including plenty of snow. These shelters might not have been as snug and warm as their Duck

Winter 1921. Dick Wood and E.J. Dailey pulling supplies into Headquarters Camp at the end of the Cold River Trail. Weeks later Wood wrote: Our "larder now having diminished to the usual trapper's stock of fresh meat, tea, sourdough bread and more meat, I could see a faraway look in [my] partner's eyes, a look of green fields and sociable friends in the lowland country." *Photograph by Richard K. Wood. Courtesy of Inez Wood Buis*

Hole headquarters, but they were at least insulated by the great piles of snow that provided an emergency barrier to the elements.

A French writer had provoked the men's first argument shortly after they disembarked at the train platform. When Dailey, the Adirondack guide, saw his partner from the southland begin to pack a set of four books into some precious space on the toboggan, he blazed, "That crap won't save a life nor catch a fur!" His colleague snapped, "Balzac's a master to be studied. It'll be that or nothing here. I love to read." To the guide's disgust, Wood refused to leave the books behind.

Wood invented names when he chose not to divulge actual identities. It deflected possible problems; "...nobody can get insulted..." he wrote. On one trip they had met and struck up a semi-translatable conversation with a man Wood called "Trapper Louie" in Brown Brother's Grocery and Trading Store while waiting for the train to Lake Placid. Trapper Louie's reports of abandoned river drivers' camps were vague: gestures directing them south, diagrams in the snow, "and shrugs, nods and lumbermen's technicalities by the old French-Canadian who had been with a U.S. lumber company 20 years previous." The men listened and watched carefully to learn where the best trapping grounds were to be found.

Harold Brown told the men Louie's long time camp was far down the Raquette River, but word was he also had a newly constructed trap line shelter with a bark roof and puncheon pole floor somewhere in the surrounding forest in the Calkins Brook country.

Wood and Dailey would tell natives and woodsmen who had been running in the land for decades that the trap lines, deer trails and abandoned lumber camps now went to whomever came along first. Yet they would meet more friends than rivals, and only once did they fire guns in ire. Dailey, exhausted from tracking down a fisher—then valued at $100 and becoming rare—was trying to sleep. Wood was sitting at a table reading Balzac. Angry, Dailey aimed his Colt Woodsman pistol, called "Lights out," and shot out the flame. "I got both of them, Dick," Dailey snickered. "The damned fisher and the damned Frenchman." Dailey had shot a hole in the book Wood was reading as well as the animal he had been tracking. Dick wasn't too stunned to react, despite complete darkness. He aimed his .303 rifle in the direction of the log wall above Dailey's bunk and fired hopefully above his head. Laughing, he shouted, "We both needed it, E. J. You shot Balzac. I shot those damned doughnuts you fried in bear grease."

They called themselves "honest trappers," but because it is often the honest trapper who loses his steel traps and furs, they discovered it was sometimes necessary to rely on ancient woodcraft. Substituting deadfalls and snares of various kinds for the steel traps was a reliable way of outwitting the "Sneakums" (trap thieves and fur pirates).

One year the duo hired a motor delivery wagon to set them down at the end of the Averyville Road. With 80-pound Duluth pack sacks crammed to the brim, the partners hit the trail. Mountain men at heart, the duo found the trail's balsam-laden air welcoming. About eight miles into the trip, Wood reported to Dailey that they were approaching an area of local legend. "A few years previously," Wood said he had learned from a local logger that "a native had become lost and wandered until he nearly starved. Only the timely arrival of a searching party saved his life. He was, when found, in rags, face scratched, body bruised, starved and on the point of committing suicide with a pistol he carried. All in a land of plenty for the person who knows woodcraft sufficiently to wrest a living from woods and waters."

Their first evening's camp was on a ridge overlooking Moose Pond. The rugged Sawtooth Range was their wilderness backdrop. They had reached as far into the interior as the headwaters of the corkscrewing upper Chubb River. Miles beyond—another day's trail—lay Duck Hole, an eventual destination where they anticipated good deer hunting and trapping.

In those days there was not much of a trail after leaving Moose Pond. Few explorers ventured toward Preston Ponds from that direction. One exception was Noah John Rondeau. During his barbering days, his standard pathway took him along Moose Pond outlet, a major tributary of the Cold River. From time to time in the company of George Smith (Richard Smith's father), he had been making his way into the country since 1909. Young and cocksure, his trial runs into the woods taught him the lay of the land, with its string of time-worn tote roads, rotten log corduroy over wet or mucky areas and the tangles of raspberry vines that grew up from the muck between the decaying log pathways. Very often this corduroy was choked

Due to rain [in January] all the snow trails "were now entirely obliterated and soft snow" caused trappers to wade through. "Between [this rainy spell] I crossed the river in front of the [Big Dam] camp, noting that an otter had during the night passed under the old dam, and set some weasel traps; also took a picture of the cabin so openly posed against the back-ground and snow-covered mountains. The Chief [E.J.] gladly escaped the confines of the cabin to rustle some fresh game, bringing a couple of snowshoe rabbits for a change in the meat diet." —Dick Wood.

Photograph by Richard K. Wood. Courtesy of Inez Wood Buis

A rest break, "having spent a half day's job having made numerous fox sets, and as many for mink," Wood said that almost every wilderness trapper he met, "was scared of darkness catching them in the woods... They timed their lines to allow ample time to get back to the home camp before dark." Wood, Dailey and Rondeau were fortunate trappers to have line camps [retired logging company buildings] fitted up for staying overnight. The shelters save a lot of needless back-tracking.

Self-photograph by Richard K. Wood. Courtesy of Inez Wood Buis with brush. The tall weeds exuded heat as intense as a greenhouse's interior, and emitted clouds of stinging yellow jackets that nested in holes between the logs.

Moose Creek outlet was Rondeau's standard route to Cold River from Lake Placid. The drainage wound through a particularly wild section in the mountains. Windfalls cross it everywhere, and its bed is often one mess of rocks of every size.

Once when Smith and Rondeau were camped by a series of pools along the moraine stream bed, George asked Noah if he'd ever "tickled a trout." That was a new one to Noah. But instead of scoffing at his chum or calling him an uninhibited perjurer, he directed Smith to show him. Gently, Smith approached a trout he had named "Albert" in a nearby pool. He very carefully ran his hand near the fish's tail and softly tickled the fanning fins. Albert indicated no alarm. Then very slowly he continued the tickling along Albert's scaly side and orange belly. Albert kind of enjoyed it! The trout turned over on his side, as though he were hypnotized. If he had lids he probably would have closed his eyes. Smith was not a bit dazed at the fish's behavior as he continued to gradually work his pleasing fingers up along Albert's side until he stuck a finger into Albert's gill and raised him from the water. Smith's lie was absolved. "Well," Noah remarked in amazement, "if anybody else had told me that they could do such a trick I would not have believed them." Seeing that the antic was a complete success, George suggested they release Albert to swim about wildly with his neighbors instead of placing him on a platter. The exhibition was reward enough.

★ ★ ★

Elric Jack Dailey and Richard K. Wood would become the first professional outdoor writers and photographers to experience the Cold River country: the immensity of its clear mountain air, the untracked bogs, the wide variety of its wildlife, the harsh rigors of its winters.

They would become the first nationally-known professional writer/trapper team to follow the winding roads of the Adirondack foothills in a flivver known as 'Old Asthma.' (Dailey traded the pelts of five blue-brown fishers that had been "trapped at the prime hour," just before the worst frost, for the new Model-T car.)

The partners were among the first to ascend the steep slopes of the Sawtooth Peaks to lay trap lines, the first to report in popular periodicals of good trapping in the Adirondack Mountains, "where trappers are not plentiful." Their fame resulted largely from magazine articles and their books, *The Trapper's Partner*, *Traplines and Trails* and *Trapping as a Profession*. There were also years of question-and-answer columns that Dailey edited for *Fur-Fish-Game* magazine.

If you could picture yourself on a wintry night in the woods with a fireside complement of mountain trappers and guides, adventurers, a friendly hermit, lumberjacks and others who love the sporting life and woods and waters—you would be part of the setting of the vast body of writing the men put down in *Fur News and Outdoor World*, *Sporting Digest*, *Sea and River Fishing*, and other out-of-print (and highly sought-after) magazines.

As with today's athletes, endorsement had a hand in moving Wood and Dailey along the path to celebrity. For "The Trail of '57," the men were photographed standing beside a wooden toboggan that had been stacked high with a variety of canned foods, compliments of the Heinz ("57 Varieties") Company. The partners not only ate well and at little expense that winter, but reaped rewards from the product endorsement long after the Raquette River was rushing with the spring thaw.

Wood and Dailey were both fastidious note takers, entering daily observations in their journals which became the basis of hundreds of stories, most cataloged under the headings "Camping," "Hunting," "Fishing," "Trapping," and "Conservation," in Dorothy A. Plum's *Adirondack Bibliography*. The public's growing passion for their outdoor stories helped fuel their creativity. Over the years, Dailey and Wood polished their writing skills so that their stories glimmered with the excitement of their adventures.

Listen to Dick Wood's love for any place wild:

> *The time was late winter, the place the heart of the Adirondacks, as far back as it is possible to get in the woods. And late winter in a deep snow country is a caution to trappers..."*

"A hard pull on the Cold River Trail, with one big loop around Mountain Pond and another around a mountain peak for martin." —Dick Wood. *Self-photograph by Richard K. Wood. Courtesy of Inez Wood Buis*

The words hold the charm of classic Adirondack Mountain scenes, of the kind of pictures he snapped in the wilds of the Cold River country. Wood's and Dailey's enlightening tales convey every reader and collector, camper, backpacker, canoeist, and woodcraft enthusiast back in time as they leaf through pages depicting time-honored places and Adirondack figures.

A 1928 Dailey story, "Life in the Trapper's Country," sent me on a reconnaissance bushwhack beyond Coreys, in the Sawtooth Range, just because I wanted to experience the same territory. He wrote, "For many miles no other trapper was operating, and no other even existed. The nearest humans were to be found at the lumber camps north of us...'as the crow flies.' We used a line of deserted cabins down the creek and up in the Seward country, where early in the season we spent the night when making the long lines..."

Wood and Dailey loved the dim roads and deep trails found beyond the settlements in the far-back country, places where they met unique people. Both were amused by a renegade Lake Placid guide's boast. The grizzly woodsman prided himself on being able to put away large quantities of whiskey and, while under the influence, shoot his rifle with dead-eye accuracy. They watched in amazement as his bullet shattered a brier pipe clenched between a trusting fellow's teeth.

Another guide, a yarn-spinning storyteller, could recite lengthy Robert Service poems about life in the Yukon. There was also a mentally-deranged trapper who never talked to anyone except the postmaster, and this only because he sent his furs out for sale. They knew a thieving guide named Wood (no relation to Dick) and his two sons. The guide boasted to city sportsmen that if he wanted to catch fish, "I can catch 'em just as well where they ain't as where they be." This meant he wouldn't hesitate to poach on private preserves.

And then there was the man many Adirondack devotees call "a treasure." Dailey and Wood knew of Noah John Rondeau. He was not yet known as the Cold River hermit. Every child of Northern New York who read stories of mountain adventure knew the names of E. J. Dailey, Dick Wood, and Noah John Rondeau, known as "Old Whiskers," or the "Old Man" in the men's stories.

Wood held Rondeau in high regard for his woodcraft skills—and his choice in smoking tobacco! Tucked in a March 1921 article titled "Trail Tested and Right," Wood, managing editor of the magazine *Fur News and Outdoor World*, tells his readers:

> *For many years I was deceived in thinking I smoked the only real tobacco that ever was cured; then one time far back in the Adirondacks I ran out of the weed in any description. For a week I stood it; then I grew weak, or thought I did. I heard of an abandoned, unlocked hunters' camp a few miles away and Pard [partner E.J.] suggested giving the place the once-over for cached tobacco.*

Dailey told Wood the owner had gone out but was a particular acquaintance of his and that "he would explain." An innocent deception. In reality Dailey knew Wood would never have gone snooping had he known the hut was used by the Old Man, but all worked out well. "And that's how I came to try out a box of Edgeworth Cut Pug, which is a tobacco to please the most discriminating pipe smoker." Following his return to the city, Wood shipped to the Coreys post office a carton of Edgeworth with a note to postmistress Catherine Petty to pass it on to the owner of the hut. Wood ended, "I consider I got the best of the deal."

Wood was content with the "fur nest" he had staked out a safe distance from Louie and Rondeau. These were the two trappers who planned on trapping different areas in the Cold River country, Wood knew. The previous year Louie had been in the green bush of the Sawtooth Mountains but abandoned it for better grounds. That allocated E. J. full rein this year, for no one else claimed the territory. Louie's two days of trap line was blazed and set between his cabin and Seward Peak.

Rondeau's territory fanned out from his hut near Peek-a-boo Mountain to Blueberry Pond. According to local legend, Louie once tried to put a stop to Noah when he first moved into the region. Upon finding the traces of a rude camp with a cheap sheet metal stove in what he maintained was HIS province, Old Louie declared to the community of Coreys, "Sacre bleu! Louie will put an ax to who ever built 'is wigwam in my territory."

That had been years ago. Since then the men had met, developed a mutual respect, and stayed out of each other's way.

In his exploration along the Cold River Trail, Wood noted two other abandoned shanties. Those he planned to make into line camps. Both were strategically positioned. Designated No. 1, the first outlying camp was located a short distance off the haul road. Less than a mile's walk southwest

Dick Wood in talking about reaching abandoned Santa Clara Lumber Camp in Ouluska Pass. "That up-hill stalk was one to be remembered. I found the mountainside a great deal rougher than it appeared from a distance. Besides I had not been in the woods long enough to get toughened up to the trail."
Photograph by Richard K. Wood. Courtesy of Inez Wood Buis

was 15 Frog Pond. In the distance, Seymour Mountain rises above Frog Pond. Noah's temporary encampment was further downriver, sited at the mouth of a huge flow created by a high log sluice dam.

Late in E.J.'s life, when one could allow an aging trapper's memory some latitude, he recounted to his friend Jack Anderson his fondest recollections of the vanished era of traveling in the 'Dacks. In Anderson's book, *Goodbye Mountain Man*, E. J. Dailey tells of the senior trapper, Rondeau, who had inhabited Big Dam Camp. "He scraped like a madman on a broken fiddle. He once killed a bear with a homemade longbow and sometimes fired any weapon that was handy at folks who approached the place."

The younger trapper took Noah seriously. They did not make light of the solitary man who used the site seasonally. Dailey writes in his book, *Traplines and Trails*, "Nearly every trapper advises others to keep out of the business. This may be natural, as they do not welcome competition." He also understood and lived by the unwritten code that said one should stay out of another trapper's territory. If Noah Rondeau did not move to Jungle Camp near Peek-a-boo Mountain in the winter, and had he in its place taken over and stayed at Dam Camp instead, Wood never would have designated the Big Dam site as his furthest line camp out along Cold River. (Wood actually referred to Rondeau's leaving for the winter as his "annual vacation."

In Rondeau's later years, he grumbled that Dailey and Wood weren't the slick trappers they made themselves out to be in print. Instead, he claimed the duo's greatest success at fur harvesting was their ability to catch the numerous field mice that scampered willy-nilly in the Dam Camp.

Dailey's and Wood's readers were treated to tales of these and other unusual characters, as well as to vintage outdoor life scenes—traversing the waters, trail hikes into the woods, mountain climbing, angling, hunting and trapping. Because of their writing, I developed an everlasting inquisitiveness about the more distant and wilder Adirondack lands—and a voracious hunger for more knowledge of Adirondack history. Sitting on my steel-runner Flexible Flyer sled, huddled over a homemade cook stove fashioned from a discarded three-pound Maxwell House coffee container, I would warm a can of Campbell's pork and beans, roast a hot dog, and warm an apple as I pretended to be Dick Wood.

Dailey's and Wood's readers were not only treated to tales of the partners' roamings in a mountainous land, where silent nighttime predators stalked at night, but also enjoyed the drama of the natural world around their trap line through the pictures that accompanied their stories. Wood's vintage early-20th-century photographs display the men's battles against wilderness snow and cold. There are scenes of the trappers returning to camp from explorations across the Seward, Santanoni and Sawtooth mountain ranges, where hardship, hunger and danger were commonplace.

Shown in a self-portrait, relaxed in the frozen wilderness, McNaughton Mountain rising in the background, Wood sits on a canvas tarp. His snowshoes lean against a wooden toboggan. His lunch is spread out on the top of a Heinz Tomato Soup crate. On the back of the photograph, Wood wrote: "Since the days of the early fur traders, when beaver pelts were the medium of barter and exchange between trader and trapper, there has been an almost irresistible lure to follow the trail and the trap line."

After enduring profoundly cold temperatures, cabin fever, hunger, injuries, a swig a day of Dr. Jordan's Pain Killer (guaranteed not over 92% alcohol!), and other perils of the trail, Dailey and Wood went on to join the first few of their profession to advocate for strong conservation laws. As New York Governor Lehman's trapper delegate, "Adirondack Jack" Dailey went to Washington, D.C., to speak at an historic First National Wildlife Conference to save the endangered marten and fisher. Perhaps it seems ironic, but the men had the sense to realize, way before their time, that "extinction is forever."

Dailey and Wood shared a simple philosophy: they valued independence and freedom above all. Dailey summed it up in 1971 when, at the age of 81, he was asked if he had any plans to retire. "The way I figure it," he mused, "there's a time to come and a time to go. I enjoy my work and I can trap as I want to...I don't owe anybody a dime and I can do it as I dang well please."

E.J. Dailey's and Dick Wood's stories, articles, technical books, and photos were an invaluable addition to the media of their time, yet there was practical advice for sportsmen, hunters, and trappers, and much of it still holds true today. More importantly, their work preserves an era of

Adirondack history and allows even 21st-century adventurers to step back in time.

Wood's several Cold River trapping seasons satisfied his Cold River fever, which had been set in motion by an old guide. He said the experience in the remote trapping ground in the Adirondacks gave him "valuable first-hand experience." He mined these experiences when he wrote numerous magazine articles with accompanying photographs, and Bette and I used these on our overland river trail. We both found it interesting that the Northville-Placid footpath follows the same route the Santa Clara Lumber Company developed as it meanders in the general course of the river for many miles to the west. While the tote road bridges are gone, there is still evidence of the former lumber camp's locations along and off from the main river drivers' road.

The lumber company's Cold River trail is the same avenue Rondeau had planned to snowshoe over the winter of '47—a planned walk over snow that

A trapper's reward. "Standing on the summit of one of the [Adirondacks'] higher mountains, and viewing the woods for miles around, one can easily believe that a million dollars worth of valuable fur-bearers have their winter-quarters within reach of the eye." —E.J. Dailey. *Photograph by Richard K. Wood. Courtesy of Inez Wood Buis*

instead turned into an unexpected helicopter lift from the frozen surface of Cold River Flow. As biographer De Sormo described it, it was Rondeau's "Air Lift to Fame."

Noah penned this notation over a photographer's picture of him landing:

> *Saranac Air Port—Feb. 12th. 1947. 21 below 0: Noah John Rondeau, Adirondack Hermit arriving from Cold River by Helicopter. Mayor of Saranac Lake and Ranger Orvil Betters bring Greetings.*

It was an experience that caused his budding reputation to blossom and changed his life.

On February 12, 1947 at 8 a.m. a little red helicopter landed on Cold River ice—150 feet from Noah's wigwams. *Courtesy of New York State Department of Environmental Conservation archives*

ADIRONDACK WILDS
Exploring the Haunts of Noah John Rondeau

Section V

Noah
Out and About

Chapter 17

Celebrity-Like Status

FOR SIXTY-THREE-YEAR-OLD Noah John Rondeau, 1947 was a landmark year for four reasons: (1) he took his first helicopter ride; (2) he made his first National Sportsmen's Show appearance at the New York City winter show at Grand Central Palace; (3) he talked to thousands of people about his thirty-five years of life in the wilds of the Adirondack Mountains; and (4) he was kissed by movie actress Arleen Whelan when she took him on a tour of Paramount Studios.

Rondeau attended his first Sportsmen's Show February 15–23, 1947, with his friend, Orvil Betters, state forest ranger. The two had agreed to represent the Conservation Department's Division of Education, which included in its exhibits a replica of Noah's habitation as a means of acquainting New Yorkers with the recreational facilities of the state's vast Forest Preserve. Because of his appearances and exposure in the media, large numbers of curious hikers sought out Rondeau's digs throughout the summer and fall.

The spectators' interest in the elaborate displays put on by the various states, plus the hundreds of booths crowded with rods, reels, tackle, guns, boats and other "impedimenta" of the field and sports had something to attract every visitor, as is evident in the column reporter Don Stillman of the *Tribune* wrote:

> *There was a raw hint of approaching spring in the air yesterday morning, when a group of enthusiastic sportsmen began assembling before the entrance of Grand Central Palace for the opening of the tenth annual National Sportsmen's Show. The doors were not scheduled to open until 11 o'clock, but before that hour the crowd had*

grown to such size the management decided to open the doors ahead of schedule. Within the hour the building had begun to fill and the line before the ticket office extended a half-block in either direction…

Farther on, he continues with "Noah John on Scene."

The Conservation Department's exhibit consists of a replica of [Noah John Rondeau's] lonely cabin in a setting which is virtually an exact reproduction of the spot where his real cabin stands. The foreground is the summit of a high bluff from which one gazes down into the river valley. In the background loom Seward, Seymour, the Sawtooths, Panther, Santanoni and Henderson Mountains. Two raccoons climb the tree stumps and frolic around…

Noah John was reported to have "charmed" even urban sophisticates with his brand of folkish wild world. During and following the show in the Big Apple, the Adirondack hermit was the focus of some articles about his role

Noah wowed crowds with his remarkable marksmanship at the Grand Central Palace's Sportsmen's Show. *Courtesy of Richard J. Smith from Noah's photo album*

as Mayor of Cold River and how he survived year after year in his remote hermitage. He had to put up with many repeat questions from the lines of people waiting to meet him that stretched past other booths. Commenting on the crowds who met him sitting in front of his tiny mountain hut mock-up, where he answered their questions, he said it was apparent that the simple life he led had "much more appeal when" the audience "learned that my living cost amounted to but $100 a year." Rondeau was also surprised that pictures of him in the media; such as the image of him repairing the rawhide webbing on a snowshoe; featured on the top of the sports section in the *New York Times*; could blanket a region far beyond the city.

A special highlight of Noah John's departure from his wilderness was the Conservation Department's plan to extract him from the mountain retreat by helicopter. Portions of two Adirondack newspaper articles summed it up:

> *The problem of getting Noah John Rondeau, bearded hermit of Cold River Flow, out of his remote Adirondacks retreat is a headache for the Conservation Department's Division of Education. Noah's personal transportation was one thing, but the job of moving a sundry collection of...belongings over 19 miles of wilderness trails buried under five feet of snow was another.*
>
> *The whole thing started a couple of weeks ago when Bill Petty, the department's district forester at Saranac Lake, parachuted a note from a plane asking Noah whether he'd consider coming out of the woods long enough to help out with the department's Sportsmen's show.*
>
> *Petty, who was traveling with pilot Melvin Bettcher, reported that Noah "...spelled out [by tramping] a big 'YES' in the snow..."*
>
> *Two years ago, the frail Noah John snowshoed out to Saranac under his own power for supplies. But it took him four days for the round trip and his vitality hasn't been the same since. This time he'll have to be helped.*
>
> *"...If we can't get him down to New York," said Clayt Seagers, in charge of the Department's exhibit, "I'm gonna itch plenty in a beard."*

Of the air flight to pick up Noah and his belongings, the hermit exclaimed the 55 minute round-trip flight was "...the easiest way I ever came out!"

For Noah, appearing before the public was something that was very unusual compared to the solitary life he had long lived, but he clearly enjoyed his new audience, his new image, and the media attention he drew.

That first New York City show was only the beginning of his period as a backwoods celebrity. In March and April he entertained thousands of people as he continued to travel with the Conservation Department's exhibit. Everywhere he went he related anecdotes and stories of the Cold River region, signed thousands of autographs, provided information about the life of a bona fide hermit, ate and slept in strange surroundings and got around in noisy cities far removed from the uninhabited Adirondack wilderness. The *Essex County Republican* concluded, "Noah John Rondeau is fully equal to the situation, continues in good health and is giving pleasure to new-found friends."

Writing to the *Essex County Republican* weekly newspaper, the celebrated Adirondack hermit reported:

This is Noah John Rondeau, Adirondack Hermit, screaming to Essex Co. Republican, Keeseville, N.Y. and saying "Hear Ye."

March 13th, I was at Gloversville, a.m. I visited The Daniel C. Miller Glove Co.; and p.m. I visited Sir William Johnson Hall at Johns Town; and evening, I had supper with Triangle Club at YMCA and spoke for an hour to about 50 members and a dozen guests.

Mar. 14th, I went to Buffalo for 9 days with Conservation Commission's exhibit at Sportsmens Show. And while at Buffalo, I made two trips to Niagara Falls, and I addressed two High Schools, in each, about 1,000 students.

And I also visited The Great Water Falls of the Niagara River. The Falls were in winter dress, snow and ice and frozen foam—

Actress Arlene Whelan took Noah on a tour of Paramount Studios in New York City.
From Noah's photo album. Courtesy of Richard J. Smith

contrasted by the broad sheets of liquid torrent from the aquatic mixture from the great lakes above the falls.

There were many clouds and few glimpses of sun shine; and the dense mist above the water at the foot of the Falls—held a perfect Rain Bow on its curtain. It was all beautiful.

I was on 2 Radio broadcasts. Spoke and dined at several clubs.

Mar. 24th came to Albany by train, then by Buss to Elizabethtown. And put up for the night at [Ranger] John Longware's.

Mar. 25th, called on Old Friend Oliver Hathaway—then with John Longware motored to Westport—Spun old and new yarn with Ralph Vougan and Frank Gibson.

And then we gass-sputtered to Saranac Inn.

Now; (at Saranac Inn) I'm resting and writing. And in next few days will hit high mark at Saranac Lake—Lake Placid and Ausable Forks. And Apr. 5th to 13th inclusive will be at Rochester Sportsmen's Show.

Noah was increasingly mentioned in the media, primarily because he was such an interesting character. He saw himself in the role of entertainer, as evidenced by his own description of himself at presentations:

...I presented myself in Cold River style. My worn out pants were full of breezy holes and cute red patches and my old rubbers had the "holes" but no patches. And my deer skin vest, decked with my mountain club emblems, hinted "Adirondack Air" as appropriately as a green Shamrock on St. Patrick's. And my home-made muskrat cap appropriately topped the climax...

Noah thought about returning to Cold River as spring moved toward summer. He also reasoned it was time for him to temporarily give up the limelight. He had earned more income from his performances in a few months than he had ever made trapping. And he hated the idea of not being able to fish Cold River in June. So he decided to temporarily bow out of the scramble for recognition and money, but kept his options open for being a sports show figure and lecturer.

He was also enjoying life closer to home. On May 1 he attended the Saranac Lake Fish and Game Club with Bill Petty. Following a short business meeting, Noah spoke to the club members for 50 minutes. The subjects? Page 122 in his yearly journal reports his talk addressed "Cold River; Sportsmens Shows, City Belles, Trail Full of Old Maids," and written in his secret code he said, "*following Mrs. Irene Pfeffer's kiss*, I draw ticket to get D. L. Bushey 30 qts. of Gass."

Following the drawing, Bill Petty showed a moving picture of the first helicopter to ever land on Cold River. At the conclusion of the viewing, Noah was presented with a certificate that recognized him as a lifetime honorary member of the fish and game club.

May 15 found Noah collecting the mail that had accumulated in his box at the Coreys post office. "Got a cheque," he noted in his diary, for his May 4 "We the People" radio appearance for "CBS—109 W. 39th St. 100 dollars."

His diary reports:

Wednesday, May 21, 1947
Cloudy, breezy and a sprinkle of rain. Ampersand Park to Cold River [Drove] To washout near Ward Creek Lean to with Frank Blanchard; Then I walk to Cold River. Saw Deer at height of

land east of #4 and other Deer east of Mt. Pond. And other Deer south of 15 Frog Pond—and 2 Deer in Buck Slough at Cold River. Some one broke Town Hall Lock—left comb. Little water Frogs after dormant winter,—cuddled in mud—under Sloughs of water—have their Pianos in tune.

Life was good. The hermit had returned home.

Noah and Don Latimer on Cold River Hill. "This photo was snapped just before Halloween 1934. Following lunch, Noah slumped in his chair saying he had 'a fine meal but oh those dishes—Hard Times.'" —Donald Latimer. Courtesy of C.V. Latimer Jr. M.D.

Chapter 18

Rondeau's 1947 Summer and Fall Season

Tuesday, February 11th, 1947
Clouds and Sunshine-Winter Day. "W.E. Petty drop letter and package from Air Plane. It came near spoiling my snow."

THIS IS AN EXAMPLE of Noah John's mind-set 34 years after he began living in the mountains. It's a deep winter cold. He hasn't seen a soul in months. And a plane arrives, roaring overhead. From it, his ranger buddy drops a note. It asks if he would like to attend a Sportsmen's Show, stand in front of "Pictures, Recorders, News Reels." To boot, Rondeau would fly out in a helicopter high over Ampersand Mountain to a "waiting crowd of 200" or more at Saranac Lake air field before boarding a Colonial Airways plane that would whisk him to La Guardia airport in New York City. Yet, all Noah had to say in his diary was that the plop that Bill's package made when it hit the frozen flow ground practically blemished his snow scenery.

The New Year of 1947 began a wonderful period of his life. It was the year he made his breakout-out-from-the-mountains move. He loved entertaining the crowds at the Sportsmen's Shows. Those paying trade shows were the scenes of many unforgettable times.

His success during the winter and spring ultimately spurred him to create a display that surpassed what the Conservation Department had built. Believing his new improved model might help earn him more attention and additional money, he fired off dozens of letters of inquiry to show bookers, hoping they would say yes to his hermit spectacle. Many did. By the close of the summer of '47, Noah was prepared to hit the road—as well prepared as any circus or carnival person. But before that "Hi-de-doo" stage-like promotion bumped up and opened up new vistas for him, Noah the hermit wanted to return to Cold River City to relax, unwind, and enjoy the simple life without all the reporters and cameramen rolling behind him.

On a "cloudy, breezy" day that saw intervals of sprinkles, Noah returned to Cold River Hill. He recorded this the following day.

Thursday, May 22nd, 1947
Much rain L.N., River high. Perfect May.
At Cold River Town Hall
While I was away (99 Days) Mice raised hell. I overhaul, Town Hall. Clean Shelves, Jars, Dishes, Burn Papers & etc.

A Robin is building nest in Wig Wam. THE GODDAM BEAR EAT 1 GAL. BEAR BAIT & DEER HAM & LEFT WHITE SHIT & SMASHED BRUN...I see 3 Deer on Fly Dope Hill and 5 Deer in Buck Slough.

Beginning on May 23, volunteer pilots from the Lake Placid Flying Club began their chain of air drops—packages Noah had arranged to have flown in. He notes the first delivery contained "29 items including Food, Clothing, Stationary & etc."

The second delivery arrived at "9 a.m." while he was outside working. "I spade Garden, transplant 70 wild Daisys to south banking of Hall of Records. Shad Trees are in bloom. I spring clean...6 Deer about Camp Grounds."

He continued through May to work in his gardens, entertain himself by playing the violin, spring and pick up his traps, and fish. May 27.: "1st fishing. 5 trout."

The weather wasn't the best on Tuesday, June 3, 1947, but on the heels of a heavy rain that fell the night before and raised the river level, Noah recorded, "very high water. Darn cold, at Cold River," the big event took place after noon. "2 P.M. Richard Smith arrive from Tokyo." Later that day Noah noted, Richard "...go fishing to Seward Pond—get Trout. RICHARD COME."

In early June Richard Smith wrote Don Latimer apologizing that Noah and he did not find the time to "fulfill the invitation to lunch at Camp Seward, and we are sorry, as we would have enjoyed it very much...Maybe we will be able to make it in the fall..."

Further on in his letter, Smith told about Noah's newest method of getting supplies into camp: "This summer Noah has been receiving packages of food dropped from the air." With some of the money he had earned, Rondeau purchased canned and dry food and hired Lake Placid pilots to deliver the goods. Rondeau paid for the fuel; the pilots donated their time when they had some to spare. No parachutes were used. The light planes just dropped low over the hermitage on Handsome Hill, as an assistant pushed the boxed-up provisions out. Smith said the two of them often spent an entire day picking up the contents that "scattered far and wide" when a crate broke open. A note from the pilot was included in the fourth drop, Smith told Don, "saying that it would be the last they could drop so I guess he will have to once again pack in anything else he needs."

Noah parlayed his short exposure to celebrity status and fame into lining up bookings for paid speaking engagements that, from time to time, drew him away from his Cold River Valley hermitage. *From Noah's photo album. Courtesy of Richard J. Smith*

Wednesday, June 4th, 1947
...big rain...I SHOW RICHARD BLACK BEAR'S WHITE SHIT. I write Essex Co. Republican. Richard Smith recently returned from Tokyo—fish Seward Pond—2 Trout His effort. REDHEAD FROM TOYKO-STAY.

Thursday, June 5th, 1947
Cloudy and mild...At Sun Rise,—I out to the Garden—Rake surface over and sow 10 20 foot drills; And 5 minutes after I complete job—an old Doe walked across every drill. And early P.M. the Doe came back and walked about, for 30 minutes within 30 feet from Camp while Richard Smith took several photographs. I cut and peal 3 maple Poles to make Wigwam frame... RICHARD STAY.

Saturday, June 7th, 1947
...I have my SPECIALIST from TOKYO DIG SHITHOUSE HOLE. I cut Poles and SET UP SHIT HOUSE...Richard STAY-fish Seward Pond; 2 fish for Effort.

On Sunday, June 8, after Richard and Noah transferred firewood poles from the surplus stack to the Beauty Parlor wigwam very carefully to avoid disturbing the baby robins in the "...Robin's nest in Wigwam...," the partners took a small trip.

Richard Smith's most vivid memories of Noah that summer and autumn revolve around Cold River. One such incident involved a fish fry.

> *Noah did overeat at times of plenty. I recall a fish fry we had on Seward Brook, where between the two of us we devoured 40 brook trout, cooked by the tumbling waters. We didn't exactly get sick, but we sort of put a damper on fishing trips for the rest of that summer, but those little speckled trout, cooked to mouth-watering brownness at streamside was beyond doubt a banquet fit for kings.*

Next day Noah stayed in bed and finally in later afternoon emerged from the Town Hall with a sheepish grin. When I asked if he was sick he replied, "Yes Richard, but of my own making, but I feel better now, and wouldn't have missed that cookout for anything. Wasn't that a humdinger of a fish fry!"

Monday, June 9th, 1947
Cloudy...then Sun Shine At Cold River City. I write MOTHER. [It's assumed he met 46er "Mother" 00Gowie.] Richard STAY-fish SEWARD POND. NO fish. Little Red Plane drop 2 pkgs... Snow spot on Couchsachraga vanish.

Ranger Petty's visit followed Richard Smith's departure.

Wednesday, June 18th, 1947
...At Mid Day—Wm. Petty call in June Grass, Dandelions and Violet Flowers. And He brought my mail and we had a Mountain Lunch: And the hundred minutes talk –like The June Day, need no—Professor's Polish. [Later in the day] I make a Balsam Bed in Old Lady's Wigwam and I watch parade of a Doe at Sun Down.

Following a comfortable sleep on his new mattress inside a pole wigwam shelter, Noah sent the *Essex County Republican* an essay he titled "A June Day."

Weeks passed and Noah was riding high. Friends and curious others stopped in to camp. Fred McClaine continued to make air drops of supplies, including a "sweet salt lick I put out," Noah noted in his hieroglyphic code.

There had not been too many times in Noah's life when something seemingly insignificant had led to something momentous, but after having been flown from his Adirondack home by Mr. Rideout, of the Plattsburgh and Rouses Point Seaplane Service, for appearances in a wide variety of functions at the five-day Rouses Point "carnival show," an idea to improve his stage presence came to him. He would not act on it until September.

It is believed that the success he attained at the Rouses Point Independence Day celebrations on Lake Champlain led to his brainstorm. While staying at the Anchorage Hotel there, he said that as Mayor of Cold River he made a "Proclaimation" that "July 4, 1947—Shall be on Friday." In a solemn ceremony, the mayor of Rouses Point presented Noah with the keys to the city. The hermit met and talked with Boy Scout Troop 42, addressed the Kiwanis Club, marched with the band "to Tombola Tents," flew "in Hydro Plane with Pilot...talked and wrote autographs," sold post card photographs of himself, "poised for pictures and answered questions." His closing remarks included "Tombola: Good Show at Rouses Point... Good enthusiastic crowd..."

Thursday, July 17th, 1947
Clouds, Sun and sprinkle of rain
At Cold River City. I write 3 letters. I work in Garden.
2 Raccoons came to camp last night; They investigate, knock dishes off table and grease their mustaches with Boot Grease.

The raccoons continued to call throughout the summer. Other animals didn't fare as well:

Thursday, July 24th, 1947
...I shoot Red Squirrel off Pyramid of Giza. 1st handful of Raspberries. 9 FISH. HAIL HITLER. JUNE BUG.

Richard Smith said the use of "Hail Hitler" was Noah's equivalent of saying "Up your nose." He wrote the expression next to many of his fish takes. It harked back to his "miserable existence days" when he was often forced to get by on only a little corn meal, flour, deer meat and fish because of the war-time food rationing.

The following day, "17 Scouts" hiked upriver from Long Lake to visit the hermitage.

July passed. On August 9, Noah began packing gear in canvas bags for a camping trip. "Planning to go fishing at West Canada Lakes," he told his diary. As he sewed "pieces of canvas" he watched "humming Birds call to please the Flowers."

September 4 found him staying at the Conservation Commission's headquarters near Saranac Inn.

I write Article to Adirondack Record [newspaper]...received in the mail 1 pr. of Maine Hunting Rubbers from L. L. Bean.

It was during this month that he took steps on the brainchild he had hatched while at Rouses Point.

I learned this from Richard and from Adolph Dittmar, who gave me old Kodak slides of the project Noah built, as natural as it could be. Right in the middle of all the activity, fever-pitch excitement and bedlam, one thought sprang into Noah's consciousness, perhaps flashing like a neon sign:

Hey, Ole Whiskers. This is it. Here's an idea to pitch yourself to radio and even national television. Build a grand version of your Cold River City exhibit on a raised platform that can be taken around on wheels. You couldn't buy a better chance to grab at the brass ring than this. Now take this idea and run with it.

For a few months people would plunk down cash for their admission ticket, and on top of the entrance fee pay fifty cents for an autographed souvenir postcard showing Noah holding his bow. Noah even went so far as to place a false bottom in his pack basket, seeding the inside with coins and dollar bills he borrowed. Spectators got the hint they were to toss donations in for the poor hermit. This is what a bit of commercial success did for Rondeau—it taught him to think on his feet. Over the years he came up with countless things to sell at shows or following a lecture. The Cold River Hermit was a quick learner and that's exactly what he did during the month of September to prepare for the day he would resume his Sportsmen's Show circuit.

Wednesday, September 5th, 1947
Cold morning, Sun and Clouds—nice day at Conservation Headquarters near Saranac Inn. I paint, cut wigwam poles, set

up second Platform, install stairs. I start...Town Hall...Grease new bear hunting shoes. TOM DERBY WITH MEN START (building) RAMP.

Saturday, September 6th, 1947
I assemble Relics to take out from Cold River...I paint Clouds on Old Oil Painting...

Monday, September 8th, 1947
I PAINT WHEELER WASH OUTSIDE. I VARNISH 4 LARGE PHOTOGRAPHS, 3 DRAWINGS, 1 OIL PAINTING PAINT WHEELER. Raccoon eat raisins and spill Corn Meal L.N. 2 WOMEN, MAN CALL...from ST. HUBERTS VIA COUCHSACHRAGA. I GREASE FISH BASKET.

Noah following an attack of "skilletitious" (overeating).
Courtesy of Richard J. Smith from Noah's photo album

For the next six days friends of Noah's continued to transport "load out" including his prize rocking chair. Noah noted in code that he "hid Yale KEY in Black Cherry tree." This key was to the lock on the Town Hall cabin door.

September 17 marked Noah and F.G. Quigley's "auto drive" adventure from "Moose Creek to Fish Hatchery," Rondeau wrote on a "perfect Sunshine day." Leaving the dense forest was a true adventure for Noah, and bound to be an exciting experience. Noah loved the wild, shady, scenic and remote Cold River country, even though as he got older the challenges were greater. Leaving home might have felt somewhat strange, but Noah was clearly at home by the time he had eaten supper at the Conservation Commission Headquarters and had bunked down at Saranac Inn.

> *Thursday, September 18th, 1947*
> *...I spend the day at Conservation Commission headquarters,— and evening with Pettys. I over haul Suit Case and do some writing. 1 HAIRCUT-BEARD TRIM-1 BATH. AUTUMN APPROACHING.*

Autumn had begun to move over the countryside surrounding Saranac Lake. Armies of bright-colored leaves marched over ridges and across valleys, circling Upper Saranac Lake, brightening rocky summits, and leaving behind gloriously-clothed mountainsides. This was the magnificent country outside of Cold River where Noah had lived on and off for years, particularly during the winter. He called the place "headquarters," partly because it was a lodging for the rangers, but was more than that, it was going to be Noah's "corporate outpost"—where he would develop his exhibit and make marketing decisions.

> *Thursday, September 25th, 1947*
> *Quite cloudy, stingy sunshine near Saranac Inn Station. White pines never so loaded with cones. Autumn colors coming on slow. Harvest of apples, squash, corn and pumpkins renew memories of their habitat In gone by years.*

Noah was still working on his new exhibit by the time October rolled around.

Saturday, October 4th, 1947
Frost L.N. to day Summer Like Sun Shine. At Conservation Commission Headquarters...I work 9 hours on Cold River Replica.... Marilyn Petty call with White Rabbit... Marilyn hid my Square. I have a good notion to put Her in Tom Derby's Cement Mixer.

From October 10 to the 30th, Noah continued living "At Headquarters at Saranac Inn Station" while he performed the final tasks on his exhibit. As he worked, reporters stopped by to take pictures, "...a School Bus full of Kids call to see the Hermit" and on October 18 "Dr. Dittmar call with His Mary and Uncle H. Ray Williams...And we inspect Cold River Replica." His diary entries during that time describe the effort he put forth to give a top-notch show.

October 10: ... Paint Fabric; build a table.

October 11: ...work 8 Hours on ...Replica. I build a Bed & etc.

October 12: I set up the Replica for temp[orary] Show...Replica. BRING GUIDE 150 CENTS.

October 13: Jerry's Lounge and DEW DROP INN. Wrote autographs... Got LOG SCALING BOOK from College of Forestry, Syracuse.

October 14: I paint Sky Blue on 4 large Curtains. ART WORK...Reporter call and take pictures. Afternoon I START MAKING A STRONG BOX.

October 15: I make a Strong Box and I outline Mts. On Replica Large Curtain. I send 2 PHOTOGRAPHS TO VERN STEELE. A LITTLE DRINK IS GOOD TO TAKE.

Newspaper articles about Noah that appeared earlier in the year had hinted that Rondeau could be a bit of a salesman—and his work on the new exhibit proved he was proud of it. His ambition was to sell his hermit life—and indeed he did sell his story.

On October 28 he admitted in code that he hadn't taken a bath in three weeks until that evening, when the code revealed: "I stink up & dress pretty." And no wonder why! The next day he paid a visit to the Saranac Veterans Club where he met a "Cuban Lady." While there he "…put new bridge and strings on violin and tune[d] it up."

The last thing he needed to do on the 29th took all day: "I work 8 hours,—I put wire on Raccoon Cage-put Hasps on 2 Boxes and chains & etc…"

To celebrate the completion of the project on October 30, Noah played "The Irish Washerwoman" on his violin for "…Mr. Smith and Mr. Young…" Then came the job of taking down the exhibit and storing it.

> *November 3: I work 8 hours… MY ART PAINTING IS DAMN GOOD.*
>
> *November 8: …I put up curtain in Garage. Dance in Garage with Marilyn Petty and Beverley Dukett. …6 P.M., Electric current go off.*

Rondeau's letter to the editor of *The Essex County Republican* dated November 14, 1947, summed up his status:

> *Hear Ye—this is the Mayor of Cold River City—population 1,"*
>
> *…I am at conservation commission's headquarters at state fish hatchery near Saranac Inn.*
>
> *I just came out from Cold River; And I brought out 400 pounds of my Cold River relics including Deer and Bear skins, old guns, paddles, fishing tackle, deer horns, bear skulls, homemade rocking chair, archery tackle, violin, bear traps and many other home spun wonders.*
>
> *And now—my plan is to build an elevated platform 13 x 26 ft.*

square; and on said "platform"—a replica of my Cold River Town Hall, plus a Wigwam, plus a scenic oil painted background.

And when these major items are trimmed with old stumps and a Wilderness Floor of dry leaves and Crow Foot vines; and furnished with the original Cold River furniture—plus the trophies of next hunting season; and the furs of next trapping season, to January; It is intended that this enterprise will be the best of its kind ever put on exhibition, at any show, anywhere.

And it is clear to the Mayor, that, the grandeur of this outfit will make Noah's Ark, look like a toy, that Robin Crusoe might have made to amuse Friday while the deluge went by as a mere sun shower.

And it is also clear to the Mayor's vision that when he steps upon his platform in a large city next winter; and starts to deliver an English speech in French; and as the audience beholds the dignified step, over a rusty bear trap, and sees the musk rat cap plus whiskers and red patches—No one in audience will need to be tickled—any where—with a feather to evolve a laugh.

Friday, November 21st, 1947
Cool winter weather. 10 in. snow on ground. At Ampersand Park to Big Dam I walk to Town Hall. See 2 Deer at East end of Park. A 10 pointer hang at Ward Creek Lean-to. From Mt. Pond to camp, 12 Bear Tracks = 1 Bear.

On Saturday he reported in his diary he was "Lame and Tired after long walk."

The remaining November entries are uneventful, yet it was probably relaxing just for Noah to be in his familiar surroundings. One day he sewed red patches to "make fancy Patch underwear." Other entries need further clarification. He wrote on November 25, "I rob can AT DOE GRAVE of Red Patches…" An enigmatic November 26 entry mentions that he returned from checking "AUBEL BEAR TRAP" and did some personal grooming: "HAIRCUT, BEARD TRIM. I SPANK PANTS RED. It's winter like in the Big Mountains."

One wonders if the decipherer's interpretation is 100% accurate here. If so, we will never know what Noah had in mind when he wrote "I spank pants red."

By December 23 the hermit was again away from his mountain home: "...near Saranac Inn. I do much writing; And I read all my Poems. GOOD TIME AT [Conservation] Headquarters.

The following day, December 24, he must have decided to partially spruce up after having "Breakfast at Headquarters. SEMI-BATH. Ride to Saranac Lake...Shop about Town...Ride to D. L. B. ...by way of LIQUOR STORE. (Xmas)."

Noah enjoyed "A Satisfactory Christmas at D.L. Busheys...My PRESENT—4 Silver LIQUOR CUPS."

On December 29 he "Put up for a cold night at Phil McCalvin's." The next day he helped the McCalvins celebrate their son Gary's first birthday. Noah reported Gary, "...threw an elephant over Dee Fence."

"At 1:30 P.M. [the Saranac Lake winter] carnival opened officially..."

1940. Phil McCalvin with Noah. Rich Smith and Phil were regular drop-ins at Cold River Hill. *Photograph by Richard J. Smith. Courtesy of Helen McCalvin Sawatzki*

Wednesday, December 31st, 1947
Cloudy and moderate temperature at Saranac Lake. Call at Commo's Studio. 10 o'clock: I meet carnival-parade at Veteran's Club. 11:40 Parade start. 12: Noon at Town hall [exhibit.].
4 P.M. move Town hall to Saranac Hotel second Floor.
Today:—Parade was very good. Crowd was extra good.

After years of near solitary living, of weathering fearful bitter winters and summer storms, of working his gardens, of living with the animals that caused him moments of fits but were also considered his neighbors, in spite of the hard conditions of life, the lack of all the creature comforts, the business of putting up cords of firewood and guaranteeing a supply of food for the larder, and facing the fact that his single ready-made source of income, trapping, was subject to wide market fluctuations, Noah continued to tolerate the odds against his survival, opting to stay put rather than to try to live outside the mountains. Heaven alone knows how this man toiled and silently suffered. His hair was grey in '47, and his face deeply graven with lines. They say that wrinkles tell in cipher the story of a person's life. So his diaries tell a noble story too.

Nineteen forty-seven was a watershed year for the Cold River hermit as well as for the groupies who loved to read about him and be around him. He revealed in his discussion with Peggy Byrne about his first experience as the "Conservationers" prize exhibit at the National Sportsmen's Show in New York City that he was fully aware it had defined him as a performer with a talent for drama as well as woodsmanship. Rondeau wrote her later,

No matter what the joke is, New York City met me with kisses. They bought me ice cream; they gave me a gold-plated fob, and a dancing doll, photographs and artificial ducks. And no clergyman could comprehend more attention than I got,--with Natural History of Mountains and Vallies; even if He preached all day on Jonah and the Whale and got the fish to demonstrate...

An article Byrne wrote for the *Conservationist* magazine in 1972 summed up her family's friend and his importance to regional history:

> *...Little Noah whittling sticks and mending snowshoes before a replica of his cabin, dressed in deerskins and smelling of bear grease, became famous overnight. And though he returned to Cold River, he was asked to appear later at many other shows and meetings where the hermit in captivity thoroughly enjoyed every moment in the spotlight.*
>
> *Eventually his cabin and many of his artifacts would go to the Adirondack Museum where he "helped them set up an exhibit at Blue Mountain Lake showing his manner of life in the woods."*
>
> *The exhibit celebrates the tiny man with the long beard who protested all limits—but set himself the toughest limits of all: the disciplines of living so frugally by his wits in the harsh Adirondack climate. But his jokes and songs and dances are gone, and his wonderful laughter crackling through the forest when he played games with the raccoons about his little cabin, and talked to the bears, and whistled to the blue jays.*
>
> *For this gentle, quiet man, who loved people and animals and birds, discovered in the wilderness exactly what the new breed of ecologists and environmentalists proclaim—the necessity for living in harmony with nature, rather than trying to conquer it. While he never would have put it in these words, he was successful, and we rejoice in his success. Amen, Noey, Amen.*

In 1947, Noah enjoyed both his life as a public figure and the peace of his wilderness retreat. His circle of friends and acquaintances widened greatly, and his struggle to survive in the woods underwent a revolutionary change. There were more changes on the way, but for now nothing could dim his high spirits and the delight he took in the unexpected turn of his new life.

Chapter 19

A Town with Memories

WHEN ASKED what was his biggest regret, Rondeau would always say, "Well, I guess it's at least a dozen points of failure. When you're young, you've got ambition on something, and my ambition was good, but it was too good to succeed under the circumstances. That was the trouble." Rondeau, "decked out in his woodsman's duds and whiskers, became an overnight sensation," reported WGY radio reporter Enoch Squires in 1959. Rondeau was a "sensation, the big drawing card of the 1947 show.

But the widespread promotion the Sportsmen's Show advertisers promised throughout the hermit's late 1940s contracts didn't last long. His string of large-scale jam-packed shows ended largely because promotion dollars went to newer, bigger entertainers. In the spring of 1949, Noah took a break from the public. He told Squires, "a lot of them [spectators] came who wouldn't have come at all, if I hadn't been there." The public adulation was predictable. "Well, you expect that in a place like that. Ahh, but I didn't realize it at first, not all of it, but the fact is I held the biggest crowd every minute for those nine long days. Two things bothered Noah John. He disliked the men who crammed around him, as he expressed it, "with too many drinks down their collars," and he "disliked the hard corners of New York." Nevertheless, he was very happy with the money the folks tossed into his pack basket in exchange for his autograph or picture. Not that Noah asked for it, but from time to time he declared, "You know, I ain't awful rich."

Perhaps fed up with city life, Noah had gone home to Cold River in the spring of 1948. His diary entry upon his arrival illustrates the joy he felt when he once again was in the solitude of the mountains and away from the things he disliked about the cities.

Noah in his homemade deerskin finery. "He liked the swishing feel of the fringe as he walked," remembered Grace. *Photograph by Ed Hudowalski. Courtesy of Grace Hudowalski*

Thursday, April 29, 1948
I walk about my Town Hall and City , Robins and Juncos, Chipmonks and Sparrows. No Gas Stations, no Dogs on every Corner, no Church Bells in my Ears, What freedom alone in natural primitiveness and what unsatisfactory waste in living Civilization, serving Gods, Religions and Industrial Slavery and multiplicity of useless fool subjects. I find lost manuscript (Recollections of 60 years). 11 o'clock Air Plane drop 37 packages in my Briars. I gather supplies all day. Sundown—Deer at 1st Brook, above Dam—and 5 deer—tails gallop east in Dead Flow. Nighthawks screech. No mice at Cold River City and very few Barred Owls.

Noah's written words didn't reveal excitement, even though excitement must have been there. While no one can be sure just what he felt coming back to Cold River, his words suggest relief and contentment.

He liked "to get among people… but if I had to stay all the time, that is if I were younger and physically more able, I'd rather take Cold River all the time than the city."

As Bette and I hiked through the river valley, thoughts entered my mind about Rondeau's last years at the hermitage. The decisive last year was 1949 while 1950 saw Rondeau at camp only during hunting season—and only then until hurricane winds struck the mountains. Might Noah John have sensed his days at Cold River City were numbered? The diaries do not make known his feelings. What he recorded only provided more about the Noah John Rondeau Adirondack hermit story.

Rondeau's 1949 record begins with a reminder…

LEST WE FORGET 1948 IN 1949
The days went one by one—1948 is done
Now it's a Random Scoot around the Sun;
And 1949 is just begun.
But We have a Diary with us yet,
Lest we forget,—Lest we forget.

Lest we forget Dear Roosevelt
Billions in the "Hole" are with us yet;
Roosevelt is dead-riddance hard to get
The Democrats are with us yet
Lest we forget, Dear Roosevelt.

Roosevelt. Roosevelt, Roosevelt
Everlasting X, President Elect and running yet
Would be Roosevelt if He was not dead
But since He's dead and gone to hell
We can't forget- Bills not paid yet- Dear Roosevelt.

Noah's 1949 "footprint" in time appears with each daily memorandum. Readers can clearly see a continuing story linked by events, just the way the writer recorded them.

Rondeau's thirty-sixth season, 1949, was spent less in the Adirondack wilds than in the past. Noah John wanted to cultivate his newfound calling of Sportsmen's Show lecturer for as long as it would generate an income, yet he still wanted the independence of Cold River.

His writing confirms the uneasy security of life in the wilderness for a man in his sixth decade of life. Trapping, fishing, hunting and growing his own food had become much more difficult and unreliable. Noah seems to have been trying to salvage his former life while getting more help from friends and engagements on the Outside.

Rondeau spent the winter at 4 Alpine Terrace in Saranac Lake with his friends, the McCalvins. With two years of experience at Sportsmen's Shows under his belt, Noah was flying high on a bubble of euphoria. As the New Year began, he made preparations to set up his miniature replica of Cold River City. The show was to be right in his own backyard.

January 2, 1949 Sunday
Quite cloudy and wintery At Saranac Lake, N.Y. I set up Wigwam at Saranac Town Hall. I go to Lake Placid. I write and overhaul old Xmas cards and letters.

January 3, 1949 Monday
Rather cloudy, cold winter day At Saranac Lake, N.Y.
I call at Guild Craft. Shop at Grays. Confab with W.E. Petty—
Conservation officer. Set up Wigwam at Town Hall.
Campbell-Fairbanks offer $800.00. I write Boston show.

By this time, Noah John had appeared in a number of sportsmen's shows. The American and Canadian Sportsmen's Show described their March 18–27, 1949, event as "an international exposition devoted to hunting, fishing, boating, camping, touring—and other wholesome recreational pastimes enjoyed in the great outdoors." Noah had contacted the director, A.W. Newman, late in 1948, hoping to secure a booth in the public auditorium where the show was staged annually in Cleveland, Ohio.

Noah was an articulate, witty, and authentic Adirondack hermit; the crowds loved him and he loved the attention. Reporters scooped him up. He was interviewed on talk radio and on newsreels. Wire services ran stories about him across the country. Articles about his life filled newspaper columns.

Recognizing the potential to earn more money in one week than he had ever earned in a year, Noah worked the crowds with the skill of an enterprising huckster. Business cards were printed and handed out. The Saranac Craft Guild worked with him. There he posed with bow and arrow, selecting the perfect images to be printed on souvenir postcards he sold. For an additional fifty cents he'd personalize each card sold with his flourishing autograph and drawings of trout.

He recognized that The Establishment had laid a golden egg right in his lap, and he took quick advantage. To encourage onlookers to leave a donation for a "poor hermit," he arranged a pack basket toss-your-money game front and center in the miniature Cold River City display. Bills and coins were generously tossed in.

Noah entertained the crowds by telling tales about living in the wilderness. He displayed native animal pelts and demonstrated leather-making. He validated his expert bow and arrow marksmanship by shooting at a target.

He said the children who talked to him "were a great pleasure."

"Tending Bar for Gary McCalvin." —NJR. Noah and Gary McCalvin at 4 Alpine Terrance, Saranac Lake, N.Y. *Courtesy of Helen McCalvin Sawatzki*

Noah did a lot of rocking, reading and contemplation as he puffed his meerschaum pipe, given to him by his friends, the Billy Burgers. *Photograph by Ed Hudowalski. Courtesy of Grace Hudowalski*

I found through talking to a great number of people who met the hermit at shows that each man, woman and child walked away with a different impression, depending on their age, their receptiveness, and perhaps on Noah's mood at a particular time.

Jim Tomczak, Leona Raymond Warner and her daughter Bonnie, John Hickey, Stephen Klein Jr., and Richard Benson were among the dozens who shared their memories of meeting the Cold River Hermit. Each expressed a different point of view. Those whom Noah had singled out or paid particular attention to had memories of rejoicing. Others remember vividly a spirit of cheerfulness. Other onlookers came away with a bigger-than-life image. All were mindful of his humanity. His bushy face of whiskers did not conceal Rondeau's slight shyness. His kindness and his interest in the forest creatures that populated his world showed through the gray growth and bushy eyebrows that framed his small face. Leona Warner expressed it best when she said the crowds "…in turn accepted him for exactly what he was…a warm, capable citizen of this planet."

"You can't go home again" is an old saying. To me it means that returning to an old stomping grounds is like seeing a once-familiar place as you might view an out-of-focus old 8-millimeter home movie shot through a foggy lens. Nothing would be exactly as you once knew it.

Rondeau's diary continues.

January 4, 1949 Tuesday
Thawing—a perfect day of Sun Shine At Saranac Lake, N.Y.
I work on Town Hall Stage (Trimming Hermit Replica).
7–10 P.M. First ever Sportsmens Show at Saranac Lake.
I write Autographs—sell photographs and give 10 minute's talk.

January 5, Wednesday
"…7 to 10 P.M. at Sportsmens Show. I give 30 minutes talk—
"Year With a Hermit". Mrs. Bartlett kiss my hand."

On Friday, January 7, the final day of the Saranac Lake show, Rondeau wrote "I make a King's Staff; and a Queen's Bouquet. I attend a Ball at Hotel Saranac...[At] 11 O'clock: I crown King and Queen At Hotel Saranac."

In his Saturday mail, Rondeau received a reply from Philip D. Perkins of Campbell-Fairbanks Expositions, Inc. The letter read:

> *Dear Mr. Rondeau:*
> *This is in reply to your letter of Jan. 3, 1949.*
>
> *It has always been our policy to book acts and feature exhibits, such as yourself, at a price which included items as you have indicated such as: bus fare, taxis, board and room. When we talked with you and you quoted us a price of $600.00, we naturally thought that this price included those items. In our last letter we agreed to pay you an additional $200.00 to cover the transportation to and from Boston of your exhibit.*
>
> *After careful consideration we feel that we cannot agree to any additional expenses in connection with your appearance at our Boston Show. We will, however, pay you $800.00 for your appearance. $800.00 to cover the transportation of your exhibit to and from Boston and all expenses incurred by you such as: bus fares, taxis, meals etc. We will, however, furnish the labor for the setting up and dismantling of your exhibit.*
>
> *Will you please let us know immediately of your acceptance of this proposition?*

Rondeau's entries rarely describe such a lovely scene as what he recorded on Monday, February 21. His everyday descriptions say much about how he perceived the world around him. "After cool night-sunrise catch-twirling crystal celestial show and reveal colors like Zodiac sifting rain bow dust below. At Saranac Lake, N.Y. 9 A.M. I call at P.O. –among floating crystals. I call at Conservation office. I write Beatrice Hathaway 4 pages. Tom Clark here for dinner. I sew on Boston garlent." [Could he have meant garland?]

On April 4, the U.S. Mail delivered a letter from Shirley Miller, one of Noah's admirers.

Dear Mr. Rondeau,
I'm learning how to type and that's why I'm typing this letter. I really can't wait till I see you again. Soon we will have our Easter vacation. We have a week off. Did you notice my name on the front cover? Ella went to New York and Jim got her a Chihuahua. I wish it was summer so I could climb the Mt's with you. Did you really mean it about going out to camp? When I finish this letter I have to clean my goldfish. Please write soon.
So long for now.
from Your Honey Bunch Shirley Miller

On April 9, Noah was picked up by his nephew Chester. "Quite cool and cloudy…Ride to Black Brook with Chester Rondeau. Supper. 8 o'clock to Wm. Rondeau's Lodge for night. Another supper—then a dandy Deer and Bear Hunt that lasted passed Mid Night."

On a "gloomy and cool" Wednesday, April 20, a misfortune occurred at 4 Alpine Terrace: "…6:30 P.M. Seth McCalvin shoot Himself within 10 ft from me with 30-30 caliber Winchester Rifle. SETH MCCALVIN TO SAINT LAWRENCE HOSPITAL BULLSHIT."

The next day's entry read: "Quite cloudy and cool at Saranac Lake, N.Y. I stay alone at 4 Alpine and take care of [baby] Gary from 4 to Mid Night. Richard Smith call [at] 8 p.m. [and stayed] to next a.m."

Seth's son and his wife were apparently holding vigil at the hospital while Noah stayed with Gary. As is rather typical of Noah, his entry does not elaborate on how he felt about watching Seth McCalvin shoot himself—or whether it might have been intentional. He did disclose the result, however. Glued below the entry is a clipping from the *Adirondack Daily Enterprise.* It reads in part: "Seth McCalvin, 62, died suddenly at 6:30 o'clock last evening at the home of his son, Phillip McCalvin…with whom he had resided for the past few days…"

In late spring, Noah went back to Cold River. Maybe he decided he'd been in the entertainment business—or just living among other people—long enough. On April 25 he packed "up notions to go to Cold River."

June 26, 1949. Transplanting flowers the week H.V. Homes was in camp.
Courtesy of Richard J. Smith from Noah's photo album

April 26 Tuesday
I call at C.C. office. 100 spinach seeds Thanks, Mrs. Brown. I buy groceries—127 at Bill Mullen. I put up 37 packages at Bill Mullen's to go to Cold River. Planning to go to Ampersand [Park] tomorrow.

April 27 Wednesday
Sunshine-clouds and showers…5 A.M. ride to Coreys with Phillip McCalvin. Walk to 2nd. Gate. Ride to Ampersand Pond with Frank Blanchard. Camps all broken by Bear. Spring music is here. Night Hawks, Robins, Northern Flickers, Juncos, Blue Jays, and Water Birds.

The weather was mild, spring-like and balmy as he rode to Ampersand Park. He and Blanchard would have shaken hands warmly and caught up on interesting things that had happened. The old gentleman custodian told about a bad-tempered bear that had broken into the outlying camps. The hardened ruffians of the woods must have felt quite jolly during their visit. It had been almost six months since Noah had seen Blanchard.

Rondeau probably took all his baggage into Bear Camp, the shack he most often used when staying in the private Rockefeller preserve. Fresh trout might have been on his mind for his morning meal, but the weather did not make it easy.

April 28 Thursday
Cold, cloudy morning,—snowed 1 inch
Ampersand Park—Cold River
Fishing Reel frozen—Hands freeze catching Breakfast Fish.
2 Ampersand Trout for breakfast. I walk from Ampersand Pond to Big Dam Cold River. Just enough Old Snow left to make one Snow Man.

To many, Noah might have skidded off the Northville–Lake Placid footpath. Maybe Noah himself thought he had spiraled somewhat out of control. His comments on April 29, 1949, after returning to the hermitage, suggest he was anxious to regain a sense of peace he had not felt Outside, and closely mimics his comments of a year earlier.

April 29 Friday
Sunshine and clouds
At Cold River Town Hall
I walk about my city,—Cold River. Chipmonks and Sparrows. No Gas Stations—To hell with them. No Dogs on every corner—To hell with them. No Church Bells in my Ears, To hell with them. No one speeling for God—To hell with the Myth. What freedom—alone in natural primitiveness; and what unsatisfactory waste of living in civilization—serving Gods, Religions and industrial slavery.

In all of Noah John's many public appearances, he hyped Cold River City. No hotels. No road into it, no cars, nothing. Richard Smith said the mayor himself offered to everybody the key to the city. He meant, along with Noah's chatter about his wilderness home at Sportsmen's Shows, that he put forward an open invitation to any and all to drop by. "The welcome wagon had already appeared" by the summer of 1949. And decades later, those who took the challenge and entered his forested country claimed it was still easy to see Noah John's face in the light of his campfire during the cool evening and hear his voice on the breeze "loud and clear." Cold River City was a town with memories. It was a location visitors would always remember, and hermit Rondeau was a man they would never forget. "Noah lives everywhere," frequent Cold River visitor Bob Bates claims.

Charles E. Thomas remembers visiting Noah "while he was still there enjoying his uncontested position as mayor."

Reading the ripples. The water was still cool and the brook trout were on the bite.
Courtesy of Richard J. Smith from Noah's photo album

"I was on my first canoe trip and was with a large coed group from the Schenectady YMCA/YWCA called the Otyokwa Club. We all started out from the beach at Long Lake village together and stopped at Shattuck's Clearing...Here we split into two groups. ...the group I was a member of hiked up the trail to Cold River City. We ate lunch with Rondeau and our counselor, Dr. Lynn Stauffer."

Al Faustin of Oakland, California, was another member of the Otyokwa Club party. He recalls that "Noah was quite old when we were there. He took us through the beauty parlor, Mr. Rondeau's sitting room, the kitchen wigwam and Mrs. Rondeau's boudoir and I have forgotten what other teepees he had. He had a very large log in the middle of town—how he moved it there I have no idea. He used it as a backdrop for a small perpetual fire he kept going for his cooking.

"...My most vivid memory is of Noah's beloved violin. It was horribly out of tune—probably half the proper frequency. Mr. Stauffer, who was our chaperone, was also a concert violinist. He tuned it properly while we all held our breath for fear that a string would snap. It didn't. Noah played it a couple of minutes, then returned it to the slack tuning he had in the first place. He never told us whether that was to avoid breaking strings or if he just preferred the lower registers..."

NOAH JOHN RONDEAU
ADIRONDACK HERMIT
SARANAC LAKE, NEW YORK
FREE LANCE EXHIBITOR – LECTURES
NO BOOKER
WRITE, OR SEE ME PERSONALLY

Chapter 20

A Poet at Home

THE SPRING RAINS had washed the last vestiges of snow from mountain slopes. The snowshoe rabbit was losing its white winter coat. Noah scanned the river's edge for the tell-tale green patch.

"I like all the seasons," the Adirondack hermit admitted, "but I guess I like spring the best of all. It's the time of life, the most inspirin'. The birds come back and get busy buildin' their nests, preparin' for their young."

Noah was often in the wild alone—months at a time. Isolation did not bother him. He'd say, "I could go the whole day, into the evening and the night"—weeks on end. He wasn't alone, after all. The sky and the water were with him. The insects, birds and animals were with him, albeit impersonally. He'd point out when asked, "See that nuthatch half hidden in a tangle of leaves? The pink cherry blossoms nearby? And those yellow buttercups? And that one? Hardly alone."

Courtesy of Richard J. Smith from Noah's photo album

As the snow melted and new plants sprung forth, Noah's spring fever turned him into a prolific writer. He enjoyed trying to describe spring's great awakening in his rough poems. There was so much natural transformation every day, and he didn't want to miss a single sight. He saw a resident buck. The deer's hairy outline was a fair target. When the first snow came, he would be easy to track and easy to hit, as his body would make a bold outline against the surrounding whiteness.

For Noah John, the hunting of the deer and bear was necessity. For his friends who would begin arriving in October, it was exclusively a sport.

April 30 Saturday
Robins "cheer Up' early morning. I find lost manuscript ("1st. Debut"). 11 o'clock Air Plane drop 37 packages in my Briars. I gather supplies all day. Sundown,—Deer at 1st. Brook—above Dam—and 5 Deer—Tails gallop east in Dead Flow. Night Hawks screech. No Mice at Cold River Town Hall. Very few Barred Owls. Barley dropped from Air Plane at Spike Birch.

Noah John's entries furnish more than enough proof he had a flexibility with words. The many occasions when he addressed fraternal organizations further illustrate that he could also speak as imaginatively, credibly and humorously as he wrote.

While there is no disagreement that Noah John's attempt at poetic prose sounds simple and early rhymeless, it is nonetheless sincere and typical of an untrained pen. Despite the fact that there is hardly ever any genuine effort at any form of rhyme scheme or pattern, and it lacks traditional treatment, his form of poetry does communicate, unexpectedly well, his nature observations. There is no lost point in "Springtime Scramble."

When the calendar says, "Spring at Cold River"
Among Lofty Major Adirondack Peaks
Nights below zero still feel like winter
And hard packed snow is four foot deep.

After the Winter, the Sun and Earth change node,
It takes half of Springtime, to melt the snow.
The day is longer, the sun higher than before;
And the first bird to arrive is the crow.

And a fortnight later comes the Song Sparrows.
A barred owl hoots in the swamp's cedar groves;
A northern Flicker pulling his Machine Gun String
Plays resonant tattles on rock maple limbs.

And as we advance a month into Spring,
Ducks return, singing whirls with their wings.
April reserves patches of snow to greet May,
And launches the rest, to make vapor for rain.

And a Hawk over the sylvan mutely glides.
A sunny morning, brings Brown Butterflies.
And three Robins arrive, in afternoon glow.
On a patch of bare ground, surrounded with snow.

And now reddish soft Maple Buds can be seen.
Collectively, giving purple casts to the scene.
This is May Day among major Adirondack Peaks,
The vallie attitude -nineteen hundred feet.

Elder buds are the size of a egg of a sparrow,
But not a leaf has really started to grow.
The north-side of knolls, have patches of snow,
And grass is slightly greening along by the Cold River Flow.

And the birds are hanging cradles for babies
To rock and swing little Susie's and Jay's
And very faithful is the wind in attendance
While old birds collect and mince worms

And the ruby throated hummingbird
Stands in midair and darts with a whirl
He visits the flowers about the wigwam
And he keeps returning all summer long.
Now blue violets are blooming in little hollows
Often near little brooks of liquid ice snow
And on bordering banks tender ferns unroll
While the turkey breaks part in trios

Shad Flowers with five long white pedals
Are in bunches like laundered cotton
In the woods the Gold Thread is blooming
And Strawberry Flowers are in the clearings.

And next as we advance into May
The yellow violets bloom by the way
And everywhere in tender green-like lawn
Inlayed like growing suns are the Dandelions

Now Bluets bloom as neat as Quaker Ladies
Jack is in his pulpit, a flowering Spadix
White Pedaled Flowers are on Pin Cherry Trees
And Wake Robin Blossoms nod in the breeze

Panzy Flowers are a show by the cabin door
Foxgloves a foot high have a yard more to go
Catnip is as high as a cat's tail is long
And an old Doe has two spotted Fawns

And now deciduous foliage is half size
Making the forest trails a shade more dark
The clearings wood border daily densifies
And Mountain slopes are in summer style

Early Flower Pedals and Bud wrappers are falling
Sunshine has a new faze through tender green
This is Springtime at Cold River Wigwam
With fried trout and boiled dandelions

The Star Flowers are indeed blooming stars
Often in pair on single plant stock
Among all flowers they are stars well named
With perfect white pedals seven or eight

Blueberry Bushes have cupped flowers in bunches
To congregate the berries for the pickers
They grow green berries all through June
And summer Sunshine… ripens them blue
And the Bunchberry Plants are blooming
A quartlet of white pedals and deep leaves
The White Pedals might be called sepals or trimmings
Flowers for red berries are at center premeditating [sic]

Welcome May Day, and perfect Sun shining.
Purple finches arrive with songs for singing.
And a Kingfisher darts over the old Dam,
As a Churping Sparrow arrives on pebbles and sand.

Now Pussy Willows have Kittens and inch long.
With Stamens and yellow pollen all around.
They look like thimbles,- a little like Bumblebees.
But more like Pussy Willow Flowers on tiny Trees.

And now, Tag Alders, Catlins, are two inches long.
And trios and double pairs, hang like tassels of brown
On the river bank wild Spirea Leaves are peeking,
Just enough to speckle the border with green.

Now Bluets bloom as neat as Quaker Ladies.
Jack's in his pulpit A flowering spadix.
White pedaled flowers are on pin cherry trees
And Wake Robin blossoms nod in the breeze

And the Water Turtles come out on the banks
Trusting sunshine lay their eggs in the sand
And even birds with family cares don't cease to sing
While poplar leaves spin like coins hanging on strings

Stitchwort Flowers are all about camp
And their five clefted white pedals appear as ten
The leaves make tender picking for hens
And the vines are weak prostrate and bent

Now screaming his double voluminous music
The Scarlet Tanager comes late into May
He's seldom seen at very close range
But his notes are as sure as his scarlet joy

...Now fireflies have lantern parades at night
Like minute men they go flashing their lights
They think they are willow-o-wisps or a shooting star
Smarter than flies without lights to go out at night

Whitewood sorral is my last flower this Spring
Five white petals with reddish purple veins
I found the first flower The last vernal day

Guiding H.V. Holmes catching big fish.
In nineteen forty-four On June 21 at nine three A.M.
The sun entered Cancer
For northern terrestrial atmosphere Summer begins
And that is the end of the vernal spring "Springtime Scramble"

Noah John Rondeau's "Springtime Scramble" followed spring to the first day of summer. The hermit's concern is with the comings and goings of Mother Nature—with the melting snow and river rising, the birds and creatures, the rocks and trees, the greening plants and emerging insects and the fragrance and sounds, with cloud formations and with all that mattered springing directly from the mountains and the sky bending over the nearby peaks.

Nowhere, he must have thought, is a better place to observe and study these events, because in his small world there were so many mixtures.

Rondeau retrieved a gift of food from the fishermen at Doctor Latimer's camp placed in the usual cache near the Big Eddy May 1st. "I find Ham, Bacon and Salt Pork...also a Bag of Potatoes...I split 48 loaves of Rye Bread and dry them in the Sun—Hard Tacks for an Old Man without any sons.

> *May 14 Saturday*
> *...9 o'clock 3 Men arrive from Plattsburg. I escort to Seward Brook and Fishermen go to Seward Pond. 5 o'clock: Fishermen take pictures; I play violin. Evening,—very cool. We gaze astronomically.*

"I got an idea to go fishing." —NJR. *Courtesy of Richard J. Smith from Noah's photo album*

May 16 Monday

...Raccoon...call last night—rattle cans and took a 9 inch Trout, and 2 fish heads from an Earthen Jar. I saw its Eyes with dim light. I apply Muslin and White Paint to my Town Hall Table; while, Birds sing and Dandelions bloom and reddish- wrappers fall from Black Cherry Trees.

May 20 Friday

...Dandelion Greens—chief on menu. I make an Open A Tent. I knock down old shit house frame. Shoot at 2 crows. Make 1 fly slow. First humming Bird come to my Town Hall Door and buzz his propellers like Humming Birds years before.

The morning of May 29 was "cold, rain, snow...Panther Peak is white,—viewed from Cold River Wigwam. Man call from Schenectady. We view the River and the Hills; The Snow on Panther, The Spot on Couchsachraga. I put on Mittens to keep from freezing. At Camp: about noon- Snow Storm dance on the Roof like corn."

Now that Noah had established a trend of spreading the word about his life in the Adirondack backcountry since the first Sportsmen's Show in February of 1947, his sales of Cold River souvenirs held up pretty well, and sightseer traffic to the hermitage increased considerably from the unremarkable results of his attempts in the early twenties. There were frequent children's camp groups and adult visitors. Requests for him to make personal appearances at functions increased. More offerings of guest spots meant an improved yearly income. The whole character of his hermit life did an about-face within two short years.

June 4 Saturday

Breezy and hot Sunshine At Boy Scout Camporee, near Ithaca, N.Y. A happy long day at Scout Camp Ground. 9 P.M. I speak for an hour- at Scout's camp fire. 1,000,022 Grass Hoppers. Big Bear died about 1920 and he's been dead ever since.

Decades of living in the deep woods of the Adirondack Mountains continued to sharpen Noah's spirited observations and rather earthy anecdotes amid stinging, biting insects. "The dear little Midgets are hot footed on this 13th day of June."

> *June 16–20, 1949 Thursday–Monday*
> *A big Doe visited at Old Ladies Wigwam. 3 Fishermen call,—on way to Black Hole. I wait all day for Au Sable Valley A.D.K.'ers. No come. Oscar's Express from Saranac Lake arrived at Las Vegas, Nevada. Black Berry Blossoms at Standard best. I gather Beaver Sticks,—pebbles and spikes. 4 People arrive from Tahawus. 5 Trout at Seward Pond for the effort. Good Camp Fire—Big Bear Stories. At Dusk: A Deer call near Beauty Parlor. [Monday] Up at 5 A.M. Breakfast—pan full of fried Trout. 6A.M. Party go to Tahawus.*

> *June 23 Thursday*
> *Nice Summer Sunshine and variety of clouds At Cold River City Spreading Dog Bane blooms. 1:30 P.M. as I write: between Mrs. Rondeau's Kitchenette and Old Ladies' Wigwam an old Red Doe stands 30' from Me—near Beauty Parlor—and blows at Me.*

> *June 24 Saturday*
> *Clouds and showers; and pesky flies At Cold River City*
> *9 o'clock: Breakfast. 12-Noon at Seward Pond. Long easy shower. 3 o'clock: back to camp. Luncheon—Beauty Nap. Splendid Supper (with 4 Adirondackers: Hogue, Dodge, and 2 Dittmars). Gossip on street at Cold River City; A lot of talk about anything: The Reserve at the Dam, The Gore, Lumber camps—Good Movie Reel about Hermitage. How monkies pick fleas off each other—"no," says one. "Monkies don't have Fleas. They pick dry scales off skin." Another, "Dear me, I thought it was Fleas!"*

Between June 27 and July 2, Cold River City was raided by Public Enemy Number 1.

Last night: A raccoon eat Fish Heads—tumble tin cans—I step out with Flashlight—Coon climb on top of Old Ladies Wigwam. 3 A.M. Raccoon came Again. Tumbled milk and Bouquet of Daisies off the Table—He climb Tripod—eat boiled pork out of Dr. Dittmar's gal. can.

The Raccoon came again last night and walked on Mrs. Rondeau's serving Table within 4 ft. of flash light—He stood on hind feet and gazed to see what hellfire bug that was. Again he came—climbed tripod—got 2 slices Bologna from a pail that hung on tripod.

And again…

Last night Raccoon investigated for 2 hours at Wigwams; He comes within 3 ft. of Flashlight and stands on hind feet to make sure it's a Light.

July 3 Sunday
Hot weather—Deer Flies continue. The day before the 4th. At Hermit City 3 men arrive—Roy Lash Party—from Schenectady. Party to Seward Brook. Chicken dinner at Cold River Town Hall. 2 P.M.—Party go to E. Moose Creek. 7:30 P.M. E.S.T. an 8 Point Buck appear at Old Ladies Wigwam and look me over for 5 minutes; I sit near Smudge 25 ft. from him; Then he walk to Beauty Parlor and observe for few minutes.

July 4 Monday
Sunshine—clouds—10 P.M. showers. Peace—Beauty—Tranquility At Cold River City
Hurrah—Fourth of July! Let fools celebrate theory of Independence and tolerate bondage; and let other fools dress in colorful—tights and run a footrace,—for paper medal and American Blab; Let other fools go on a Hill overlooking the town; and shoot a fool Cannon as if bloody war was on. And for lucky Dart a good cigar. But give me the day alone in the wilds, by a River among

Mountains, even with Deer Flies. And the giddy may have Reminder of War—and "good cigar" and to hell with drunken shout—"Fourth of July."

July 17 Sunday
A nice day at Cold River
I heard Raccoon–tumble dishes last night. Did not get up. He's an Old Story. Morning proved he pushed my plate and spoon off the Table and He ignored String Beans I left for Him. The dear little Deer Flies are with us yet.

July 27 Wednesday
Clouds, Sunshine and Thunder Shower
The Raccoon got some corn and sleeked his mustache with pork fat last night. 6 P.M. Mr. and Mrs. Mc Kenzie from Middletown, Conn. arrived at Cold River, Town Hall. McKenzie paid 25 dollars to C.V. [Latimer] for paint on mountain top. {Received] Gruyere cheese—gift from Mc Kenzie. 3 P.M. thunder shower.

From a letter addressed to:

Noah J. Rondeau
Mayor of Cold River and
President of the Common Council and
Recreation Council

From:
R.G. Wiezel
Socony-Vaccum Oil Company, Inc.
P.O. 163
Athens, Greece

Dear Squire,
It is with a feeling of remorse and self-reproach that I take up pen

in the long overdue gesture of acknowledging your encyclical bull promulgated from your hermitage at Cold River some months ago. I was especially pleased with the excellent likeness of yourself which you enclosed. I notice that you have compromised with your holy resolve to only get converts by leading an exemplary life of meditation above the Swamp Cedars on the Flow and that you are now going forth bringing your message to the masses in no uncertain terms. However, I gather that at least during the summer you take up your abode in the old Cold River haunts and keep company with the denizens of Seward Pond.

The drought which has been visited upon the mountains this summer must really be a sad occasion for an old woodsman. I hope that it breaks before any serious fires get started. In any case, I can't believe that it will happen two years in a row and am looking forward to the mountains being there all fresh and green next year.

Big Horn Camp, Shattuck Clearing built by the CCC during the Great Depression. Cold River is in the valley behind the log cabin. *Photo by George Widill taken on October 30, 1945. Courtesy of Richard J. Smith from Noah's photo album*

Thanks to Grace Hudowalski I am still getting at long intervals my ADIRONDAC, in which occasional reference is made to your Cold River Bishopric as well as your appearance among the cities of men. I am still waiting to hear someone sees to it that your epic "Spring Comes to Cold River" gets into print. Hope to be writing you later upon my return to Turkey and would also appreciate hearing from you again.

Sincerely,
R.G. Wiezel

The McKenzie party returned on July 30. Rondeau met them "...at Cedar Swamp's South Bridge. They (will) take my mail to Bomyea's on Their way to Ward Creek Lean To."

July 31 Sunday
Rain half inch last night. Today: cool and cloudy.
At Cold River City
I put up New Tripod for Flower Caldron. Raspberries are at standard best. Thanks, July, for 31 days; Come again but not too soon—I'll be busy for 11 months; wait, until after June.

August 3 Wednesday
A nice Summer Day At Cold River City
Raccoons get Pork and Rice. 3 Handfuls of Black Berries. Umbellatus Asters begin to bloom. Last night a large Deer walk 6 ft. from my Bed. Mid Day Peter Ward—priest from Lyon Mountain and 3 young Men from Potsdam call to climb Couchsachraga Mountain. And without scientific philosophy,—what handicap is education, in a multiplicity of useless fool subjects. For instance:—A man over 500 years old building an Ark; and a man in a Fish in the Sea; And later the same man preaching to Nineveh. That's a mystery of Holy Blessed Trinity when you understand it, have an Onion. When you don't understand it, try 2 Onions.

Peter Ward described his group's trip in "Our Days in the Cold River Region." The article appeared in the May–June 1950 issue of the *Cloud Splitter* magazine. Ward, a frequent visitor to the hermitage, beams in his story.

> *"Noah gave us some 'broth'—contents: cold Ralston left over from morning; corn from a can opened in the morning and exposed to sun's rays; bouillon cubes; package of dried chicken noodle soup. Darned if it wasn't delicious! Hot, tired, dirty, thirsty—almost anything would have tasted good."*

"51 years ago to day, [August 8]," Rondeau remembered, "I ran away from home—Flew the Coop, 1898.

> *August 9–13*
> *I make 5 Canes. Mountains are wonderful—Vallies too. Golden Rod is blooming and so is Meadow Rue. Dr. and Mrs. Dunham and daughter, Jo Ann from Evansville, Indiana call. Crickets are well tuned up. I write. Put up New Maple Poles for clothes Line. I gather Crimson Cross Seeds. Another Brooklyn Man call on way down River. River Dale School call. A Humming Bird courts his reflection in the Mirror in Hut Gable. The raccoon called last night— first time in a week. Several Air Planes Soar. Raspberries are all gone. Blue Jay says "Thief! Thief!"*

> *August 31st Wednesday*
> *Cool and breezy after rain, perfect sun...in Cold River Valley. Last night: 2 raccoons get mouse in water pail. They come within 3 feet of flash light. Raccoon shit cherry stones on my grave.*

Edward J. Fox from Charlottesville, Virginia came into Rondeau's camp September 3rd. He referred to his group's Cold River trip as the "William J. McRoberts Memorial Hike." He said he remembered "Noah taking out a violin and playing for us. Phyllis Lynn, Irma, Ann and I thought it [the performance] was rather interesting." Fox was also treated to the hermit reading his original poem, “To a Fox.” Fox recalled, “It was an amusing affair.” The subject dealt with a frisky, clever fox that had survived the hermit’s trap. The poem is interesting as an illustration of Rondeau’s level of education, and the refinement of his mind, despite the rough verses.

To A Fox

“Fox,—You’re a Fox,—a very Foxy Old Fox;
And You’re as pretty, as You are wise;.
Your Fox Tail following with equal grace,
Your body’s perfect glide along a trail.

…And as smooth as on a single Skate,-
You Moon Light Trot the Frozen Lake.
And watching Your shadow, the Fairies think,
They drive a span, across the bay.

…But You’re not just Foxy—pretty and wise,
Sleek, full of philosophy—cunning and sly;
You have all this, and fire in your Eyes,
And you call a Hermit Trapper “a City Guy.”

…And not satisfied, you come right back,
And on the snow You leave Your Card,
Between the pan of my New Trap,
And Snow Prints of Your Autograph.

…If it takes all winter with a double st,—
You Imp from hell. I’ll catch You yet.
Watching Your shadow, on my New Trap,—
Straining to stink in bright Moon Light.

You’ll be surprised, from within the snow.
When my other Trap spring, and catch Your toes.
And you hang in briars—by metal Hook,
That will change Your foxy jubilant look…

Snippets from September 4–13 entries.

32 People call. Air Plane (makes) 2 circles over Cold River City. Chipmonks cart Cherry Stones. Raccoons eat Fish Heads and Deer make tracks at door. The River is high. [Editor's Note: In response to a statement from an Instant Maxwell House Coffee clipping he has pasted in his journal— "Makes about as many cups as a pound of regular coffee."—he pens: "Not quite true."] Briars and Deciduous Forest show insinuation of Autumn Rust. I went west of Seward Pond and got a Bear Trap. Saw a quill pig S. of Seward Pond. A dozen Bouquets of Crimson Maple Leaves garnish Seward Pond. 2 packages. Violin case of books I carry to Ranger Bomyea's near Moose Creek. Two men raft down flow. Noodle soup and coffee. Briars and deciduous forest show insinuation of Autumn rust.

September 25th Sunday
Some clouds—lots of sunshine, gentle breeze. I dig a 200 pound boulder out of path and put it on north end of Pebble Tray against Permanent Boulder on my Ashes Ground...

Noah referred to his grave as the "Ash Ground." It was a site he had prepared in advance of his death. His belief was that some person would someday come along and find him dead on Cold River Hill. Funeral instructions were left in a visible location tacked on the Town Hall wall. The label on the envelope read "If at My Wigwam you find Me Dead." Noah instructed the finder to stack all the wigwam poles into a funeral pyre, place his "carcass on combustible bulk" and "cremate to vapor and to dust."

When October arrived, the recorder first painted an autumn picture before squashing the 15th-century sea captain Christopher Columbus in typical Rondeau sarcastic style.

October 1–7
Frost, Sunshine, Perfect breeze. At Cold River City. At Seward

"Charging Dee Fiddle, 1946. An interested and captivated listener." —NJR.

Courtesy of Richard J. Smith from Noah's photo album

Pond—many Soft Maples are Sunshine yellow, not usual crimson. Frost shrouded briars with white; and blanched greenest grass and crisped foliage on bordering trees. Then, Sunrise poured a shower of leaves. Tree tops are getting nude.

October 12th Wednesday
Clouds and Sun; very breezy,- wind sweeps Autumn Leaves around the Hut. At Cold River City. Columbus Day! When Columbus landed (he) made a law to "put to death" whom dare say "He was not in India." A few hours later: Made another law to "Put to death whom dare to think "He" was not in India. Great Man? Great Mind? Great India? ...

A picture with the Cold River hermit was a frequent request. This photograph, with an unidentified couple, is believed to have been taken in front of Crandall's Hardware Store in Marathon, N.Y. on March 25 1950. *From Noah's photo album. Courtesy of Richard J. Smith*

October 18th Tuesday
Frost last night. Today: Sunshine
At Cold River City. I call at Buck Slough. Beauty walk in Dead Flow. The bunch on my arm is worst. Swollen. Sore.

The late fall attractiveness was disappearing by October 19 when he noted he took a "Beauty walk in Dead Flow. I sit on Browning Grass near the Flow and watch the colors come and go..."

With the arrival of frost, Rondeau decided October 22 would be a good time to visit friends living outside the river. "Breakfast with Lucius Russell [at Shattuck Clearing.] Dinner at Adirondack Coffee Shop. Supper at 4 Alpine Terrace, Saranac Lake [where] I tune the Violin and warm up the Irish Washerwoman."

He continued to remain busy traveling between Saranac Lake and Au Sable Forks between October 24–29. "I write "Fire Prevention [essay]" for Shirley Miller. Call at Gray's Cheeman, laundry, P.O. Turkey supper and slide pictures-speaking; Good Time. Call at Dittmar mansion. Mary Dittmar take me to Dr. Spranz and to [my sister] Priscilla McCasland's. I paste 30 photographs in Album. I hunt north of Ampersand Mt. with Bill Hooley and Philip Mc.Calvin. Prepare to go to Cold River."

On November 1 Noah returned to Cold River City on a "Nice late Autumn day;...

Clouds and showers. Park car 3 mile mark. See Hunter on Rondeau's Hill. 11 A.M. at Peek-a-Boo Cabin. Noon: Look for Bear Trap on top of Hill. 3:30 P.M. at Camp Wild Cat. Fancy Supper in 2 Tin cans; and Fancy Bed by Calkins Brook. Rain during night 3 miles through wet Spruces. At Dark (5 P.M.) set up camp in Jungle. Night: wet, cold, snowed—1 inch. Up at dawn in snow Jungle (code). Walk to Chattock Clearing by compass. Dinner at Twin Bridges cross Cold River at dusk. Supper and Lodge at Big Horn Camp.

By November 3, "the mountain Scenes are winter-like; and the feel of Valley Air verifies 'winter like.'"

At this point in the month Noah began "commuting" between the hermitage and Ranger Russell at Shattuck Clearing.

November 7–13: "…I carry pack to Big Horn [camp]. I hunt 5 hours on Sugar Bush Hill…I carry Bill Petty's Basket to Jack Ass Gate.

For several years the Clarence Whiteman deer hunting party pitched their camp near the Big Eddy. Clarence volunteered that his party arrived with the regularity of a well-turned grandfather. "Our seasonal visits with Noah made it extra special for us. It's hard to explain why we derived so much pleasure from so much work. The hermitage was a long ways back in the woods, but it was worth it. I suppose you would have to have been a participant to really understand what it was like."

November 16 Wednesday
Ice last night. Today: cloudy, cold. Mountain tops are white. At Cold River Town Hall. 2 P.M. 1 eye at Alexander's stand. 3 P.M. A good shit in Fancy shit wigwam. 10 A.M. 3 hunters call from (Clarence) Whiteman camp. I hunt 3 Legged Swamp. 2 to 4 P.M. I watch at mouth of Seward Brook.

With the arrival of the winter of 1949–50, the hermit closed camp and headed out for the McCalvin family's home in Saranac Lake on November 27. That night he wrote: "Quite cloudy and cold…I read and write. Very quiet at Saranac Lake. I shop in catalogues. 4 P.M. I talk [on the telephone] with 'We The People.' [Penned next to a clipping for the *Poultry Tribune*: "This (catalog) cost me 2 cents…"]

Late November found the Cold River hermit in New York City.

November 29–30 Tuesday–Wednesday
Very cloudy and mild. At Saranac Lake - On the Train and at New York City. Motor to Lake Clear—Set up Hermit Replica and take pictures—Open Fire, Hunt, Set Traps, Mix batter and

handle rifle. 9:53 P.M. leaving Saranac Lake on Sleeper for New York City "We the People." Up at dawn in my little apartment on Sleeper. As train moves along the Hudson River—feeble dawn and flying gulls. Belmont Plaza Hotel is a splendid Satisfactory place to stay—any time while in N.Y. City.

December 2 Friday
Cloudy, mild, noon—showers
At N.B.C. International Theatre—"We The People" Television Rehearsal at 3:15 and 6:15 P.M. Broadcast at 8:30–9:00 P.M..
"Yipee-i-Yi, Yippee- i- Yay!"

"I'm not sure exactly what day he came to be interviewed," Dorian St. George said, "but I can tell you with absolute certainty that never have I been so delighted as an announcer at ABC in New York than the year I was assigned to attend the Sportsmen's Show in 1949…and find [Noah to interview] for a late evening sports program…"

December 7, 1949
A letter from WE THE PEOPLE
Madison Avenue
New York, N.Y.

Dear Noah,
I want to thank you for the splendid performance and wonderful cooperation in making last Friday's WE THE PEOPLE such a successful one. I hope the strain of all the rehearsals required by the combination broadcast and telecast was not too great and that you left with a warm spot in your heart for WE THE PEOPLE. If we can ever be of assistance to you please don't hesitate to call us and again many thanks.
James Sheldon, Producer, WE THE PEOPLE

By December 9, Noah was back in the Adirondacks and living with the McCalvins, readying for the Christmas season and preparing for new challenges in 1950.

> *December 9 Friday*
> *I shop. I write 15 Xmas cards. I call at Saranac Supply store—*
> *Give Bill Mullen a kick in the seat—later: found a big Red Apple in my coat pocket.*

Chuck Dunham's most vivid memory of Noah revolved around a chance encounter on a winter day, one he loved to tell about.

> *My only personal contact with Rondeau was in the winter of 1949–50, when I was advertising salesman for the Daily Enterprise. These were the years when Noah was the star of the annual Sportsmen's Show in New York City and elsewhere.*
>
> *Well aware of Noah's reputation after his lifetime of living on Cold River, I recognized him one day walking toward me on Main Street of "the Village," as we called Saranac Lake. He apparently recognized me, or thought I was worth greeting. He had an almost European courtly manner, as he bowed slightly at my approach. There was no conversation that I remember.*
>
> *Why should he have taken any notice of me? I've wondered. But looking back, I was a tall lad of 20, well dressed, and as I had no car, I made it around town in quick, long strides…I must have had an odd appearance. (When I went into Charlie Green's Store 40 years after my winter in Saranac Lake, the old man immediately recognized me: "You used to work for the Enterprise.")*

Dunham said he thought but emphasized that he did not know for certain, "that Noah lived, at the time, in the Berkeley Hotel." He remembered it might have "been on the corner of Main and Broadway" and that it might have been a three-story frame structure entirely occupied by "permanent guests, not transients…"

December 13
I call at 14 Academy Street. Confab with Richard Smith, Anna Rice, Frank Baker and Mrs. Vosburg and Mrs. Bray. 2 o'clock I attend Rites for Charles Middlebrook Palmer. I guided Irving S. Cobb in Palmer's Party July 6, 1923.

December 15 Thursday
Snowed 1 inch last night. Today:—calm and sunshine with 1 inch snow on ground I mail 7 pkgs. and 60 cards. Santa Claus is busy and so is Old Saint Nick. 8 P.M. Philip McCalvin go to picture show.

December 17–18
Received 2 letters, 5 cards. I write 2 letters. Herman Bova from Ogdensburg call and leave a gallon of wine. Anna Pettnato came to 4 Alpine Terrace and played pinochle. We drank the gallon of wine. I sew 5 skins of floss on checkered shirt. I help Philip and Helen McCalvin set up the Christmas Tree—and trim.

December 31, 1949 Saturday
The last of 1949. 3 inches of Snow cover the ground At Saranac Lake I read and write. Got letter from V.J. Steers in Alaska. 12 Mid-Night 1949 is done. The days went one by one. Now it's a random scoot around the Sun. And 1950 is just begun.

Noah John ended his diary with a future event he and other amateur astronomers surely looked forward to with great anticipation: "Beginning of 1950. There will be a total Solar Eclipse September 11, 1950."

★ ★ ★

The week before Bette and I left on our week-long Cold River vacation, I remember I darted back and forth from home to our camp on the Tug Hill Plateau. I would start a fire in the cobblestone outdoor fireplace and sit, randomly flipping through Rondeau's diaries (I have copies of all of them), stopping to read what Noah had written on a particular date that marked an occasion in my own life. For example, on Wednesday, September 18, 1963, my last year in high school, Noah recorded: "To Day Perfect Sunshine; and perfect Autumn Colors, coming to climax." He continued in code that has since been deciphered: "Put down 1 pint of Good Deal Soup. I cook Slam Bang. I get 5840 cents [from] Mr. Welfare."

Almost one year later, during the week Bette and I were making final plans for our wedding—and our subsequent Adirondack honeymoon at Blue Mountain Lake—Noah jotted "Monday, 24 August 1964. Overcast at Singing Pines. I go to Wilimington. Call at P.O. and at Melvin Peck, and Eleanor's Restaurant. I taxi to Mrs. Dodge. National Democratic Convention open, in Atlantic City-N.J. I sit at TV and scribble Notes of convention. I Taxi home at Mid-Night."

That late August afternoon, I placed Post-It Notes on the pages I liked best, and thought about the leaf changes on Tug Hill and how much more fall color might be showing in the High Peaks.

Listening to Bette's questions and seeing her enthusiasm as we hiked in "Noah's country" in the fall of 2007 got me thinking of all the one-of-a-kind photos I wanted to show her in Doc Latimer Jr.'s Cold River photo album when we returned. I was also struck with a rather obvious thought: I should try to find a way to share more of the common entries in Noah's yearly journals. I knew the daily recordings were not remarkable, nor did his coded entries reveal anything earthshaking. Yet each one continued to trace his life—from the woods to the Outside to his passing. And, I knew there are people who find his life in and out of the Adirondack wilds intriguing.

The hermit's life is a legend, the likes of which the Adirondack Mountains don't produce anymore. The Adirondack Forty-Sixers and the Adirondack Mountain Club have their hiking and service volunteer enthusiasts. The Adirondack Park has its vocal preservationist supporters. Adirondack folklore has Noah John Rondeau.

I remember one fall I was at Singing Pines with Richard Smith. Sinking sunlight glistened on the vibrant leaf carpet that was as solid as it was colorful. I told Richard that I thought a place can have a "presence." I felt that aura when I camped on Cold River Hill and I felt it at Singing Pines. He agreed.

This "presence" is an air or general feeling. It's not always dependent on an appearance. The presence of an object at a specific place is also not necessarily needed.

Noah's hilltop impresses me as peaceful, and his diaries, although they may seem simple, also evoke a particular feeling—a presence. His 1950 journal did not let me down.

Bette O'Hern at Cold River Hill. The former site of Rondeau's hermitage has a feel of peace and tranquility. *Photograph by William J. O'Hern*

Chapter 21

The Ex-Mayor's First Outside Year

THE LANDSCAPE OF COLD RIVER country is "handsome," as Noah has said, but the humans who were part of the landscape were what made it interesting. To me, those who dwelled in the corridor of the lumberjacks' Cold River Trail brought life to the territory. Maybe the fact that I knew some of them personally makes a difference, and maybe it's also that I knew so much about them, and so understand more of what went on. Or maybe Bette is right when she tells me Cold River's rhythms are a part of me. I'm not prepared to give a definitive answer on just why I'm drawn to this Adirondack land. All I wanted to do when we returned from our backpack trip was immerse myself in Noah John's diaries. I wanted to set aside the fall scenery, the weather, and our accomplishments and concentrate on what exactly happened to the man who left it all behind.

Noah returned to Saranac Lake from the mountains by way of the Ampersand Park route, according to his November accounts. He toted a backpack of staples and necessaries, often through tangles of downed trees.

By the second half of the 20th century, 37 years after Noah Rondeau had left Lake Placid and moved to Coreys, one would assume he'd successfully made the transition from dissatisfied barber and restless wanderer to trapper and woodsman. According to Richard Smith, somewhere inside was a man who was the picture of a life of solitude removed from society, who felt more comfortable out-of-doors enjoying nature's soft sounds. But he had no sooner begun to settle in around the Raquette River than he began to grasp the fact that in order to survive it would be necessary to guide an occasional sport—a mountain greenhorn—in order to earn cash for needed staples.

He might have squawked that he was "no slave to industry," but he was also a realist. When proprietor Fred Woods called on him to act as an occasional fishing and hunting guide for the guests at Foresters Inn, Rondeau's practical side came into play.

Rondeau's friends have consistently reported his goal of living on $100 to $200 a year. He claimed that was all he needed. Trapping was a stable livelihood and one way to earn money, but of course it would take amazing luck to accumulate enough furs to rely on trapping alone, particularly with constantly fluctuating prices. Add to that Richard Smith's assessment of Rondeau's preparation of hides: "He lost money because his fur stretching and preparing was never done with great care. Yet, he didn't mind."

It seems Noah John was typical of some trappers who were just glad if in return for their furs they got provisions, ammunition and clothes enough to last them through the following year. After all, he lived mainly on greasy fritter flops, simple bread, soup, sauces, his notorious Everlasting Stew, and

Cold River beyond the Big Eddy. "We moved on through a picturesque river valley toward Cold River Hill. I told Bette Noah knew his bearings well in this territory and that Bob "Cold River" Bates was really the only other person in the whole world who knew the inconspicuous places as well as the hermit had." —W.J.O.

Photograph by William J. O'Hern

wild meat, and his living habits were almost always rough. That is part of the simple style of the hermit business, the part that comes from living alone in a place where survival is more important than gourmet provisions or stylish dress.

"Noah was a level-headed fellow," Smith put forth. "His way of getting by, as you can imagine, would give most people a scare." He was a practical don't-you-worry-about-me kind of person. Smith also said with one hundred percent certainty that Noah had scanty confidence in the people he guided. "The most of them, he told me, drank too much and talked too much."

And probably because the Conservation Commission would not issue him a guide license after his run-in with the law in 1924, he gradually started to get accustomed to a rougher sort of life, and little by little he fell in line with the idea of living back at Cold River rather than having any social life with greenhorns he didn't care much for anyway.

Clarence Petty confirmed Rondeau's position on guiding parties. Petty weighed in: "Rondeau never said much of anything about the parties he took out. It was not unusual for him to avoid addressing the people he spoke to by either their first or last name unless he was specifically talking about someone."

Petty continues on the issue of Noah's lack of eagerness to solicit work.

> *As for Noah guiding parties, he never cared very much for very many of the people who asked him to guide them—mostly hunting parties in the fall—and he would take a few of them but his disregard for money and care for some of the things he had is exemplified by something he told me he done one time. He had an auto loading rifle, I think it was a .30-.30, and he was on one of his traplines up on the side of a mountain back of his camp and he got tired of carrying the gun and decided to leave it. So he just took the stock and drove it into the top of an old rotten stump and left it there. A year later he said it was still there. I don't know if he ever went back there to get it or not.*
>
> *Noah didn't take very good care of the furs that he caught. After skinning and fleshing them out and drying them he would*

very often leave quite a bit of the stuff on the hide and then he sent them out, usually to some place in St. Louis, one of those places where we used to deal with the furriers. He would just double them up rather carelessly and put them into a bundle and ship them. We were rather careful on how we handled the furs because we felt we could get more for them, but Noah never cared too much about money. He never seemed to look ahead in life very far, although he did recognize that he would probably die some day and he rigged a place up there at the place he called High Banks where he said he would probably be buried and yet he never seemed to realize that the time would come when he would be physically unable to be there, which was rather unusual, I feel, for someone who had spent a lot of time talking about astronomy and things of that nature.

★ ★ ★

Noah's 1950 diary begins the last phase of his life story, the part that happened outside Cold River country. The bitter cold of the 1940s was not experienced in the Adirondack Mountains in the decade that followed, but there were still clear nights, howling wind and plenty of foul weather to enjoy from the safety of his newfound home. Ever the philosopher, he wrote this entry followed by his day's activities.

The headnote "Belated Monkies" seems to be one of Rondeau's favorites. It is repeated in several diaries.

"Belated Monkies"
In Evolution, there were Men and Monkies, without Gods, for millions of years, before Bible, Myth, Liar (God), presumptuously made a 'First Man' from a handful of dust that was not a week old.

Let Fools be Fools, and liars—liars; Even the kind of Monkeys that go to Church with Bibles.

Lest We Forget

The days went one by one, 1949 is done; Now its a Random Scoot around the Sun; and 1950 is just begun. But We have a Diary with us yet—Lest We forget Dear Roosevelt.

Roosevelt—President Elect, Everlasting X and running yet—would be Roosevelt if He was not dead. But since He's dead, and gone to hell—riddance is hard to get-the-Democrats are with us yet, Least We forget—Dear Roosevelt.

[Noah began many years with an entry about Roosevelt, who he found objectionable.]

January 1, 1950 Sunday
Calm, mild and Sunshine. A nice winter day At Saranac Lake. Mid-Century:—at end of 1950. For many this is "the day" after the night before. Petty at the Conservation office, Methodist Food sales, worked with the Saranac Lake Winter Carnival committee, much chatting.

When jack-of-many-trades Rondeau had first come to Saranac Lake as a laborer at the turn of the century, it was just beginning to emerge as a fashionable destination resort that would eventually be served by two railroads and multiple taxi companies and would boast of personalities such as Mark Twain, Robert Louis Stevenson, Albert Einstein, Jack Dempsey, Al Jolson, and Somerset Maugham, for starters. Dr. Edward Livingston Trudeau's sanitarium became the Western Hemisphere's foremost center for the treatment of pulmonary tuberculosis.

It was vastly different by the time Noah returned in 1950. Saranac Lake had continued to grow and develop. According to an article at www. wikipedia.org, "The development of a pharmaceutical cure for tuberculosis in the 1950s brought the curing era to a close and set in motion the village's development as a family resort destination. The cultural amenities once demanded by recovering patients lived on in emphasis of education and the arts."

There must have been times when Noah John wondered if he had left all semblance of his frontier homestead behind him in Cold River, where his life had been so vastly different. As an old man he loved hearing boat builder Henry N. Allen, local artist and instructor of painting and drawing at the Saranac Lake Study and Craft Guild Ray Ridabock, and Seth and Pearl McCalvin tell about the village's earlier days.

Throughout January, Noah lived in one of the McCalvins' spare bedrooms in Saranac Lake. Noah John invested some of his prior year's earnings in several photos that showed him posing with some "hermit fancy." His favorite picks from those professionally produced images were turned into personalized post cards. Rondeau ordered 3,000. Buoyed by the successful sale of his earlier personalized cards, he wanted to be prepared to continue the income they generated at this year's shows, dinner parties and the gatherings he would attend.

Besides the energy he put into his hermit-related business, his journal records the usual and mundane. Noah went to the movies, ate dinner with the McCalvins, helped care for their baby boy, scanned cover-to-cover agricultural catalogs on the presumption that on some future day he might like to raise bees and poultry, read and wrote letters, attended funerals, shopped, and confabbed with friends.

His remarks throughout the year seem quite commonplace. "Splendid supper cooked by Herb Williams." "Chat, wrestle and dance with young fellows." "I spoke 'On Trip to New York City.'" While the entries are ordinary, they illustrate the changes the long-time woodsman was beginning to make as he shifted to a life outside his mountain hermitage.

[Rondeau's diary entries are not always self-explanatory. Notes with further matters of general interest, correction and comment are within brackets; amplification when he wrote in code appears as caps.]

January 16, 1950 Monday
Heavy Rain last night. Today: Sunshine, Bare Ground, Cold wind.
At Saranac Lake, N.Y.

I call on Photographers-14 academy. Call at C.C. office. Shop at E.L. Gray's. SADIE SHUMWAY COME AND TELEPHONE. CUTTING PORK. Evening: Willets come and play cards. Agent call-selling JESUS ON A CLOCK. Philip McCalvin & Helen Duprey Married 1946.

January 27, 1950 Friday
I call at P.O., Saranac Supply, Adirondack hardware and Methodist Food Sale. I SELL 2 PHOTOS & GIVE AWAY OVER A DOZEN...7 to 10 P.M. at [Saranac Lake] Town Hall-Carnival Show Meeting. Special Meeting. 1 BATH-26 DAYS.]

Noah wasn't making much money at appearances, maybe a few bucks a talk, but the praise was worth more than money. "That was a real good talk, Noah." "We'd like to have you come back." "Maybe next time you would read some of your poems." That was pretty heady stuff. The money went quite a ways for a former hermit's needs in those days, too, but it was mostly the people he enjoyed. Everybody wants to be loved; I know he wanted to be loved, and talking got him the attention he'd never gotten any other way.

February 7, 1950 Tuesday
I work 4 hours at Town Hall trimming Cold River Replica. 7 to 10 P.M. I listen to an American Fool Radio until I renew my vow "never a Radio in My Home."

Here perhaps he should have qualified *never to own another* "American Fool Radio." As much as Noah crowed that the radio was nothing more than a "screech owl," and of the emerging television, "A bay window with a screech owl," he was continually exposed to both when he lived outside the hermitage. His primary complaint about the electronic media was the number of advertisements and the manner in which the product propaganda was squawked at listeners.

February is reliably snowy in the Adirondacks. Winter temperatures back in the mountains had always been Noah John's enemy. Blizzards were

Incoming vacationers and sports would follow the dirt road that curled through the hamlet of Coreys in Clarence Petty's and Noah's day. *Courtesy of Clarence Petty*

his greatest danger when on a trap line. The fall of heavy flakes obliterates snowshoe tracks and wipes out visibility quickly.

February 8, 1950 Wednesday
Last night 24 degrees below zero. Today: Calm and Perfect Sun. At Saranac Lake, N.Y. I purchase a Pot of live Flowers for a Queen; And I trim 2 canes. 7:30 I crown King and Queen [at the Saranac Lake Winter Carnival]. I SELL 2 PHOTOS & GIVE AWAY OVER A DOZEN. 1 BATH IN 26 DAYS. LETTER FROM OSCAR [Burguiere].

February 12, 1950 Sunday
...I work 5 hours at Town Hall taking down Exhibit—to ship to Lake Clear. I see a few American Fools from Paul Smith College (Smart Alex). I autograph 25 Photographs.

Some would describe Noah John as an "earthy" man. I guess there were also those who would describe him as sharp-tongued. "Cagey" is another term I have heard. His English was faulty. He would pronounce a word wrong now and again, and he peppered his dialogue with French. Perhaps he seemed dim-witted to those who didn't know any better. A rube might say, "Oh, I can take him." Then they didn't take him. He was ahead of them before they even opened their mouths. He was razor-sharp with horse-trader sense; he fooled them. They walked right into his web!

Along with Valentine cutouts that are pasted on his February 14 page is this thank you letter.

Dear Mr. Rondeau,

On behalf of the Saranac Lake Chamber of Commerce and the winter carnival committee we wish to extend our appreciation for your time and effort which you expended in the 1950 winter carnival. We would appreciate your further cooperation if you would be kind enough to stop into the Chamber of Commerce office...

and express any ideas or suggestions you might have that might be incorporated into the 1951 winter carnival.
Robert J. Brennan, Secretary
Chamber of Commerce

Noah's diary entries let us know he participated in the Winter Carnival parade four times: 1948, '49, '50 and '51. During the 1950 pageant he held the privilege of crowning the winter queen and king. Not only did he enjoy standing on the platform of his miniature Cold River City display, pulled through the main avenue by a slow-moving Caterpillar; he said he enjoyed the cold, crisp air and the beauty of moonlight that reflected on the ice castle, the snow-covered streets and lawns and frozen Lake Flower.

February 21, 1950 Tuesday
At 4 Alpine Terrance. Water Pipes froze.
I PAID $10.00 BOARD. I talk with H. V. Holmes
over the wire IN MARATHON, N.Y.
I GET DISTEMPER-GERMS FROM GARY [McCalvin].

February 22, 1950 Wednesday
Cloudy, cold
At Saranac Lake
Again: I have to listen to an American Hateful Fool of a Radio; Never a Radio in my Home! 7 o'clock: Again, and yet, the Radio is still Advertising in my Ears. Ironized yeast, True Love Story by Walker. I'm sick of American weak minded Radio Whoop.

Noah penned a letter on February 17 and addressed it to *The North Creek News.* It appeared in the March 1, 1950, issue. Rondeau's rambling discourse attempts to poke fun. It's an example of the philosophy of a man whose background was different than most—a rough gentleman of the mountains.

Gentlemen:
I've just been reading the last issue of North Creek News; and

find—17 suggestions as to what is news and, after searching my stock and store I found very little up to date news because;— I did kill a few pigs but not in last ten years and,—shot a "wife" perhaps just because "I never got married."

I "borrowed a stamp I loaded a stamp," but it's a long time ago and the stamps were all paid back–and—Slate Clean on both sides. There is fresher news in astronomy, the trees on one acre or the growing moss on one mountain boulder. For a hermit I made many speeches but it's been days on end since I took the platform for forty-five minutes. I never robbed a bank and come to think I can't give a good reason why not. Perhaps never knew enough. A hermit is very dumb. I never sold a dog and never lost a wife. Gone fishing many times and never caught a fish that was bigger than the pool; I was most places but as far back as can't remember committing suicide, if I did it was not successful because I am still

December 29, 1939. Noah with a post-Christmas group showing off their fancy clay pipes at the Billy Burgers' Pipemakers home in Westport, N.Y. *Courtesy of Jean Burger Cushman*

thinking. Here people are wrong on two sides. They say I thought I was dead and when they are dead they don't think so. "Drowned a cat?" No, I killed wild cats a long time ago but never drowned one. "Been away?" Always from most places: but as far back as I can remember I was always somewhere and once I did not know where I was, I went to the woods for a week and forgot to take my compass and later—I got my compass and it took me two weeks to go back and find out where I had been. And, that's better than Columbus ever did when he came here. He didn't know where he was going and when he got here he didn't know where he was and when he got back home he didn't know where he had been. "Take a vacation?" Not me. When I was fifteen I left the house to get a pail of water and was gone three months; and fifteen years later I was so fed up with the handicaps of civilization. Bookish Education, and Lack of Common Practical Sense. I went into the woods for 33 years but never thought of it as 'on vacation.' "Got licked?" Maybe. Always but mostly just vocally behind my back. "Made a bet?" And—LOST. Well—a long time ago, I used to bet up to forty thousand dollars but it was only vocal expression to go higher than the other wager—and-so-I got as rich by losing as by winning. And that's all the news for today except that I might find a bit more news by sticking my nose in others people's business. I didn't know that Mr. Thomas Kelley or Mr. Charles Egor of Tahawus ever killed a pig; but I know they were away from home today because they called on me at Saranac Lake and in spite of the fact that I was with them for the day in 1949 we are still not on speaking terms today, well we talked quite a lot, the trouble was we wanted two hours and only had thirty minutes. Threats were made on both sides to take hold again at first opportunity.

Noah John Rondeau, Adirondack Hermit
Written at 4 Alpine Terrace.
Saranac Lake, NY
March 15, 1950 Wednesday

...I telephone Billy Burger. 3 O'clock: ...I go with Him to Pipemakers [name of the Burgers' home] on Lake Champlain near Camp Dudley. 8 to 9 P.M. I speak to Westport Hi Wi FOR 60 MINUTES. 3 KISSES FROM 3 BELLES. 5 P.M. MRS. LILLIAN BURGER SPREAD BLANKET OVER ME. She said "Nothing like it for us Old People."

Earlier in March, Noah had received this letter:

I received a telephone call from Mr. Holmes of Marathon this week informing me that you will be free to come and speak at our Sportsmen's Banquet March 28th. He told me the charge would be $25 and your expenses. I sincerely hope you will drop me a line confirming your ability to come and the fee.

This will be a great occasion for us sportsmen in Bainbridge. There are quite a few men in this locality who are acquainted with you and are eager to visit with you again.

Mr. Holmes and I are attending to the details of transportation from Marathon to Bainbridge and back. It is a short distance.

Trusting this finds you in the best of health & I may hear from you in the very near future, I remain,

Very truly yours,
William R. Burton

March 24–26, 1950 Friday–Sunday
Mild,—cloudy; lots of snow slush. On Train to Syracuse and Bus to Marathon. 2:10 A.M. at Utica—wait 100 minutes for train to Syracuse. 7–8:30 A.M. on bus to Cortland. 9 o'clock at Cortland Hotel. 10–11 with H.V. Holmes from Cortland to Marathon—14 miles. Lunch on way. Afternoon: Beauty Sleep at H.V. Holmes. 8:30–9:30 I speak 60 minutes to 373 people. Sold several photographs.

I entertain at 3 stores and 6 houses in Marathon, N.Y. I greeted customers. Several People call at Holmes to see Hermit. I draw ticket from box for Lady who win a good Fish Pole.

I go with the Holmes; car ride of 25 miles-in beautiful Vallies among beautiful Hills. Called at Old House where John D. Rockefeller Sr. was born.

Mrs. Holmes play piano, Mr. Holmes play a saw, I play Violin. A good visit. Happy Day at Marathon.

March 28, 1950 Tuesday
...At Marathon and Bainbridge...9:50 to 11:05 p.m.
I give 75 minutes, Lecture on Hermit Life and Hermit Debut.
I SELL ABOUT 68 AUTOGRAPHED PHOTOGRAPHS.

On Thursday, March 30, Rondeau was using the power of the radio to hawk his Cold River exhibit at an upcoming show: "...1:30 on the air (waves) 15 minutes advertising Tahawus Sportsmen's Show tomorrow."

By April the bitter cold had abated. The air continued to be clear and the light breeze promised continued fair weather.

Noah's "Replica Exhibit," which he first set up along Route 3 at the Coreys Road turnoff. This mockup of Cold River City was next moved to a location along the Whiteface Mountain highway and later to a number of other locations.
Courtesy of Richard J. Smith

Phillip McCalvin's mother died April 19—one day short of the date her husband had died in 1949. Noah accompanied the McCalvins, who gathered at Richard McCalvin's home in Lake Placid.

April 19, 1950 Wednesday
...I go to lake Placid with McCalvins. I call at Clark's Funeral Home. I call at Richard McCalvin. I SEND FLOWERS FOR MRS. MCCALVIN. I BUY 1 LITTLE BROWN JUG...

When May arrived, Noah knew he would have no trouble keeping warm even on the coldest of pre-summer nights. He made arrangements to secure, rent free, space where he could once again unroll his bearskin blankets, hang up his steel traps, go off into the woods to shoot a couple of rabbits, and with their meager flesh prepare his well-known "Everlasting Stew." The opportunity to live throughout the summer beyond Saranac Lake was almost too much for him. His excitement mounted daily. Soon he would be signing autographs and be in demand. Perhaps he thought he had tumbled out of bed and awakened from a dream. Just a few years before, he'd been scrounging around for a dime for a sack of dried beans.

May 9, 1950 Tuesday
A Perfect Vernal Day
Saranac Lake—Corey's, Eklund
Robin cheer cheer—cheer up! I find dead Wood Thrush. It seem,—killed by Telephone Wire. Car ride to Corey's Road. I work 7 hours cleaning camp ground. All day: Robins "cheer-up." Work: cutting brush, raking dead grass.

The Stony Creek setting of Coreys is a short distance east of Highway 30, a working man's land of the past, a portion of the Adirondack region that was once part of the lives of guides and loggers now long gone. It was at the entrance to the hamlet that Noah John was allowed the use of a vacant triangular chunk of property to set up the replica of his Cold River hermitage, a business venture in which he had great confidence.

For many people, I believe, there is (at least) a single experience, one defining moment, when confidence replaces the self-doubt that most of us wrestle with in our lives. For Noah, that might have happened in late spring of 1950, when he was given temporary use of that land to live on free and clear.

All the way through May, Rondeau's entries tell of "Clouds and Sun" and "Perfect Vernal Sunshine." Spring was moving toward summer.

The sun rose and set and the moon rose high and grew full, and each night there was a bit less of spring's chill. Coreys had lost its mysterious sense of the past that the Petty family had known decades earlier. In time, Coreys would grow into a community of second homes and camps, like many other Adirondack places, and would build for the newcomers a legend of its own. The ebbs and flows of the little hamlet's past would weave into its trees, rocks, water and landscape, and become as much a part of the atmosphere as the crisp mountain air.

Rondeau's May turned toward June.

> *...Ride to Corey's with Philip McCalvin. We set up the Wigwam. First: on camp ground. Dinner in Wigwam. I sleep in Replica of Town Hall. I set up Karl Eklund's tent. I cut Balsam and make Pillows. Build stone fireplace.*
>
> *...I get 200# fertilizer from Tupper Lake. I plant 90 cucumber seeds and 25 summer squash. I put new canvas on Town Hall Replica. I make new cherry handle for mattock. Mass. Party call.*
>
> *June 9, 1950 Friday*
> *Very hot weather*
> *At Corey's, N.Y.*
> *I work 5 bows to temporary finish. I fletch 13 arrows. Set up first archery target and shoot a few arrows. I make a smudge pail. Mail comes from Corey's. I get 2 boxes of balsam from Halsey Payro. First Fire Flies. After hot days,—screech owls, screech, and summer ozone fill the Atmosphere.*

As the approaching summer's warmth began to spread over the mountains, Noah completed setting up his Cold River exhibit on the ground bordering the state road and the Coreys roads. Likely as not, he thought the location would be ideal to hawk his handmade souvenirs and hermit trinkets, warm up his fiddle and tell living-in-the-mountains stories to tourists passing by.

Throughout June, he planted and worked his garden, listened to the birds, enjoyed nature and continued to improve his hermitage replica. He entertained guests who stopped by and sold handcrafted balsam pillows, painted boot jacks, souvenir "eyebrow pencils," and homemade arrows. He also sewed novelty leather goods from scrap leather he purchased from the Berman Company in Minnesota. Buckskin bags and coin purses were the most popular. And of course, he also sold autographed postcards of himself. Friend H. W. Holmes gave him used canoe paddles, and he painted trout on them and sold them. Long Lake business owner Roy Lash furnished him deerskins. Occasionally he'd be invited to speak at luncheons and other functions and would often drive to Tupper Lake with Karl Eklund, who purchased the old Pat McCormick property, include the land where Noah had been permitted to set up his camp. On July 18, 1950, Karl was operated on and found to have cancer. "3/4 of his stomach was removed," Noah noted. (The Eklunds' property was sold to a Brooklyn plumber named Fontana who operated it for many years as The Cold River Ranch.)

June 25 at Rondeau's mock "Hermitage Hotel:"

> *Callers: Saratogan Party; Young English Woman write notes for Saratogan...I WASH...SUNDOWN. WHITE THROAT SPARROW SINGS WHILE I CHEW VENISON.*

Between June 20 and July 30 Noah's guests increased steadily, but he wasn't getting far with his public appearances. He hadn't appeared at any money-making functions, and mostly sold trinket souvenirs. He wasn't exactly swamped with the kind of success he had envisioned.

> *July 5—..Callers...22 from Syracuse University. I PUT MY ARM AROUND OLD LADY. I SHOOT ARROWS FOR 2 LADIES.]*

July 6—I am 67 years old...Karl Eklund bring me a Bottle of Pepsi Cola. Acrivlelis bring me a slice of Slam Bang. Callers: 2 Mrs. Hollenbeck and Carol, and Danemora Party, and Priest. Bus Tour from Tupper Lake. Mrs. Acrivlelis make me a Birthday Cake—we celebrate Evening at Snack Bar. Last Night a Deer within 50 feet of Cold River Town Hall. Noah John Rondeau born 1883. I PUT MY ARM AROUND OLD LADY...

On August 1, Noah John accepted a wonderful job for a major North Country company—Santa's Workshop, an "...enchanted village a short distance up Whiteface Mountain." He had arranged for "my brother Bill," said Clarence Petty, "to take over the management of his money" following receipt of his payment at the first Sportsmen's Show in New York City. "Bill continued to manage his money until the end of 1950. But money was not considered of much value to him and as a result he [eventually] became dependent on welfare, which seemed like a sad way to end a life of independence that he treasured."

When Rondeau began working, he took Bill's offer to store whatever personal property he didn't take to Santa's Workshop in the old Conservation Department's Saranac Inn Headquarters, where Bill Petty and his family lived when he was District Forest Ranger and later Regional Supervisor. With the hermit's "riches" safely tucked away, Bill said something like this to Rondeau: "Do what they say and have a good time."

The elder mountain climbers who continued to explore and revisit the Seward and Santanoni peaks and then descend from the summits to Cold River were aware of the debt they owed Noah John. Anniversary celebrations usually aren't a part of climbing and backpacking, but several members of the Adirondack 46ers club did honor Noah in his absence when they stopped by his unoccupied hermitage that July. During the summer of 1950, Peter Ward's climbing party found the register cans on the Seward Range summits, signed in, then headed down into the wild Ouluska Pass, hitting the old lumber road that would lead them to Cold River Hill. Noah's absence was certainly noted, but the missing hermit was duly honored.

Some of the July talk had to do with Noah's partnership with the valley and river. It had been assumed by many of Noah's friends that the "Grand Ole Man of the Mountains" would never again live at Cold River because of his age. Noah never said he would resist change should it become necessary. Many assumed that as a senior statesman of hermitdom, Noah would live out his life in the mountains.

While Noah was out at Coreys trying to improve his financial status, working on his public presentation, and participating in change, the Ward party enjoyed themselves at the hermitage. Noah was a living example of the old saying, "You can take the man out of the mountains but you can't take the mountains out of the man."

> *July 25—Clouds and Sun. 10 drops of Rain on Tent…I make 2 Best Blue Balsam Pillows. Callers: Geo. from Schenectady—we shoot arrows.* LADY WHO SAW ME AT BAINBRIDGE CALLED. I MAKE AN AWL AND FURUHE. 3 INDIANS

Noah wasn't a bona fide hermit because he enjoyed socializing. Following months of isolation, winter slowly loosened its grip. He looked forward to a long-awaited homecoming for the anglers, backpackers and mountain climbers that arrived with better weather. His summer would bustle with life for a few frantic weeks.
Courtesy of C.V. Latimer Jr. M.D.

FROM ST. REGIS CALL. I SEND REQUEST TO FLOSSIE WHITE. SUNDOWN. YUMMY GOOD FEED OF SLAM BANG. STAINS BY ANVIL IS VENISON. I WASH... AMEN. July 30—Sunday. A.M. Cloudy—P.M. Sunshine. At Corey's, N.Y. Hazel Party call. They collect my arrows from Target. Indian Girl call with party. Peter Ward Party on way to Seward Range call. Mr. and Mrs. Bush—newly wed Party call. Expert Fox Party shoot arrows in Tent Roof and loose one in grass.

Following the Ward climbing party's "trials and triumphs," as Peter Ward declared, his group hit the trail on a "hot August tramp into Ward Brook" lean-to and thereafter "...right down into that wildest of passes" [Ouluska Pass], where the "going was bitter and exhausting..." The following day the climbers followed the same route to the hermitage as Bette and I did 57 years later.

Peter Ward wrote about many of his days in the Cold River region. Today, those descriptive trip write-ups can be found in old copies of the Cloudsplitter magazine.

Rondeau's August 5 entry tells:

Saturday. Cloudy, Bits of Sunshine. P.M. Heavy Rain and Hail Stones. At Corey's, N.Y. 8 o'clock I ride with Mr. Julian J. Reiss to Santa Claus City, at North Pole, in White Face Mountain. The ride is beautiful.

I put on Santa Claus uniform and I'm Santa Claus for 9 hours. I greet thousands. A thousand cameras shot at me. I hold up hundreds of little tots for pictures.

This was Noah's trial run at being Santa. His journal describes the days following his acceptance of the position as temporary Santa. He packed his "Wigwam and Archery Target, the Cold River City replica and moved it to The North Pole amusement park where "5 men set [it] up for me" along one walk in the North Pole village. He signed contracts for his exhibit to appear at future Sportsmen's Shows; met with old friends Karl Eklund, who had returned from the hospital, and Dan Emmett; dug "a pail of Potatoes;" visited the pharmacy; and did some shopping.

Noah's diary describes his first days on the job.

> *August 12—Perfect Weather-Perfect Business. At Santa Claus City, North Pole, N.Y. I do the Roll of Santa Claus 8 1/2 hours. I HUG 50 YOUNG GIRLS, 20 WOMEN. KISS 10. Florence Menne brought daises. A little Tot. SANTA CLAUS SINCERE.*

> *August 13—I autograph and sell Photos. Audrey bleach my beard and hair. Santa Claus make up—cream, rouge, paste and powder. I do roll of Santa Claus for 8 and a half hours. I do my own cooking and get along very good in a crowd of 14,000 for the day.*

> *August 17—...I HUG A FEW LADIES. I autograph Photographs. I GET 25 CENTS FROM HOLY DAD...*

> *August 21—...I do the Roll of Santa 8 and a half hours. An American Thief took the Horns off my white deer skin today, and he got away with them; he wants a relic souvenir to hang on his wall to remind him that he is a Thief.*

> *August 24—...Up early...Callers: Bill Petty's family. I autograph and sell Photographs...HUG MANY LADIES.*

Noah glued a label that reads "This shade is Raven Red..." to this page with this note written beneath the colored brand name. "Rouge for Santa's Nose."

August ended:

> *August 31—Thursday. Showers last night. Today: a.m. cloudy, p.m.:downpour At Santa Claus City. I discover someone stole one of my canes about August 25th. An American Fool, about 35, peeled bark from a Silver Birch and give it to His young Son and Daughter—as he explains, "What a fine souvenir he got them."*

In one of his poems about an approaching autumn, "Information to September," Noah had written:

September, you're between August and October
You make the Earth, and sun change node;
And you paint the forest, in poly colors;
You bring the Deer, a brand new coat.
You bring the South Pole, new morning light;
You bring the dawn, of her six-month day;
And after her six months night,
  you paint the surface, of her concentric spin
You send the woodchuck back to bed;
You spread sunshine from pole to pole;
You make many, an apple blush red,
And you turn the pumpkins into gold...
...you bronze the Ferns, like Foxes tails;
You dropped the acorns, from their pans,
And with the leaves you carpet the trails.
You put snowflakes on mountain tops,
And you also bring a...harvest moon;
You bring the vallies frost at night,
And you bring many a sunny noon.
You're satisfied with thirty days,
And also in schocks you bind the corn;
You retard the moon, to light night parade,—
And you strip the velvet from old bucks horns..."
But, little September, don't you cry;
You'll have the seasons that now are June's...

While Noah did notice the sunshine and what he considered the desecration of a silver birch, he had little leisure to write poetry.

September 12—At Santa's City, North Pole, N.Y. I autograph at my Wigwam. Callers... [A couple from Coreys reported] "Your Squashes are running across the Road...."

September 25—Morning Roofs are white; Ice on water pail in Wigwam. ...Brilliant Sunrise. I'm Santa Claus... Chat with Grace Hudowalski at North Pole. ...I watch Penumbra of Earth's shadow advance on the Moon; But Atmosphere is too hazy for Eclipse to be worthwhile.

Twenty-one years earlier, in 1929, Noah had entered his truly sequestered year of isolation with no doubt about his future or the dire times that lay ahead. His plan had been to drift between temporary employment and the trapping grounds, where he could polish his craft. Certainly those years were tough compared to Noah's easier days working at the North Pole as Santa. Bill and Clarence Petty never thought Noah was such a talented raconteur, even though the hermit had given them the impression that he knew how to turn a buck. Bill and Clarence did, however, feel he made a good Santa because of his beard and his interest in children. And both men took their children to Santa's Workshop to visit their family friend.

Bill and Clarence weren't the only ones who found Noah well-suited to his role as Santa. From the *Knickerbocker News*, Friday October 6, 1950:

"No Other Hermit"
...Noah, it became known today, is a substitute Santa at Santa's Workshop, a much ballyhooed commercial project up Whiteface Mountain way. Noah isn't a full-time Santa. He isn't heavy enough and sad to relate, Noah may never be Santa again just because this news is in print. A spokesman for the workshop today said that if news of Noah's new job was published it would shorten the term of his employment. Maybe so, but we are betting against it because if Noah is fired it is sure as shootin' that the workshop will be picketed by the international association for the protections of hermits who have given up their hermitages to be substitute Santa Clauses.

Rondeau's October writings continue to outline his season at the North Pole.

> *October 13, 1950. Wind, cloudy, snow in Atmosphere…Fire all day in box stove. Wood fire is appreciable (feels good, smells good). It's pleasant to meet the many children.*

With his bona fide beard, wire-rimmed eye glasses and winning way, Noah John ably filled Santa's boots. Accepting the job was a deliberate move toward supporting himself.

Oscar Burguiere's father received this special Christmas offering from Santa Noah, taken when he worked at the North Pole in Wilmington, N.Y. *Courtesy of Richard J. Smith from Noah's photo album*

Noah could not have picked a better role than St. Nick to develop a special image for himself, but since he worked only part-time as Santa, he filled in his other hours in his original—and real-life—role as hermit, employing his Cold River City replica at Santa's Workshop in Wilmington, along Whiteface Mountain Memorial Highway.

October 25—...I PUT 600 DOLLARS IN BILL PETTY'S CARE. Deer Hunting Season open[s].

The income a hermit-become-entertainer can realize is obviously limited. It ranged from a bare livelihood for performing at local functions to the level of twinkling star status at the nationally-known Sportsmen's Shows. He was in demand for personal appearances, which increased his chances to earn a living income, but whatever Noah did earn was never enough to keep up with the necessary expenses he was faced with in living on the Outside.

The changes in his lifestyle were modest. Up until 1949, the only entertainments he had had were playing his fiddle, reading and writing, and visiting with the people who wandered into his camp. Now it was possible to afford an occasional movie, not that he went hog-wild spending money. Bill Petty tried hard to help Rondeau stretch every last dollar.

Clarence Petty offers one of his remembrances to illustrate Rondeau's disinterest in money.

My brother Bill got Noey out of Cold River for the Sportsmen's Show largely because the Conservation Department was looking for somebody that could actually relate to the Adirondacks and Bill thought Noah would be the one to do it. Bill would put the money in the bank that Noah earned and largely because Noah didn't have a bank account and he didn't care as long as it was in a place where he could get it later when he needed it. I remember him telling Bill that if St. Peter calls before I come for the money you do whatever you want with it.

Being frugal is not so bad. According to those who knew Noah, even though he lived sparingly himself, he was never stingy. From the time he began earning money from shows, he bought lots of canned food. This way of eating, according to Smith, was "a gradual start on his getting accustomed to a less rough sort of life." Little by little he fell in line with the way people living outside Cold River provided for their meals and other expenses. His journals mention eating in diners and restaurants, renting a steam-heated room in a Saranac Lake hotel, buying candy and little toys for children and taking in a picture show now and then.

Bill Petty's daughter, Joanne Petty Manning, remembers Noah as a thoughtful, civilized hermit. When she got to know him he was in his fifth decade. He was already well known far and wide. He was older than her father, but both men had known one another for the last thirty years.

Joanne Manning shared:

> *...I have several personal notes from Noah John to me, dating back to 1954 when I was six years old, that I cherish. When I graduated from Saranac Lake High School in 1965 Noah John sent me a letter of Congratulation, a picture of himself, "five pictures of George Washington" he wrote, [five one-dollar bills] and, of course, his outstanding signature!*

Her uncle, Clarence, also recalled Noah's generosity. When he and his brother were children in Coreys, and Noah had just begun his life in the wilds, Noah sometimes visited the Petty family. Clarence remembered that Noah would make his hand disappear into his pocket and pull out coins that he handed to Bill and Clarence, even though he could clearly have used the money for some needed ammunition or some other provision.

During Christopher Angus's research for his 2002 book, *The Extraordinary Adirondack Journey of Clarence Petty*, Jean Freeman recalled her childhood remembrances of hermit Rondeau, with whom her family was clearly familiar. Her grandfather, Harry, and father, Ross, were both guides on the Indian Carry. Jean has never forgotten Noah walking past her home in the early 1940s. She commented to Angus,"He would pull little toys from the pocket of his deerskin suit…" as hand-outs for her and her siblings. Angus reported Jean "scoffed at the notion" that Rondeau was a match for what people thought of as a hermit. "He was the most sociable hermit I ever heard of," she said.

When Noah worked as Santa at the North Pole, he repeated this kind of generosity again and again.

On Tuesday, October 31, Rondeau ended his employment at the North Pole on a "Perfect Sunshine; Like summer day without Bugs."

> *"With plenty of help I take down Wigwam—Town hall and move to Lake Clear and Saranac Lake. I Saw a Rough Grouse on White Face Mountain Highway. The Ridge from North Pole to Lake Clear and back to Saranac Lake was most perfect; calm, warm and clear; Ausable River and Mountains are most beautiful…"*

The following day found him once again at the home of his friends Philip and Helen McCalvin in Saranac Lake. His journal records say he offered a hand laying "linoleum in the upstairs Bath Room." Later that day and into the next he readied for the next escapade: "I pack and store Hermit Riches." Wednesday's newspaper reported news of interest; he glued a photograph of George Bernard Shaw with the caption "The Voice Is Stilled" onto his Wednesday, November 1, diary page, complete with this footer: "…The 100 per cent American is 90 per cent idiot…fortunately, the more I insult them the more they adore me." Shaw's picture bears a striking resemblance to Rondeau's own face. Besides noting the death of the century's "most famous playwright," he also remarked, "This afternoon:—Two Puerto Ricans made desperate attempt to assassinate President Truman." He also noted that word had arrived that his Shattuck Clearing ranger friend, Lucius Russell, "kill[ed] a very large Bear."

Quiet times were Noah's again once he left his employment and moved back with the McCalvin family. One day as he and Phil stood looking out the window, Noah shared this sentiment, which I've loosely reconstructed: "When I'm alone in a hotel room in the center of a city, I sometimes stand at the window and look down at the streets and the people, and I find my heart returning to the few things that lay claim on my memory—a patch of land near Cold River, the simple but good life and all I have experienced."

> *November 5—...Trying to storm...Phillip McCalvin... go hunting. DEER GOOD TO EAT. 1 DEER HAM... I PLANT ONIONS AND GARLIC BULBS.*

By this time of the month, deer hunting season in the Cold River wilds was calling Noah. He began shopping at Bill Mullen's combined little general grocery, hardware, candy, and paper store for the last of his food staples, packed his gear including snowshoes, and readied for the day he would head back to the hermitage.

Noah had no idea it would be his last hunting season in the land he had called home for so many years.

Official Camp Seward guide—lead hunter—and honored guest. Noah on Seward trail just before heading into Laughing Buck swamp to begin a deer drive.
Courtesy of C.V. Latimer Jr. M.D.

Chapter 22

Final Hermitage Days

DOCTORS C.V. SR. and Jr. had treated Rondeau as an extra special friend for years. Members at their camp were warm and complimentary toward their upriver wilderness neighbor. He was apparently everything C.V. Jr. says: "Rondeau was humorous, he was helpful, he looked after our camp." All his characteristics "were directly in front of you. He said what he thought," without restriction. C.V. remembers the last years before late November 1950—"in the time of the Big Wind"—as a good period. He attributes Rondeau's upbeat attitude to his celebrity, which seemed to place him above requirements considered normal in woodsmen affairs. Other hermits were much worse off than Noah. Latimer figured they ranked lower in the wilderness caste system.

Richard Smith thought the public's interest in Rondeau's wilderness lifestyle was the beginning of the end of Noah's mountain-dwelling days. "I think he enjoyed being the center of attention" and amusing people and also sharing his outdoor experiences. Smith reflected, "That was just a long chapter in his life." Noah had some great times in that Adirondack back country. "All of us did," but 1950 was just the year that marked the time for him to move on, to begin a new chapter of what he hoped would not be a boring life. Noah "had simply grown too old" to remain trapped in the woods, especially in the winter, but there was one thought he could hang on to: The old hermitage was still there for shelter should he return for a short time each June to fish. Noah certainly knew it would have been foolish for him to continue to live at Cold River out of a mistaken sense of devotion to wilderness life. "He used his good sense and got out," according to Smith.

Smith was referring to Rondeau's decision several years earlier. Considering the amount of time Noah planned to spend outside following the success of the 1947 Sportsmen's Shows, Noah John began a slow process of emptying the contents of his hermitage. His biographer, Maitland C. De Sormo, reports the beginning of his move from Cold River in *Noah John Rondeau, Adirondack Hermit.*

> *Noah with the help of several Rangers, packed up about 600 pounds of his belongings and toted them the nearly five miles of the Northville-Placid Trail to its junction with the truck road. On this trip Noah's burden was his cherished rocking chair.*
>
> *Those and other assets were transported to the New York State Conservation Department headquarters at Saranac Inn for short-term storage.*

Richard Smith pointed out that the account reads as if Noah had pulled up stakes immediately, but he said Rondeau didn't completely empty the hermitage in '47. The move took place over two years. Smith launched into what he knew for a fact:

> *With the dump truck at Mountain Pond we (there were four of us) hiked to Big Dam while Noah made loads of piles to tote out to the truck. His three donkeys—our private joke—carried them. Each of us made several trips hee-hawing throughout the day. Back and forth from Big Dam to the dump truck we went, stopping now and then for hay and oats. By our calculations we each walked around 30 miles. We did have quite a truck load of curios and things Noah thought he wanted with him on the 'Outside.' I'm sure he felt a little heartbroken as he left the hermitage. I was beside him on the last load. At the Gate to the City, he turned and said, 'So long old friend, I will be back.'*
>
> *He knew he had to leave, but he did entertain the thought he would come back one last time. I can't say he had tears in his eyes that very last time. I know if I had been in his shoes, I would have.*

At first it gave me a sad feeling to listen to two of Noah's best friends reminisce about Noah leaving his long-time home, but then everything has a beginning and an ending. Rondeau's diary entries and an interview that appeared in the February 1, 1951, *Marathon Independent* newspaper describe his November 1950 movements. His journal entries confirm he hadn't been living full-time in the boondocks.

It's believed Phil McCalvin drove him to Helms's Dock at Long Lake about November 7, where he joined up with some deer hunters. The men shared the cost to charter a four-passenger floatplane. Helms taxied his passengers the short distance up the lake, where they disembarked at Plumley's Point House. Noah's memo tells that once they arrived he enjoyed "…coffee, cookies and gossip with Ladies in kitchen." He then hiked to Shattuck Clearing, once the site of a tumble-down deserted sawmill along Cold River that the State of New York converted to an interior ranger station. There he found "Lucius Russell and Rev. Morgan skinning a Bear."

Before evening set in on November 8, Rondeau had arrived at his much-missed hermitage. Noah recorded:

> *Wednesday, November 8, 1950*
> *Shattock [to] Big Dam. Up at 4:30—Breakfast at dawn. I go and skin a Bear's Head and salt the Hide and then walk 7 miles up old River Trail. A Bob cat hang on Pine Limb at [Harold] Rightmyer's camp. 2 Large Bucks hang [at] Camp Seward. I see large Deer in Cold River at mouth of Seward Brook.*

Thursday and Friday found him working "at Cold River Town Hall. Big Dam." They were days of chores. While he boiled a bear's head for chowder, Noah burned the old bough bed, refreshing the frame with a "New Bed of Blue Joint [grass]." He spruced up the camp, washed the dishes, picked up a wigwam that had collapsed, "...drove out mice and set a trap…[and] I look over my city streets—Cold River."

By the end of the second day he had his hermitage running "in city style." The anticipated "finger bowls and paper napkins" supplies finally arrived, being dropped from a "Cub plane" whose home base was the Lake

Doc Latimer Sr. and Noah near Laughing Buck Swamp. Noah's Camp Seward friends knew the stupendous difficulties of day-to-day living in Cold River Country. In the Adirondacks, the journeys were sometimes troublesome and could be really dangerous. No one walked on paved roads, but just as in any mountain range one could slip and stumble, sometimes on trails, sometimes not; through forests, quagmires, across water, and over rocks; harassed by frost, storms, insects, snow, hunger and illness. But, at any rate, Noah always got by. *Courtesy D.V. Latimer Jr. M.D.*

Placid airport. The air drop caused some of the cartons to break open and scatter. He found a "Pick Axe near [a] 9-foot boat…" By evening he was settled in and feeling at home once again. He believed the mice, in next to no time, recognized his authority as mayor, dog warden, tax collector, and pest exterminator.

Life at Cold River continued as it always had. Rondeau sat up enjoying the Hunter's Moon, after the shadows of the trees melted into dark.

Deer hunting season in the Adirondacks had opened. Animal cries sounded clearer in the crisp mountain air. He observed deer, buoyed by a dense mantle of hollow hairs that seemed to make their bodies float as they used their broad, splayed hooves to speed them across the river.

Rondeau was pleased with a shot he had made at a large buck. In a letter to H. V. Holmes he said he had spotted the buck across the river a fair distance away when he saw "sun glint from his antlers as he pussyfooted among the trees."

He was enjoying life back at his old diggings. November was a time of renewal. He revisited some old haunts, hunted, and otherwise savored the pleasures of his previous wilderness life.

He wrote on Tuesday, November 14, 1950: "9 a.m. I shoot from Town Hall Door and kill a 12 Point Adirondack Buck. The last 3 years: I saw the Buck about 100 times near camp, and recorded him a score of times in my Diaries. And I knew 9 of his beds…I fed him Bread, Pan Cakes, Salt, Sugar and Oat Meal. Today 2 Bullets took Him almost instantly—at Standard best. Deer Hair [was] blown on snow by 2 Bullets."

He was still as annoyed as ever by wildlife regulations.

> *November 15—…I skin a Deer's head and neck. I boil a can of Slam Bang. I prepare American Fool Tags to comply with American Fool Law…*

Until November 16, Rondeau might have viewed the weather as "well-mannered." That day he recorded that the run of decent days began to change from "Breezy, very cloudy" to "Growing colder." On the next day, he noted:

> *November 17—…Blustery-winter like…Hunters…[arrive]. We canvas Roofs of the Town hall and the Hall of Records. THEY OCCUPY HALL OF RECORDS.] I cook a slam Bang Gullion.*

The weather was cold—cold enough that several inches of snow had fallen and remained, covering the ground by November 21. Of course, cold and snow were to be expected, and Noah was not complaining, merely recording the change of season from late fall to the beginning of winter.

> *November 18–24—Breezy…Growing colder…I bank Town Hall with Soil, sticks and cobblestones. I boil a pail of Bait…take 6 traps*

and pail of bait to Seward Pond. Wigwam at Pond is half submerged by Beaver Tide. 4 hunters call. Coffee and Hunter's gossip...Deer make tracks in plastic snow on Cold River golden stairs. John Stepyro and Francis Eibert carry out 60 pounds for me. 4:30 p.m. 2 Couchsachraga climbers return on way to Duck Hole.

C.V. Latimer Sr. and Jr. recalled that Noah would often contentedly sigh, "Happy Days at Cold River." It was one of those expressions that summed up his mood and everyone else's during the fall hunting season.

Happy days indeed. If Rondeau had been clairvoyant and had known that a terrific land hurricane would soon hit the Adirondacks and create unprecedented devastation beyond anything ever experienced in New York State's history, he might not have used his favorite phrase that November. Then again, it might not have changed his attitude. If you love a place—or a person—you just love it, despite anything.

The 25th of November 1950, the final morning at the hermitage, was a day Noah would never forget. He was tired because of an uneasy sleep. High winds throughout the night had made him feel uncomfortable. Like all woodsmen, he had seen the worst of storms throughout every season of the year and had prepared for bad weather before he settled in for the evening.

As the gale raged hour after hour, all night long, he knew this storm was different. The canvas on his roof flapped with a fury as air infiltrated the opening and caused part of the roof covering to balloon. Bucketing rain accompanied the gale-force wind. The wigwams leaned. Poles not attached together were tossed around. The sheltering log walls of the Town Hall kept Noah dry and gave him a relative sense of safety in the face of limbs cracking outside and branches swishing overhead. Everywhere he heard trees rubbing against each other. The woods were full of creaks and groans and branches dropping from the trees. Rondeau was a veteran of nature's tempest, but this all-night storm was different from any other.

By morning's light, he decided to rejoin friends at Ampersand Park, taking his shortcut through Ouluska Pass Gap. At Ampersand Pond, saws were buzzing through downed trees, axes were chipping at limbs, people were shouting, and a few of the most stimulated were swearing in the best form he had heard in a long time.

He wrote:

Saturday, November 25, 1950
Cold River-Ampersand Pond.
Cloudy and fierce wind. Snow all gone.
I recanvas Town Hall roof where wind raise hell.
I find 1 gallon glass jug full of sugar hid since 1934.

I walk 8 miles to Donkey Lodge. 4 to 7 p.m. Stop with Marcellus Hunters. 7 p.m. to Ampersand pond with Frank Blanchard…Hunting Season close.

It would be interesting to know if the Marcellus hunters' Donkey Lodge was a canvas-wall tent. The occupants certainly would have experienced one hair-raising night. The eight miles Noah recorded would suggest the camp was near Ward Brook outside Ampersand Park's boundary line. Noah was within the boundary of Ampersand Park, where a tree struck a sheltering outbuilding. He heard from eyewitnesses that trees started falling down, then suddenly there was a hole in the ceiling, and then the rain came in.

On the next day Noah wrote:

November 26, 1950 Sunday. Still Breezy after 35 hours of worst, Forest Destroying wind ever in Ampersand Valley. BUCKS. I make 3 canvas MONEY bags. I bake a pot of beans and get supper for 3 men working to clear fallen trees from road. Happy Day at Ampersand Pond resting after a Cold River Hunt and Mastering a 12 Point Buck. 3 BRANDY SLINGS…

Thanks to a letter Noah wrote to H. V. Holmes following the Big Blow, we know that by the time he was near the end of the former lumber road that went through Ouluska Pass, he approached the southern boundary of Ampersand Park. There he discovered modest amounts of damage compared to a number of troublesome spots between Donaldson and Seymour Mountains and the government trail. The slash required turning off the old tote track to avoid small tangles of downed trees.

On the other hand, west of the Rockefeller parkland all along the four miles to Stony Creek Bridge, the woodland was a jungle of jackstraw-piled trees "six feet or more in depth." The Park caretaker and his assistants, along with "a dozen hunters and about 20 Conservation Department men" worked for two days to cut down trees and cut back slash in order to open the roadway. "Most of the familiar landmarks had been obliterated," he reported. It was difficult to even recognize where he was.

In all directions Noah saw only trees with broken dangling limbs, uprooted trees, trees with snapped tops, trees braced by other trees, trees piled on top of other trees high off the ground. The scene created an impenetrable barrier. It looked like an impossible clearing job to all but the most skilled lumberjacks.

Children were a particular joy to the Cold River hermit. Noah with Gary McCalvin, December 19, 1949. *Courtesy of Helen McCalvin Sawatzki*

De Sormo described the heavy damage in plain words, adding how the blowdown would also affect Rondeau's future.

> *A later assessment of the damage caused by the unprecedented destructive storm showed that more than 400,000 acres had been seriously affected—from 25 to 100 per cent leveled. So vast was the area and so great was the danger of subsequent fires that the whole region was closed to the public for more than three years. That edict, plus the realization that he was then, at 67, too old to ever seriously consider the resumption of the uncertain ways of the wilderness, ended forever that phase of Rondeau's life.*

What is also known is that nearby Coreys residents were absolutely shocked by the devastation that had occurred in the area because of the storm. Between the downed trees and wires and road blockages, volunteers began working under truly bad conditions. All the men and women went above and beyond to check on people and help control the situation. It took the better part of the next three years to clear the tangle in the thousands upon thousands of mountainous acres of Forest Preserve just in the Cold River region.

The extraordinary storm was so violent, so intense, so fast and so vicious, that the force can only be described as having the power to damage and destroy as only hurricane gusts can do.

Rondeau's diary describes the following days. There is some dried flora pressed on this page. He noted they were "Ferns and Moss from Buck Rock-Ampersand Pond."

> *Monday, November 27, 1950*
> *Quite cloudy, calm and mild. At Ampersand Pond.*
> *I make a Canvas Bag.*

It's curious to speculate about how unmoved and very matter-of-fact Noah was in his diary remarks about the windstorm and the hellish trip out to Ampersand Park's line shack. He seemed to take the wreckage in stride. I suppose it just goes to show what a good woodsman he was. The strong wind and blowdown were worthy adversaries. It probably would not have made a bit of difference to him, however, if he had been warned what to expect. Even though he had no inkling of what was in store for him until he began to crawl around blowdowns in the north gaps of Ouluska Pass, he had already planned to leave the woods at the end of hunting season. But there was a bigger surprise waiting—one he could not have imagined.

It wouldn't have surprised him that all the newspaper reporters and newsreel cameramen later came on the scene to take pictures and write about the damage and subsequent salvage, but he surely would have been stunned to learn about the Conservation Department's decision to close the woods to all recreational use.

The ring of seriousness can be heard in the "Blowdown Aftermath" report written by P. Schuyler Miller that appeared in the July-August 1951 issue of *Adirondac* magazine.

> *...The principal closure—for an indefinite period—is 60,000 acres in the watershed of the Cold River. According to Commissioner Duryea, this is too remote for salvage by contract and too big for immediate attention by the department crews, who are concentrating on damaged areas in the campsites and along roads and main-traveled trails, where public use and consequent danger of fire is greatest. The Cold River area is out for this summer so far as hiking and camping is concerned. The department has pointed out that quite apart from the fire hazard of having even the most experienced campers at large there, the blowdown has made it nearly impossible to get anyone out of the region in case of sickness or accident...*

Rich Smith weighed in with what he remembered hearing Noah tell him:

> *The big blowdown...caused damage in the watersheds of Cold River, Moose Creek below Moose Pond, Ampersand Brook, and the tributaries of the Raquette River and Long Lake between Plumley's Camp near the north end of Long Lake and Stony Creek Ponds*

near Coreys. I understand Donaldson Mountain was in the center of the hazardous area...The areas that I knew best, the Cold River, Calkins Brook, Duck Hole, Bradley Pond, and Preston Ponds were all off limits. Trails were impassable and there was all sorts of talk about the risk from fire.

By this time Noah was getting well into his late sixties. He had suffered a few miniature heart spasms, which made him realize he wouldn't be able to live out life at the hermitage. When the Government Road [Ward Brook fire road] was once more cleared for travel, he hired a dump truck and got permission from the Conservation Department to travel the gravel road between Mountain Pond and Ampersand Park. The road from Coreys to the Park was a mess of fallen trees extending into the Rockefeller's park at least as far as Ward Brook. The rest of the way in toward Duck Hole was more or less smaller hardwood, second and third growth, and didn't get the whole force of the wind. The blow hit in spots, sometimes leaving several acres untouched.

Some places, such as Mt. Nye and Wallface Mountain and for miles around, all the old trees, spruces, balsam, and yellow birch lay flat on the ground in a twisted array of timber that was almost impenetrable.

Noah's wish to fish Cold River one last time was never fulfilled.
Courtesy of Dr. Adolph G. Dittmar, Jr.

I had expected that discovering he would not be able to return to his camp the following spring would have led to some classic verbiage written in Noah's coded language. Yet, none exists. He arrived at the McCalvins' house in Saranac Lake on November 30, and that entry brings the month to a close.

> *November 30—...At Saranac Lake. I parcel Post a Deer Head to Taxidermist...I call at Conservation Commission Office. Call on Bill Mullen. PHILIP MCCALVIN: "I HAVE A SHIT POT FULL OF MEDALS UPSTAIRS."*

On a bright December morning in 1950, Noah followed the same pattern he almost always adhered to when beginning a diary entry: The month, the day, the year, and the weather. He had no inkling that he would pass another year living with the McCalvins in Saranac Lake before he would move to Hill Top Ranch, the home of his sister, Percillia McCasland, in Au Sable Forks. He also had no way of knowing that while boarding at Hill Top Ranch he would begin a new act in the up-and-coming "Outside Life" chapter of an ex-hermit turned wanna-be farmer.

Tuesday, December 5, was a "sunshine and slushy" day—clear blue skies, visibility unlimited "at Saranac Lake," where it "snowed 7" Last Night" he put down. So—Rondeau listened to the radio to find out about the day's weather in order to plan his agenda.

At Cold River, the hermit had created a number of poems about the weather. The sheer beauty of nature, the brilliant sun, Jack Frost's brush strokes, snow flurries, rushing water from winter's melting ice, sparkling dew clinging to spider webs—it all caught by Noah's eye. The natural world has personality. The emotions it evoked were experiences he must have internalized. The feelings in turn were recalled during periods of tranquility and provided mind food to ponder and then write about. Looking from Saranac Lake, Noah simply knew what it was like each morning in Cold River's mountain valley.

Rereading his old diaries must have transported him quickly all over Cold River country as he flipped helter-skelter through the pages, like a housewife with a feather duster swishing high and low along all the surfaces where dust had collected.

Noah thumbed through those old journals time and again, Peggy Byrne told me. She was the daughter of John Meyers, a respected Plattsburgh resident who owned M. P. Meyers and Company, and was also a good friend to Noah. "He used them to revisit those old familiar places," Peggy said.

Peggy recalled her father had met "Noey," as she often referred to him, in Coreys. "My father and his friend Merrith Stanton went in there on a hunting trip and while they were there Pop discovered Noey had a fabulous diary that described all the birds, all the animals, all the flowers, all the seasons...everything that he saw..." Yet Noah told Peggy, "My diaries are like my poems, poor scribble..."

His "poor scribble" picks up again.

December 5—...I call at Gravy's and at Newbury's.
I BUY 2 DEERSKINS FROM DAVE BUSHEY...
INVITE TO MOOSE VENISON SUPPER 12-14-'50.]

Dec. 13—...I have civilization's distemper, that people call "a cold." I'm taking Bromo Quinine. SICK...ALL DAY LONG.

December 16—...I receive 9 Xmas cards. I send out a Doz...
I ORDER 300 SEEDS FROM BILL PETTY. I ship 2 Deer hides.
Confab with Bill Petty.

December 17—...1 GALLON. OH BE JOYFUL.
1 HAIRCUT, BEARD TRIM-4 MONTHS.

December 24—...at 4 Alpine Terrace all day. 1 BATH-25 DAYS...
I get agreement from Campbell-Fairbanks for New York Sportsmens Show. I get 12 Xmas cards...Santa is busy Trimming Xmas Tree.

The month of December seemed to move along quickly with the activities Noah John noted in his daily writings. Following a local fish and game club dinner, Noah gave a little talk. There were more visits with Bill Petty, Christmas cards to write and a Christmas tree he helped decorate. He was part of the "elaborate celebration" birthday party for four-year-old Gary McCalvin and spent time "arranging" clippings and photographs in his album and scrapbooks. Beside making plans for future lectures at Billy Burger's Westport "Pipemakers" home and organizing his exhibit for the upcoming Tahawus Sportsmen's Show, he accepted the offer from Campbell-Fairbanks to attend another Sportsmen's Show in New York City.

★ ★ ★

Cold River Hill is less than forty miles from the room at 4 Alpine Terrace where Noah boarded in Saranac Lake, but it is more than a matter of miles. It is a matter of time. Rondeau's Cold River Hill "City" quickly became light years away. When I read Noah's journals, the days in the Essex County hermitage don't seem so long ago, but they were very different from the life Noah began to lead by 1950, and even further distant from the life Bette and I lead today, so that they almost seem like a daydream.

Even the memories of many people I interviewed are disjointed—just a drop here and a dribble there, with gaps in between—but to me they are even more precious now because everyone I interviewed years ago has died.

Noah lived more than three decades in the mountains and did his "course work" (reading) by natural, candle and kerosene light. In town he had electricity and the radio "squawk box" to complain about. Saranac Lake had paved roads; he had been used to dirt footpaths and snowshoe trails. Saranac Lake had theaters, cultural events, stores and shops, medical offices and two lakes, to walk along. To most, it would seem that the ex-hermit was much better off than he had been back at his home place, but I'd venture a bet that he just wished he was able to be back at Cold River.

★ ★ ★

It seemed as though somewhere in his 1951 daily record book he would have appraised his new living conditions, but he didn't. Instead, his Outside life continued as it had throughout the majority of 1950. There was the bopping between North Country towns, visiting friends, preparing for lectures and more Sportsmen's appearances, and his June 26, 1951, move from Saranac Lake to his new digs. About all he said that was noteworthy about that change was that on June 30, he sold his first autographed photo to a visitor from Rochester, NY.

For the next seventeen years Noah experienced his famous "hard times" (though of a different sort and not so amusing) as well as an outpouring of love and happiness from his fans and friends. Everyone seemed to want him to know they enjoyed his company. When he talked about his former life, he told the audience the mountains had given him "thirty-seven hard but good years," and I believe he meant every word.

As the years went by, what was left of the little abandoned structures on Cold River Hill crumbled into the earth for nature to reclaim. Today, Noah's Cold River Hill is a state of mind. It has not lost its magic by any means, and it's still a place where there are no meddlesome game protectors, no "American Thieves," certainly no "Big Business" and "Industrial Slavery," no "Republican Stove-Top Hats" and "Jackass Democrats." It's a place where there is only a simple sign nailed to a tree. A destination where all you are concerned about once you arrive at is how long you will stay. Will you hitch up that heavy backpack and continue hiking, or pitch your tent here? What route will you take down to the river to get water? What will you prepare for supper? Oh—and did you sense a bit of Noah's presence—a friendly wave just at the edge of your vision or a small voice urging "Come back again!" as you traversed the footpath on the way home?

★ ★ ★

Bette and I passed over the Stony Creek Bridge as we drove over the seasonal dirt track that leads to the Seward Mountains parking lot, and I told her about Richard Smith's and my October 30, 1992, drive to the same destination. The snow had stopped falling early in the day. Smith had predicted, "There's a clearing trend in the making" as we drove toward the entrance to Ampersand Park beyond the hamlet of Coreys. This was a day of what Richard called "clarifying and enlightening" me. He wanted to show me how inaccessible the park would have been in 1950 when the hurricane wind walloped the territory. As we bumped along he also talked about the term "gilpin" (a young deer without spots in the fall, locally known as "camp meat"). When I protested that I didn't feel it was right to surreptitiously take a deer so young for camp meat, he countered with, "There isn't a hunter living that is so pious and straight-laced that they could say they never killed a gilp for camp meat."

He added, "I'd be the first to admit some of those little deer are better off in the pot, as they are so small, they don't have a prayer of surviving the winter." Then he broke into yet another Noah story.

> *Noah told me once he went with an old-timer around Christmas time to pick up gilp that had been too much of a temptation for him to ignore during the November hunting season. This old fellow had the young [illegal] deer well hidden in a hollow log. When the men hauled it out it was stiff as a ramrod. As they carried the deer, Noah said he wasn't acquainted with the section. When he asked his friend which way they had to go to reach the house, the man held the gilp out at arm's length with his stiff little nose pointing like an arrow indicating the direction. "That way," the old fellow said.*

After a look-see at the private entrance to Avery Rockefeller's camp, I turned the truck around and parked in the nearby Blueberry parking lot that the state made for hikers and hunters. We dropped the tailgate, pulled out a basket of food and lit up my Coleman stove. We both looked forward to some hot cocoa with our sandwiches. This was the kind of setting Smith most loved, and he particularly enjoyed being at or near a location when he related some past event closely connected with the place. He said Noah must have had an angel on his shoulder during this particular occasion.

The leaves had long ago dropped onto the forest floor as Richard and I talked about Noah's last days of deer hunting and occupancy at the hermit-city.

Rondeau had been a lifelong friend of the Petty family. Clarence and his brother Bill were youngsters the summer day in 1913 when Noah arrived in Coreys. The boys were fishing in Stony Pond when they spotted Rondeau walking down the Coreys Road pushing a loaded wicker baby carriage. The stranger's appearance and manner of travel immediately piqued their attention. They set aside their poles to better watch the dark-clothed figure as he parked the baby buggy and entered the door into their home that led to the Coreys Post Office. "I knew him from that day on," Clarence said, and there was no doubt in his mind that Rondeau had been anything other than a true friend to all the Pettys. Clarence felt that no hardship and no difficulty could disturb Rondeau's self-reliance. He was a tough old bird, and it seemed as if it would be impossible to draw him away from his "City"— until the Big Blow.

Noah John's wish to fish Cold River in June again never came true. In 1954, his hilltop hermitage was almost bulldozed level during the final phase of the salvage operations following the blowdown. Noah didn't try to preserve his past life under a glass dome, but right up to a ripe old age he continued to share his Cold River experiences with fascinated audiences.

Mopping up operation by the U.S. Bobbin & Shuttle Corporation on Cold River Hill. Loggers Harvey Carr and Paul Crofut saved one of Rondeau's shacks. It's now at the Adirondack Museum at Blue Mountain Lake. *Courtesy of Harvey Carr*

Chapter 23

A Last Look at Cold River

FALL 2007: I WAS STANDING on Rondeau's hilltop again, staring out across the river and forest, straining for a clear view of Panther Peak, when Bette joined me. I heard her approaching, nearly inaudible in her Gore-Tex hiking boots. Still, I did not need to turn around. I knew her light and steady footsteps.

She stood next to me with an expansive smile. I thought she was pleased that she had finally made it to the site of Rondeau's "City." She had heard so much about the place over the years. Bette was well aware of the price she had paid to reach the Hermitage. Over a long span of years, she had been a mother, elementary school teacher and helpful grandmother. During that time, I enormously regretted that there was simply no opportunity for us to backpack together. I was anxious to share my interest in hiking and to have mile-to-mile, day-to-day contact with her on long trails, to give her an on-site perspective into the history I'd been telling her about and the anecdotal stories I'd come home with. Chatting with her about my exploratory historical journeys after the fact is much less satisfying than the pleasure of actually climbing, hiking and camping with her. With retirement here and the grandchildren all in school, we finally had the opportunity.

Tolerance of each other's individual projects and sharing time together are two cornerstones of the commitment we've made to our retirement years. Backpacking wasn't easy for Bette. She wouldn't tell you she heard Nature's sweet melodies as she trekked mile after mile, hour after hour, sometimes for eight to ten hours with only short rest stops. Our Cold River expedition was no cakewalk, and yet getting out on the trail together was a big deal, a goal accomplished.

"What are you thinking about?" she asked as we stood together on Rondeau's hilltop.

I told her how much had changed since my last trip to Rondeau's territory. "The trees have grown so tall they almost obliterate the 'handsome view' Noah used to enjoy from this lookout," I said.

I pointed out that when Richard arrived here in 1965 and again in '67 he saw familiar sights as well as changes, but the changes hadn't been this dramatic. I read her some of Smith's notes about his 1967 trip, just after Noah's death.

> *The first thing I noticed along the Ward Brook fire control road route was the aging Black Jack top telephone poles—black as the proverbial boot black leather polish from being saturated in a creosote bath. A number of poles along the W.B. and along the road to Duck Hole had been chewed or clawed by a large black bear. I followed the path of destruction for a mile, eventually catching up to the doer. I'd say he would go over 600 pounds easy as pie. Surely it had no respect for government property or cared a damn about singing wires; in fact it must have been in a downright mood moved to destroy as many as his anger permitted. I wouldn't swear to it, but I presume it might have been the same bear that had done the Andes stove toss through the Ampersand Park cabin window that Noah had told me about. I'm not exaggerating these facts. I wasn't afraid. I was too petrified to be scared!*

True to his character, Smith's trip recollections focus on the good times.

> *As I walked down the Cold River trail from Mountain Pond I saw how the route had remained in general unchanged. I enjoyed the time alone. My caretaking jobs were caught up, and while my employers and their families were enjoying the late summer, I was doing something I had wanted to do for some time.*
>
> *As I passed familiar landmarks, I comprehended the amount of years that had passed since Tony Okie and I first followed this*

route. I paid a visit to my old cabin site and settled in for the night at the Duck Hole lean-to. The next day I sat on the deacon log of Cold River 1 [lean-to] where Tony and I, thirty years earlier, had eaten some cast-aside food. The water in Cold River was unusually low for that time of year.

On his arrival at Big Dam, Smith said, "I traced the path of Noah's Golden Stairway down the slope from Cold River Hill. I pictured Tony and me as we waved good morning to Noah."

Casting my fly below the remaining logs toward the hole that had so often proved reliable, I found that it was still possible to put a fish or two into my creel. As I reeled in a speckled trout, a doe with twin fawns stood motionless on the opposite bank eyeing me without fear. I wondered if I was the first human she had seen. The three of them watched the entire sequence: the first strike, the retrieve, the netting, and the final placement in the basket. With a nod I complimented Mrs. Deer on her family and how well she looked in her coat of red. She remained unafraid when I spoke.

Today, the only far-off views from Cold River Hill can be seen from the river.
Photograph by William J. O'Hern

Smith had been aware of the clean-up logging operations in Cold River country following the November 1950 Big Blow. It wasn't a surprise to see that the "stately, old growth yellow birches" had been harvested. "Noah and I always enjoyed touching their trunks as we walked among them toward Boiling Pond." Rondeau called his trail to the high pond "The Cathedral Walk." Smith was a supporter of the special exception the New York State legislature and the DEC arranged for timber removal in the Forest Preserve. He didn't, however, care for the jumble of remaining wood left in the wake of the special operations.

> *The salvage operation's "final indignity to the forest" was to put in a road that wiped out the men's favorite route to Boiling Pond. Bulldozers and graders carved out a road two trucks wide. Hardly a tree remained of Cathedral Walk, which wound across the rolling hills toward Ouluska Pass Brook and Boiling Pond beyond.*
>
> *One of these haul roads began at the confluence of the Ouluska Pass Brook and Cold River and eventually joined the old tote road—last used nearly a century ago—that went through South Pass Notch. The new road veered into the woods, followed Seward Pond outlet, and circled Noah's trout pond.*
>
> *The once grand birches were dropped. A log length or two was cut from each tree, leaving the tops like so many butchered bodies. In the years following the clearing operation, runoff from the road filled the pond with silt.*

And if that "irreverence" was not enough...

> *Beaver, too, had come, built their houses and further changed the appearance of this lovely mountain pond where Noah used to reel in trout from his raft, and then scoop them up in his simple landing net made from an onion sack laced on to a crotched stick.*
>
> *Saddened by all the changes that had taken place, I knew that this would be my last trip. A horse trail constructed during the 1960s when Rockefeller was governor ran parallel to the east side*

of the river near to places we hunted called The Finger, Belly-Ache and Laughing Buck Swamp. In the vicinity of Black Hole, a well-known cauldron for trout, were two horse barns and a lean-to. There was even an interior ranger's cabin at Duck Hole at which Governor Rockefeller on more than one occasion vacationed.

Smith had experienced years of steady exposure to the true wilderness, and he had an unshakable reverence for the land of his roots.

Smith said of the territory Bette and I backpacked through, "There is a beauty and a frailty in those mountains. I think if people really sat down and listened, they would be in awe of all that has transpired here, and that would increase their respect and enrich their experiences." Smith's view of the Adirondack Park was as pure and simple as that of the most down-home Adirondack character—a wild place is of more social importance to human beings than any economic good that can come of it.

Smith said of his last trip to Noah's hill, "Unless I knew where Big Dam had been, I could have passed on by. Water action had almost finished what was left of the log and stone dam. It almost looked like any other part of the riverbed. Someone had placed a simple memorial sign on a tree at the top of the hermitage's hill—an old board probably taken from the tipping, decaying Town Hall. In yellow paint they had written 'Rondeau's City.' There was very little left of what I remembered. The Hall of Records cabin had been hauled out by loggers. They donated it to the Adirondack Museum. When I left the hermitage for the last time, I hurried away, never looking back."

Smith had been speaking from his heart. His feelings were closer to a bittersweet nostalgia. For him, Cold River Hill would always represent Noah. When Noah left, nature to gradually begin take command of the place Noah had made his home, the quaint, welcoming spot that had meant a great deal to so many others.

"Nature has a way to reclaim what man has disturbed," I told Bette. Noah himself had also seen natural and manmade changes to the land over the years. Change is change. It's not necessarily bad, and can often be viewed positively.

That said, I still imagine that Noah and Richard both felt a sense of approaching homesickness during their last days at Cold River Hill. A bit of a sentimentalist myself, I feel the same way about change. For them, it was more than being connected to this piece of land, more than the wilderness life they enjoyed there. For a little space of time, it was *their* land. It could not have been easy to push aside their feelings and knowingly give up a place to which they were so deeply connected.

Surviving in the mountains, if you stop to think of it, is now a fairly easy task, with modern equipment and technology. Noah's daily struggles included warding off the deer and rabbits who snacked on his very necessary garden plants, and the raccoons, bears, and various rodents who raided the staples he had carted in for miles from the distant grocery store. Firewood supplies were crucial for survival, as was holding off the growth of brush and small saplings in the clearing so sunlight could fuel the growth of vegetables and flowers.

It's nature's way to relentlessly invade the work of man, and almost everyone who visited Rondeau over the years must have seen his burdens as somewhat pointless. Yet they valued his indomitable spirit and could easily see the pleasures that such a demanding life provided. Few in their right mind would choose to live under the going-without, making-do conditions that seemed so desperate, but Noah did.

Noah's many verses evidence the pleasure he took in studying nature's seasonal and yearly changes. Lines in his prose indicate he witnessed history, drama, romance and song in the physical world. They also indicate his perception, knowledge, wisdom, good humor and sense of beauty. He definitely kept his eyes on the world around him. Smith has said his mind was still "alert, accurate, keen" in his late eighties, when he lived, worked around, read and wrote daily at Singing Pines. "Reading, studying and puttering prevented him from getting old," explained Smith. "What's the old adage? A man who works is never bored, is never old. A person is not old until regrets take the place of hopes and plans. Work and interest in worthwhile things are the best remedy for aging."

Once again, I pulled out my photocopies of some of Noah's October 1943 journal pages so Bette and I could compare our experiences with his, in that October sixty-four years previous to our trip to the river.

October 4: *Perfect Autumn Day. At Beauty Parlor. I write verses. Enough Leaves have freshly fallen from yellow Birch and Soft Maples to cover the ground noticeably...The forest is half stripped of its Leaves.*
October 5: *Cool Atmosphere...Specks of Snow. I play fiddle and I write.*
October 7: *...Handsome View...Perfect Sun Shine continues from weeks back. At Cold River. Morning: I take a short walk in the woods. Afternoon: Mr. and Mrs. Rockefeller and Mr. Blanchard called; -from Ampersand Park.*
October 9: *Somber. At Cold River City. Many trees are completely stripped of their Leaves.*
October 10: *Wind Last Night and Very Nice Today...Deer 30 ft. from Town Hall....*
October 11: *Ice Last Night...1 Aeronaut Over Town Hall.*
October 12: *Half inch Ice Last Night—Nice Sun Today... I Play Violin.*
October 13: *Half inch of ice last night; calm and perfect Sun Shine to day. At Cold River. 451 years a go to day:—Columbus discovered America. (?) When he came he didn't know where he was going; when he got to the West-Indies He did not know where he was; and when he got back home he never found out where he'd been. He was Italian, Catholic and a Sea Pirate; He never saw America. Let the Pagans rave!*
October 14: *...I Get Wood...Wind and sprinkles of rain...I take walks each day among the Hills and Mountains. I call at Frank Walker's shack of long ago (8 miles). The River is the lowest ever. The leaves are all off the Trees (2 weeks a head of usual schedule). I see four deer. I set bear trap.*

What had been Noah's expansive view from Cold River Hill was now hampered by encroaching trees and shrubs. Talking about him and Richard, seeing the changes that had taken place, and reading Noah's writing at the same time gave my mood an alternating tempo.

By late afternoon, Bette and I had spent all the time we needed to mosey around the old hermitage. It was obvious to me that, mostly because of Richard, I too would always feel a close connection to this motherland.

Richard's and Noah's words resonated in my mind as Bette and I reloaded our packs and headed off the hilltop. I had fully explored everything I wanted to, and Bette had at last visited the place Noah John Rondeau had called home for more than three decades. As she took my picture standing where Richard's ashes had been buried, she agreed with me that it certainly had to have been an interesting stopover for sportsmen, hikers and mountain climbers.

As we headed toward the nearby lean-to and the bridge beyond that spans Ouluska Pass Brook, Bette and I picked up our conversation about which package of food we would eat for supper. I was happy to have once again returned to a favorite haunt, but it was time to move on. Closing one door means opening onto new views and adventures, new promises, and supper! All good reasons to move on.

Bette O'Hern by a glacial erratic. It's only by traveling through Cold River Country that one begins to learn the natural beauty in the homeland Noah carved himself a niche in the time-beaten woodland. *Photograph by William J. O'Hern*

Chapter 24

Beyond Cold River Hill

IT WAS DECADES AGO that Noah and his friends carried the last articles out of Cold River City to a truck they had parked at the intersection of the Ward Brook fire control road and the Northville-Lake Placid Trail near Mountain Pond. It was what most would call common goods, but each item was also a precious reminder, a useful tool, a household good or interesting thingamajig Rondeau wanted moved to the Outside. Although a lumber company soon carted his Hall of Records building out of its deep mountain homeland, the hermit of Cold River is still among us.

You'll have to go far beyond the Adirondack Park to find someone who won't perk up at the mention of "the Hermit of Cold River," "Noah John Rondeau," "Cold River City," "Big Dam," "Shattuck Clearing," "Long Lake," the "Duck Hole," or "Plumley's Point." Maybe these terms are not always associated with the reclusive Adirondack character, but they're widely known.

In a few small isolated places, you can still see or surmise some of what he saw. If you're an up-and-coming backpacker-bushwhacker, it's almost a prerequisite to say you have visited the hermitage site atop Cold River Hill. Among Noah's counterparts—Archie "Bobcat" Ranney, Moses Follensby, "French Louie" Seymour, Atwell Martin, and "Moose" Kelsey—who also lent color and romance to the Adirondack backwoods, it is Noah John Rondeau's legendary name that is most recognizable.

As Bette and I followed the same long and winding trail over which the hermit's articles were carried away, bringing us to Cold River Hill and then away, I could not think of anyone I'd rather share my time and regional knowledge with than unfussy Bette—that is, until I led her on her first bushwhack along Ouluska Brook to Boiling Pond. My wife has an adventurous side, and doesn't want to be like Ben Franklin: When he was asked if there were things in his life that he was sorry he had done, he responded, "No, but I am sorry for some of the things I *haven't* done."

Walking an established trail and bushwhacking are decidedly different, and sometimes the latter is the only way to get where you want to go—in this case, Boiling Pond.

Bette wasn't particularly interested in shoving brush and saplings around all day for no other purpose than to look at the pretty scenery I promised and to fill her lungs with fresh mountain air. She is a woman of reason who knows enough to keep my "great little adventure" trips in their proper perspective. While we filtered water at Ouluska Pass, I mentioned that I'd really like to go to Boiling Pond. "You'll love the setting around the pond." I promised. "It isn't a long hike, maybe forty-five minutes. Noah kept a wigwam shelter and log raft up there to fish from. Rich said Noah felt it was one of the most peaceful places in the mountains."

Bette was silent for several minutes, thinking about the effort the push would require. She had a very good idea about the hike I was proposing, because a number of years earlier I had taken my daughter into the pass.[1] I thought it would be fun to climb the slide on Emmons and then bushwhack to its summit, going next to Mount Donaldson and Seward Mountain. Susie's little whirl into the pass and around the summits didn't turn out to be a cakewalk; however, my wilderness passion and urging and her passion to give almost anything a try won her over.

Few people feel the same way I do about bushwhacking. It didn't take Bette O'Hern long to stop pretending to take pleasure in the experience. She describes it like this:

"I can put up with all kinds of inconveniences when I'm hiking and camping—things that aren't the most enjoyable, but they aren't anything that would destroy a normal person. The bushwhack to Rondeau's pond was challenging. It wasn't the most enjoyable thing I've ever been on, but no one forced me to do it. I knew ahead of time it was going to be hard and not like any other experience I've had. True, I wasn't prepared for the wet weather, the insecurity of an unmarked route and the heaviness of the

1. Jay's story "Celebration of Life" is included in *Adirondack Peak Experiences: Mountaineering Adventures, Misadventures, and the Pursuit of "The 46,"* copyright 2009 by Carol White.

backpack's weight pressing against me as I twisted and turned through all the dense growth. It didn't rattle me that much. I just don't care for that sort of thing. But hey, I was together with Jay, going to a place he wanted me to see. What can I say? I did it. It tested me. It was another experience. But I don't see a need to ever do it again."

When we returned to the Ouluska Pass lean-to later that week I promised I had no intention of taking her anywhere else like that. "Your feet will remain on a marked trail—well, mostly," I promised, "except when we wonder off trail to see if anything remains of Doc Latimer's camp." Still, I was anxious to share the many places and people connected with Noah—places we would need to paddle to, locations requiring river fords, off-trail "short hops" that would require us to tote our backpacks.

"Tell you one thing," said Bette, in the patient tone. "I'm rather proud of my bushwack, but I'm not about to put myself in that situation again."

Cold River's history fascinates me. The entire river corridor has a historical significance, but by the time I arrived on the scene to begin my years of investigation it bore few scars from the turn-of-the-century lumber company, from the more recent 1950s special exemption salvage operation, or from Rondeau's long presence. Nature had pulled ahead in the race, and was reclaiming the forest.

I owe a debt of gratitude to Bette, who appreciates my long-standing interest in Adirondack history, specifically, that of particular districts, like the Cold River. She knew I felt I had the potential to write Adirondack histories, and that I felt an obligation to record stories with historical import. For tens of years, Bette single-handedly managed our five growing children while I wandered the mountains in search of remarkable Adirondack characters and the stories I felt must be told.

My supportive wife has been behind all the stories that I have so far told about this wild Adirondack country that holds me so tightly in its grip. When she finally went with me in October of 2007 and beat down the same tracks I used to follow alone, her companionship made *Adirondack Wilds* much more than a personal scrapbook history.

Our intention was to make our trip a sort of "green pasture" 44th wedding anniversary as well as a centennial celebration of all the people who

Noah hoped he would die and be buried on Cold River Hill. *Photograph by Ed Hudowalski. Courtesy of Grace Hudowalski*

had shared their histories of the territory, had established their own contacts with Noah, honored his friendship, created their own traditions, and offered me so many remembrances of past times in Cold River. Their memories and collections are a powerful contribution to the mountains' history. Because of our common interests, I struck up many friendships. Bette too had met most of them at one point or another.

The river valley in front of Ouluska Pass lean-to makes a splendid autumn scene. The glimmer of sunlight that reflects off Cold River is a sight that seems to invite, "stay and enjoy me. I am a comfortable viewpoint." On the other hand, the same location is only a pick spot in the fall. "BEWARE OF THE MOSQUITOES," warns an entry in the shelter's logbook. On other pages in the record, similar words of caution are repeated time and again. It seems that staying at this site during any other season of the year is a dreadful experience.

"We should take advantage of the cover the log refuge offers," Bette said. "This grove of trees, the river, the landscape across the water all make it worth settling down for a day. It's a lovely spot—and it's clean. I'd like to spend an entire day and night here. You can tell me about the other places we're going to go."

Bette had apparently accepted Ouluska's invitation to stay, and her suggestion lent a certain amount of good sense to my plan. While I prepared supper, she scouted the woods methodically for enough fuel to keep a comfortable fire burning well into the night. Within earshot of the owls that hooted that evening and the satin sheets of water speeding over the rocky riverbed, I began jabbering about some of the people I had met and places I wanted to take her.

On the wooden lean-to floor, I laid out the National Geographic No. 742 Adirondack Park "Lake Placid/High Peaks" map and started telling Bette about what I called my "trip back in time" with Jim Plumley. She had met him and his wife, Millie. Reviewing the foot trail from Plumley's Point on Long Lake to Duck Hole seemed like the best place to start. Then I could show her, "Here is where Jim's sportsmen camp used to be. Right here along the trail you'll be able to see a wonderful panoramic view of the Santanoni Mountains," "Here is where Doc Latimer turned to reach his camp," or

"There's a great lean-to at Miller's Falls. We should enjoy the convenience before it's torn apart. All the lean-tos along the river are scheduled to be removed in the future."

"I want to try to capture some moments in time for you," I told Bette as we warmed ourselves by the crackling campfire, "just tell you some stories about the people who've lived here, and the experiences I've had too, so this map will mean more to you than just a bunch of symbols, notes of mileage between lean-tos and blue words." I hoped this method of proposing the itinerary I had in mind would make the region come alive for her, and I hoped I would seem something like a verbal photographer, capturing moments along the winding red line and rousing her interest. I began with Jim Plumley and Long Lake.

PLUMLEY'S POINT, LONG LAKE: "I know you remember Jim Plumley, the former owner and operator of Plumley's Point House," I began. "You'll recall, he had agreed to take me on a sort of 'historical' tour. We planned to revisit the site of his hostelry on Plumley's Point. Today it's a popular camping spot at the far northeastern end of Long Lake. It was once a remote haven for fishermen, hunters and recreationists who wanted to get away but still enjoy some creature comforts. He was very nostalgic about his years at Long Lake.

"The nearby Black Dock and Harper's Clearing sprang to life, having once been only names of locations, black squares on an old topographical map. The State Department of Environmental Conservation has erected a lean-to where the Point House stood. A footpath leading to a second lean-to winds over land where tiny lakeside cottages lined a rocky shoreline. Jim and I zig-zagged the property in back of the principal building. We could see vestiges of the garden plot and remains of the well house. And much to Jim's surprise, the floating steel dock fashioned from an army surplus barge and the rusty frame of a favorite truck stood where he had left them when he sold the property to the State of New York.

My favorite story that day was about Noah Rondeau's last visit in 1949. Jim and his brother pulled a terrible prank on the unsuspecting old man. I'll read you the portion of Jim's interview so you hear it just the way he told it to me.

In the early fall of 1948 or '49 Noah phoned from Long Lake. He said he had an acquaintance and asked if we had any room for them and if so would Carl or I come get them at the village. He was inquiring if there was room for them to stay the evening.

Well, we did. We didn't have any room in our main lodge but we did have some unoccupied cabins. We always looked forward to having the old fellow stop by. This time was unusual, though. He had never come with someone else. Just who the social contact was made us curious.

When Carl reached the Long Lake dock he was surprised to see a woman standing with Noah. Carl said later he couldn't help but conjure up a joke on the old hermit.

When the unexpected party reached the landing, I met Carl at the dock. As Rondeau and the woman were walking off the dock, Carl gave me a wink I took to mean I was to follow his lead.

"Right over there, Noah," Carl pointed as he walked toward the cabin near the shore. Carl swung open the door with a broad hand movement and pointed out the furnishings including the single bed. Right there I knew what he was up to.

Shaking his head, Carl said he regretted the smallest cabin was the only one available for the evening but they would find it comfortable just the same.

By then we were bursting inside but remained very serious as we watched Noah move his head from side to side as he said, "I'm sorry boys, but this arrangement just will not do."

We watched the old fellow for a few minutes. He was all nervous and fidgeting and fussing about. Feeling our little joke had just about been played out, we both broke out laughing and told Noah we were only kidding.

I told them there was another cabin available right next to this one. They could occupy both. We waived the usual $10 per day cabin rental that included three meals.

Almost immediately his uneasiness came to an end. Noah laughed and then the woman smiled and laughed politely.

Relaxing on Jim and Carl Plumley's Point House dock, Long Lake. "Saturday, August 16, 1947. Morning walked to Plumley's with Ranger Russell. I wish to hop off at 9 o'clock. Visit with guests...I join evening party. Munch, sip, laugh, and talk to 2 next A.M." —NJR. *Courtesy of Jim Plumley*

We felt the two of them took the joke in good spirits.

I don't know where the woman came from or why he brought her. We didn't ask and he never volunteered any information.

At that time of year we had some fishing guests and folks who enjoyed hiking in the area. During supper that evening Noah spotted my wife's violin hanging in the dining hall. I asked if he would care to play for the guests.

I knew Noah might relish the attention, and he did. Noah put on quite a show. The old boy put a lot of motion into his fiddle playing. He even played it upside down and still the tunes sounded pretty good.

Later that evening all the guests gathered around the hermit, asking all sorts of questions. He stayed up late entertaining them all.

The next day Carl took them back to the dock in Long Lake. He didn't know where they were going or how. Carl assumed the woman drove.

Rondeau was getting along in years at this time. We both wondered if this might be his last visit at our camp. We didn't think he was going to be able to physically last much longer back at his old stomping grounds.

I told Bette, "Landlord Plumley was patient with all my questions that day. He was never bored. He enjoyed walking around saying things like, 'Here's where the root cellar used to be,' and showing me remnants of anything he thought significant. I think he was flattered to have an interested ear. He also told me how much he enjoyed it when we got together with him and his wife that one Christmas."

Bette said, "That sounds neat. I'd like to go there if it isn't too hard to get to."

I was so happy to get her okay on Plumley's Point that I decided to go ahead and tell her about Shattuck Clearing.

SHATTUCK CLEARING: "I didn't recognize Shattuck the third time I hiked back there."

"Why?" Bette asked.

"It's like the pits compared to how I remembered it. A guideboard attached to a tilted cedar post marks the location as Shattuck Clearing, but it is a far cry from its former self. I remember Big Horn Camp, an old interior ranger station. It stood on a level spot, and was very inviting to the eye. A rail fence separated the outpost from the gravel roadway. Geraniums thrived in window boxes. There was a grand view of the Seward Range in back of the cabin, beyond the Cold River. Today the cabin, the view, the roadway, two bridges that spanned the river, they're all only memories. It won't be long before the rest of the clearing fills in too.

"While I stood there on my last trip, immersed in the small, semi-grassy area—taking in these details of change since the disappearance of the log camp and its last occupant, Ranger Lou Russell—I recalled Dr. C.V. Latimer Jr.'s story of his dad's maiden journey to Shattuck Clearing in the spring of 1919.

Dr. Latimer Sr. had come to fish. Fish he did, but his son told me he also fell in love with the surrounding country. Enlisting the assistance of the local ranger, the men selected a well-hidden site back in the woods along a long-derelict tote road between the Big Eddy and High Banks, upriver some three miles from Big Horn Camp. The doctor procured the ranger's help in the construction of a permanent camp, a green timber affair. Christened Camp Seward, the structure erected on state land was illegal, but some things were overlooked in the backwoods, and the ranger needed the extra income. Upon payment, the ranger quickly lost all memory of his carpentry work, the building, and its whereabouts.

For the next three decades, Doctor Latimer followed the law and applied for a yearly permit to set up a non-permanent structure. He came for a month—two weeks in the spring for trout fishing and two weeks in the fall for deer hunting. Noah John Rondeau became Camp Seward's caretaker. Rondeau was the doctor's unofficial guide, close friend and an honored guest at Seward's dinner table."

"I totally forgot Rondeau was a caretaker there. They must have really looked forward to those two trips every year," said Bette, adding a sizable chunk of hemlock to the fire. "Just imagine the conversations around the dinner table after they'd been out all day fishing or hunting. It will be interesting to see what's left of Camp Seward, won't it?"

"Yes," I heartily agreed, "it certainly will." Inwardly I was shouting "Yes!"

COLD RIVER, UPSTREAM FROM SHATTUCK CLEARING: I pointed out a place on the map that was just upriver from Shattuck Clearing.

"I never pass by this section of the river without thinking of Don Bowman," I said. "His road to prosperity during the Great Depression was really rough-and-tumble, a fitting part of his maverick, prospector-like existence. He wandered into Shattuck Clearing country to trap and gather ginseng.

Those conventions of self-employment both appealed to his sense of survival and placed him where he most wanted to be, in the outdoors.

"Don showed me the vicinity where he'd first met Noah Rondeau in the fall of the 1930s. We crossed the foot suspension bridge that spans the Cold River and followed a neat winding trail to a rise above the water, where the river widens. There is a cluster of small islands in midstream, all surrounded by the shallow boulder-strewn waterway.

"Don said he'd been on the prowl for riches during the darkest economic times Americans had ever seen. 'I was digging wild ginseng,' he recalled. Don was bent over in a weedy, low, dark hollow that was back from the river. His ambition was to harvest enough of the wiry green root, a mysterious substance celebrated for its medicinal powers in the Far East, to make extra cash for the holidays—maybe even find his fortune.

He said that for the longest time he felt as if he was being watched, but that it wasn't a spooky feeling because he had learned to trust his senses. 'I just felt an animal or someone other than the boys from the C's [Civilian Conservation Corps] side camp was poking around me. Maintaining my crouched position, I rolled my eyes upward and to the sides, making full use of my peripheral vision. Finally I saw a movement behind a nearby tree. It was a human. I stood up, looked toward the figure and waved in a friendly-like manner. Then, I moved a few steps toward him. The person stepped completely from the shield of the tree, and out of the forest shadows. I waved again, friendly-like. The man was dressed in ragged overalls and wore Bean rubber-bottom boots. As he approached within easy speaking distance I introduced myself. He seemed cautious, but reciprocated after sizing me up for a few minutes. 'I'm Noah,' he finally answered, 'but not of the Ark.'"

"Did Don ever say if he made any money harvesting ginseng?" Bette asked as she moved from the lean-to's deacon bench toward the fire pit. On this trip she was acting, she said, as the official fire maker-tender. I was the proud dishwasher. We shared in the cooking.

I replied, "No. But you know, he did say he thought he'd found something more valuable than the dollars he hoped to make, and that was the friendship that was struck up by chance in the wilds."

Lou Russell at Big Horn Camp, Shattuck Clearing. *Courtesy of C.V. Latimer, Jr. M.D.*

Her questioning reminded me of a joke Don said Noah John made during another time he dropped in at Cold River City. Don understood Noah had recently experienced the usual succession of hikers and Boy Scouts walking into his retreat. "That prompted him to remark, 'It's beginning to look as though the world is at last beating a path to my door' when I appeared that summer."

I promised Bette that on our return to Cold River next year I would show her some areas where I knew ginseng used to grow.

THE BIG EDDY AND OUR FRIENDS C.V. JR. AND HENRIETTA LATIMER: East of the widening Cold River, continuing upstream on the Northville-Placid Trail, the shoreline and distant scenery turn even more picturesque. The footpath follows a tote road, although time has faded the double track in most places. Pike men once walked this route, rousting beached and lodged logs back into the mainstream and unlocking log jams to return softwood to its wild ride downriver to the confluence with the Raquette River water highway.

In sequence, the real life of this road was the thump of large work horses during the early logging era, the beat of trappers, the roll of buckboards that toted gear and supplied the larders of fishermen's and deer hunters' canvas camps, the grinding pitch of rubber-wheeled mechanized skidders and trucks during the cleanup operations following the 'Big Blow' of 1950, and the rock of Conservation Department jeeps. Today, in the ever-pleasant mountain vistas, only in one's imagination, sharp and delicately tuned, can the past movements of this well-traveled backpackers' pathway be felt and heard. However, you can learn about the days past if you have an observant eye and appreciative ear. Old-timers, lumbermen, woodsmen and sportsmen of the old school, with pleasing remembrances and more pleasing imaginations, can still take one back in time with yarns of the Cold River Country when feet, hooves and wagon wheels traversed the land to distant points beyond.

"You remember when we got together with C.V. and Henrietta Latimer, Bette?"

"Sure I do. They were a nice couple."

"Remember C. V. Jr. telling us how to find his dad's camp?" I asked.

"Yes, but it didn't really stick with me at the time. It was hard to picture."

"Well, once we pass the Big Eddy, a beautiful wide pool of stillwater, there should be a mini-falls that washes over smooth bedrock in a particularly rocky section. At that point we need to look for what he called a large-sized boulder on the west side of the trail. C.V. had told us it would probably be hard to see by this time. Originally a survey marker was embedded in the top of that rock, but it's gone now. C.V. told us that boulder was one of the Latimer brothers' 'stages.' Do you remember?"

"Was it something about dancing?" Bette asked, smiling.

"Yes! After long months away from the Cold River scene, the entire Latimer party felt their spirits soar once their buckboard rolled out of Harper's Clearing and gained ground in its journey toward Camp Seward. The first sight of the Big Eddy thrilled the young men's hearts so much that they would dash to the big rock, climb on top and good-naturedly break into a short jig. It was an annual ritual for many years."

C.V. Jr. had told me that the rock marks the point where you should turn north, away from the river, and enter the forest. His dad's camp was off the State's trail by only a few hundred feet, located in a dense spruce growth.

"If you come on to a low wet area that should still have some signs of corduroy spanning the swampy spots, you will have gone too far," C.V. had

Lt. to Rt. C.V. Jr., Noah, C.V. Sr. at Camp Seward. "I remember the morning this picture was taken shortly after I returned from WWII. Noah walked into camp. He greeted us with, 'Good morning.' He was so keen to be on the move that he told us he ate breakfast standing up and was ready to set off in ten minutes." —C.V. Jr.

Courtesy of C.V. Latimer Jr., M.D.

cautioned me. "There was once a skid road that wound over to Boulder Brook and around the mountain you would be looking at in the distance."

I told Bette how lucky Chris Latimer, C.V. Jr.'s son, said he felt when his uncle Don guided him to the faint outline of Camp Seward's rectangular perimeter when he was twelve years old. It had been nothing more than the spongy, moss-covered base logs. In 1968, Don Latimer, C.V.'s brother, had returned on a family pilgrimage with his sons and nephew. They quizzically and haphazardly dug into the layers of forest duff. To Don's surprise, they uncovered a rusted saw he recognized as once belonging to Oscar Burguiere. In 1918, Oscar cooked for the High Banks Gang, a group of New Jersey hunters Noah Rondeau ran out of the territory. Noah liked Oscar, though, and thought he was an innocent, impressionable twenty-year-old who only dreamed of acquiring enough woodcraft skills to be a good woodsman. In the spring of 1919, Oscar arrived at Noah's with a new canvas wall tent that he set up at the hermitage. Following Doctor Latimer's move into the country and his subsequently meeting Noah, Oscar was introduced to the doctor and was invited to join his "Fat Man's Club." Doc Latimer and Oscar became two of Noah's closest friends.

I pointed again to the map, and explained why it was an important place to Noah.

MILLER'S FALLS, COLD RIVER: "A short distance beyond the Big Eddy, the overgrown roadway ends and a narrow footpath continues atop a high ridge with a number of gentle ups and downs to the Seward lean-to at Miller's Falls. You might have also heard me call it Natural Dam. I spent some time there searching for a spring where Noah and C.V. had sunk an old lidded iron kettle for stashing surplus pounds of butter, eggs and bacon. It was in a small clearing with a lot of exposed spruce roots. Noah set a thirty-gallon metal garbage can from a Civilian Conservation Corps side camp next to it. The container was the drop point for bread, sugar, flour and other supplies that C.V. left for his upriver hermit friend."

HIGH BANKS: Another significant spot for Noah was an esker-like ridge defining the High Banks section of the Northville-Placid Trail. Barbara

The end of the tote trail was shy of Miller's Falls. 1936. Unidentified teamster from Long Lake. *Photography by C.V. Latimer Sr., M.D. Courtesy of C.V. Latimer Jr., M.D.*

McMartin's *Discover the Adirondack High Peaks* trail guide describes the footpath as narrow and rough underfoot but the "most pleasant imaginable." Noah especially enjoyed this part of the trail and took time to appreciate the natural beauty. He had two special spots where he would sit, relax, smoke a bowl of tobacco and take in the combined beauty of the cedar forest, tall hemlocks, the enormous boulders in the river course, and the incredible views of the surrounding mountains—all easily viewed from his high, steep river bank seat.

"I never go by this spot without thinking of Rich and Noah," I told Bette, pointing out the High Banks. "I have a snapshot of Rich holding his favorite Marlin rife and looking serious as he stared across an expanse somewhere in this area."

"You'll have to show me when we get home," said Bette. "The pictures will mean a lot more to me after this trip." It was pitch dark now, and the stars were very bright and seemed close enough to touch.

"How about the lumber camps?" she asked. "How many were there? Where were they in relation to Rondeau's camp and the Latimer's? Close by?"

I explained that upstream, above High Banks, the Santa Clara Lumber Company had erected a string of at least seven or eight lumber camps. The shanties were designated by number, such as Camp 4. They were positioned conveniently for the choppers, teamsters and river drivers. With good scouting, you can still find remains of many of the camps. Two were placed at higher elevations. C.V. Sr. used the old camp by the unnamed stream that flows down Emmons as a lunch spot. Halfway up Ouluska Pass Brook, opposite Ermine Brook, was another. You can still see the remains of the corduroy roadway that worked around Emmons Peak. Rondeau's Big Dam camp was midway along the river. Two others were near Mountain Pond, one near Duck Hole and another along the Ward Brook main haul road. There was another spotted along the Bradley Pond trail.

OULUSKA PASS LEAN-TO, COLD RIVER: On the map, my finger was poised above the Ouluska Brook suspension bridge. Bette looked up at me, her face soft in the light of the campfire, but her voice firm.

"That's once place I'll long remember. I'll never go up that stream again. It's not that I couldn't do it. I just don't like bushwhacking."

"Well, think what it was like when there wasn't any bridge there. I can remember when it was like that. Anyway, I never cross the brook without thinking of Richard. He told me about crossing it one day when he and Noah were coming back from a day of deer hunting at Dismal Swamp."

"It must have been November of about 1940. The drainage had become slightly more swollen than earlier when they made their early morning tramp downstream. They had to recross it on the way back. There were adequate stepping stones, but the tricky part was to keep one's balance, especially if the surface was coated with ice. Richard told me Noah went first. He deftly 'hopped, slipped and waltzed over the ice-coated stones and landed soundly on the opposite bank. Then he turned and waited for his young deer hunting partner. Richard told me he thought it looked a mite tricky, but seeing Noah maneuver it smoothly, he figured it should be no problem. I remember him saying, 'Heck, Old Whiskers was twenty-five years older than me.'

"Richard, however, was not as fortunate in his attempt to cross. 'In spite of my youthful confidence, I was not as good,' he told me. 'My rubber-bottom soles, wet and muddy, were jolly lubricated. As I landed on a rounded crown of a good sized rock midstream, my pack basket swayed a mite too much. I juggled with the balance staff, but I lost my poise, slipped off the rock and got my paws wet. Although we were within a brisk quarter of a mile walk from the Dam Camp, Noah declared a halt at the lean-to.'"

This is never a spot to linger in July and August because the many standing kettle holes in the nearby marshes breed hordes of "mosquitoes that bedevil," but in this case it was the right time to twist the water from Richard's socks and smoke a bowl of tobacco

"Noah and Richard sat with their legs crossed and puffed blue smoke into the crisp early evening air. Then Noah said, 'You know, Quack, there's a difference between the dance steps of the nimble Cold River Shuffle I did and the Ouluska Foot Tangle you capered. Remind me to give you some instruction.'"

Bette laughed at the hermit's amusing comment on Richard's unfortunate situation.

"I can almost see the look on his face. Even though we didn't actually know him, it sometimes feels as though we did. I guess visiting his home site really helped him seem more real to me."

BEAR TRAP MOUNTAIN, DUCK HOLE: Duck Hole is at the other end of Plumley's Point. The pond is also near the former location of Richard Smith's Bear Trap cabin. Reaching the actual site involves bushwhacking. I had made an X on the map to show Bette where it used to be, and I remember her words when I mentioned that on some future trip she might enjoy finding it.

"Don't even bring up a bad idea."

I understood how she felt about bushwhacking.

It is far easier for me to walk on trails she will enjoy. Even so, I wanted her to hear one last story about the route we had been on.

"Just so you know, let me tie up, if possible, an end-to-end hike along our route. Here is Bear Trap Mountain." I pointed to a small peak north of Duck Hole. "I once rummaged around its craggy ledges for three of Rondeau's high-grip Triumph bear traps. I expected to find them rusted and useless, but I thought it would be neat to have located Rondeau's bread and butter meat traps. I had been told where the traps were cached in 1947, but a lot of evergreen needles and leaves have fallen since then, so I was unable to locate them. I also scouted the site of Richard Smith's little log shanty at the base of Bear Trap. Richard maintained a crude, illegal cabin in the woods from 1939 to 1947."

While Bette was interested in the information, she also reminded me, "But I'll never be going to Bear Trap. I'm never going to bushwhack again."

I knew exactly what she was getting at. We had tramped down Ouluska Pass in the pouring rain, and I had not covered the packs the following evening. I thought they would stay relatively dry hung under the spruce tree near our tent. I'm sorry to say I first lost my good woodsman status at 2 a.m. when I woke her up to scramble out of the tent. I had assured her we didn't need the fly. It wasn't going to rain.

"Oh," she had groaned as I quickly tossed the rain fly over the tent and staked it securely as thunder and lightning filled the sky in advance of the torrential rain that followed. "When will you ever learn to listen to me?"

By morning's light I had learned another lesson. Of course I knew better. I should have slipped the plastic bags we carried over the packs, but the damage was done. Our backpacks were soaked. "Oh, my God!" Bette groaned as she wondered if she was going to lug ten or twenty additional pounds back down the pass. Very definitely, I was going to listen to her from now on if I wanted her to do any further backpack camping with me.

Oh, do I love the Cold River country. I'll never follow the N-P Trail back through the mountains and along the river without remembering this or that right here or there. Sometimes I wonder when hikers pass along the marked line if they have any knowledge of times gone by.

I'll never pass over Cold River Hill without stopping to read a plaque a friend left at the hermitage. It reads:

Noah John Rondeau, Adirondack Hermit
The Last of the Last
1883–1967
Here dwelt Noah Rondeau

Richard Smith's Bear Trap Mountain camp near Duck Hole ca.1941. A complete record of the camp is told in *Life With Noah*. Courtesy of Richard J. Smith

A Hermit some say;
Year upon year,
Day after day;
He knew Nature's creatures,
And all of wood lore;
The Hermit he was

He is no more.
"WHAT IT IS, IS WHAT IT IS"
Anonymous
Friend of the Mountains

I didn't really know if Bette would enjoy our entire adventure in the same way I would, but out of our trip did come her new appreciation for the countless hours she has spent traveling with me to interview someone who knew Noah.

★ ★ ★

"My pioneer life could not last forever," Richard Smith recognized. "Neither would Noah's. Noah and I were treading on the very fringe of an era."

Noah tunes up the strings for Mary Dittmar. "Good evening, ladies and gentlemen," he began. "My name is Noah John Rondeau. I have the honor of being your fiddler for the evening, and I believe that tonight's music promises to be some of the most exciting in Cold River City's long history." *Courtesy of Dr. Adolph G. Dittmar, Jr.*

Cold River country was *their* land and that of the countless others who found enjoyment and happiness along this river passageway. It is a land with a personal and social history. I did my best to introduce Bette to the deep meaning it had for Noah and Richard, and to what it means to me.

★ ★ ★

ON THE TRAIL WITH BETTE: There is no hike more challenging or chancier than a backpacking trip with a bad back in the heart of the Adirondacks High Peak country—even if it is going to be a valley trek. If I make it back to the trailhead parking lot without an incident, I know I have my hiking poles to thank to some degree. To be sure, I've anticipated some degree of sciatic pain. But then I think of a portion of the conversation sixty-plus year old Noah shared when talking about his year-to-year life in the wilds of Cold River:

"Oh, it [the time] varied when I went Outside [to buy groceries]. Once or twice [a year], ...usually, I come out in April and October and buy my supplies and get them in there. It might take me two weeks to carry them in on my back." The last four miles seemed the hardest.

Once he got the supplies back to camp he "...had garbage cans to put stuff into. Mice couldn't get into them, you know, and so forth. I had that planned right to a kind of hermit's science."

I figured Rondeau had it tough. He grew up learning how to recognize edible plants. "I almost knew that from childhood," he said. His family would go out and gather greens "...wild spinach and stuff like that" in the surrounding woods.

Then there were some wild foods he didn't take a chance on. "Mushrooms, for instance. There's a class that's poisonous and they go by this and that [name] but it ain't quite a hundred percent sure [safe to eat], so I made sure! I probably missed a good mushroom but I didn't eat the poisonous ones!"

I was thankful for the opportunity to hike with my wife and have the opportunity to share our interests, laughter, and time with each other. As we walked side by side, I lifted her spirits whenever she thought she might have heard, smelled, or spied a black bear.

Like so many other wilderness visitors, Bette and I know life can be a spiritual as well as a physical journey.

★ ★ ★

Although Bette and I had seen the Rondeau exhibit at the Adirondack Museum a number of times, we decided to stop in once again after our

Lt. to Rt.: Bill Barzler, Fred Studer. Phil Rumbolt, Bill White. By 1946, Noah had gained a new audience and a legendary status in hermiting with the arrival of backpackers and mountain climbers.

He said of the new comers: "Well, they came along as mountain climbers and hikers and so forth, ah, they usually had good packs and they, the people in the neck of the woods sometimes, come in and steal my gun too, they've done that, but the mountain climbers, they'd buy a good pack and they had a job somewhere and they were refined and they had education and they were interested in the mountains. Some came a purpose for that. They were on their way to climb the next mountain; see they had already come ten miles over rough trails and had another four, five, six miles to go. And then get way back, that's why they appreciated stopping at my place." *From the 1959 WGY Schenectady Radio station interview with reporter Enoch Squires. Courtesy Fred R. Studer*

Noah pointing out the variety of plants he cultivated in his flower beds.
Courtesy of Bill Frenette

backpacking trip. The exhibit itself hadn't changed in years, but Bette's appreciation of it had. Now she knew what the difficult trek into Cold River was like, and when her imagination added a few feet of snow and the cumbersome clothing and equipment of Noah's days, she was simply amazed. Something else that hit home with her was that Moose Kelsey, another Adirondack hermit, was mentioned in the Adirondack hermit display. Kelsey was Bette's maiden name.

People say a picture is worth a thousand words. Bette had seen plenty of pictures depicting Noah's life. They might well be worth a thousand words, but the actual experience of hiking to the hermit's site had been priceless. As we breathed deeply the clear air of Noah's mountains, huddled close to the campfire on chilly star-sprinkled nights, pushed further and further into the deep woods and felt the outside world fall away, we knew that each day intensified our understanding of the hermit's remote life. Visiting the hermit exhibit at the museum further deepened our comprehension of the life and times of Noah John Rondeau.

ADIRONDACK WILDS
Exploring the Haunts of Noah John Rondeau

Section VI

Cold River Home

Jay and Bette O'Hern on a late-fall hike.
Courtesy of emanphoto.com

Chapter 25

Homeplace

KNOWINGLY OR INSTINCTIVELY, I think, most people face the question, "Where do I feel most comfortable? Where is *home*?" On the practical side, home is where you might have to make it because of health, employment or a compromise with a partner. But my question takes the search for one's homeplace into a philosophical realm as well as an actual, physical setting into which one *feels* one fits.

It seems to me people are oftentimes disconnected with where they live. That sensitivity is more or less from nostalgia, which *Webster's New Collegiate Dictionary* defines as, "the state of being homesick" and "a wistful or excessively sentimental, sometimes abnormal yearning to return to some past period or irrecoverable condition." The nostalgic are truly displaced people, obligated by circumstances to put down roots in surroundings in which they are uncomfortable. They want their homeplace but are prevented from being there, or perhaps they have never explored the question and don't even know where their true home is.

Noah John Rondeau was not one of those people. For reasons of circumstance, he understood (and accepted) his state of affairs as a result of the Big Blow of November 1950. And, while he did try to create a resemblance of his home with his Cold River exhibit and later with the comfortable place he created at Singing Pines, Cold River Hill always remained in his heart and in his mind.

Cold River Hill was the highlight of Bette's and my adventure—and it was a true adventure, an exciting experience in the High Peaks of Northern New York. The Cold River country is a magnificent territory—wild, isolated, beautiful, filled with memories. Far back from any trailhead, it is

July 4, 1949. Rondeau's log entry recorded following Charles Thomas' party's departure. "Monday. Sunshine- clouds- 10 P.M. showers. Peace-Beauty-Tranquility at Cold River City. Hurrah—Fourth of July! Let fools celebrate theory of Independence and tolerate bondage; and let other fools dress in colorful—tights and run a footrace—for paper medal and American Blab; Let other fools go on a Hill overlooking the town; and shoot a fool Cannon as if bloody war was on. And for luck start a good cigar. But give me the day alone in the wilds, by a River among Mountains, even with Deer Flies. And the giddy may have Reminder of War—and 'good cigar' and to hell with drunken shout—*Fourth of July*." Courtesy of Charles E. Thomas rugged enough to make reaching it a challenge, to demand a degree of confidence and physical ability—and we loved it. It was all new to Bette, and she found it agreeable. I immediately sensed what I believed to be that *home feeling* that Noah, Richard, Oscar, Jay Gregory, and doctors C.V. Latimer Sr. and Jr. felt each time they arrived at Cold River City. This was the forest of Noah's outdoor years. The Adirondack Mountains was an extension of that larger forest cover that he had once roamed as a child living "in the old Dewyer House on Jackson Hill, four miles easterly from the Fork of the Ausable River and among the Sylvan Hills of Clinton County," described in his first chapter of his writing, "Recollections of Sixty Years."

Entering the Cold River region was like returning to something I had known well a long time ago. It was much different than the woods of the early trapping days of Rondeau, the Petty boys, E.J. Dailey and Dick Wood, but so has everything else changed in the Adirondack Park. Still, hiking though the woodland was like reliving the long-ago days of the men and women who had spent some time in the woods with Noah John. Much like them, we spent hours on the trail, hitching up the shoulder straps of our heavy backpacks. We shared evenings at a lean-to or in our compact tent. We hiked miles to introduce Bette to old haunts that are now only a pleasant memory. But looking ahead, past the long winter and into the warmer days of next year—as if realizing Noah's dream that someday he would return home one last time, I know Bette and I will go back to burn our evening candle in the Cold River wilds.

While he wasn't wealthy, Noah had what many never find: He knew beyond a doubt that when he was at Cold River Hill, he was *home.*

Epilogue

"WHY WOULD YOU want to visit the site of a long-ago hermit?" That's what I was asked on the eve of Bette's and my first Cold River backpacking trip. I don't remember my exact reply, other than that I wanted to revisit the place where Richard's ashes had been buried and that I wished for Bette to see the location she had heard so much about. It was just important for me to go back to the river again.

★ ★ ★

October, 1993. Deer hunting season. Almost two months after Smith's death, two people stood at Cold River Hill. The bearer of Richard Smith's ashes walked through the sparsely-leaved trees and down a gravel pathway to the water's edge. Trees and shrubs covered the steep banks near the river, and the man stood on a sand ledge a foot above the river and gathered a handful of pebbles and scooped a cup of water. The second person passed the time on the hilltop. He snapped sprigs of balsam and spruce, gathered bits of crockery that were scattered around the hermitage site, and picked up a small piece of rusted ironware found near a hollow that had been the earth floor of the Town Hall.

The men looked for a particular setting along the southeast rim that was a favorite scenic lookout of Noah's and the site of his rock-sculpted intended "Ash Ground." Smith long remembered Rondeau had said it was a good place to look out on Panther Peak. At that location, Richard Smith's ashes were mixed with the collection gathered at the scene, then placed where he had requested. The men read a few verses from "Crane Mountain," Smith's

May 2012. Bette and Jay O'Hern at the intersection where the Ward Brook Trail connects with the Northville-Placid Trail. *Photograph by an unknown backpacker who hapened by*

favorite poem by Jeanne Robert Foster, related some vivid memories of Smith, and turned for a final look around the old hermitage site before swinging their day packs back on to return over the Northville-Placid Trail to Mountain Pond, where the Ward Brook truck trail intersects the N-P Trail.

I like knowing Richard's remains are right where he wanted them to be. He appreciated knowing that he would always be out there on Noah's hill site.

Richard Smith and Noah John Rondeau have been gone for years. There's no headstone for Smith, and the only marking Rondeau is ever going to have at the river is that stainless steel plaque bolted to a tree. For some years now, the hill has stood empty and pretty much bare of anything that resembled Cold River City. I was pleasantly surprised to see a few old iron pieces near the sunken hole that designated the area as the site of the Town Hall. In some ways Cold River country has not changed, but in others it has.

Smith's ashes long ago disappeared into the earth, and the memorial plaque at the former hermit's home will remain only at the pleasure and the honesty of the hiking crowd. But the hermit display in Blue Mountain museum permanently honors Noah. His memory also lives in dozens of diaries stored in the museum's archives.

As a novice backpacker, Bette feels more confident now. She has more skills and security—physical and mental. And the more security she has and the more independent she is, the less she hesitates to plan our next outing. It took a lot of work to get that confidence and security. It's going to take another Cold River trip to shake out the last of the bugs.

That's all right with me.

In fact, I can hardly wait.

Adirondack Wilds

Postscript

IN THE YEARS since "We Hit the Trail" Bette and I have adopted two lean-tos along abandoned Calkins Brook Truck Trail. The shelters, aesthetically positioned in view of the western slope of the Seward Range, were built in the early 1960s during New York State's drive to establish horse trails and shelters throughout the Cold River country.

Yearly backpacking trips have taken us to new pinnacles throughout Cold River. Our camera has never quite been able to capture the magnificent scenic views or reflect the full palette of fall colors as they look in person.

The water level in Noah's high mountain pond continues to regress, and Ouluska Pass seems to get more peak baggers using that approach to the near-by summits. An interesting man who has spent years ferreting out the location of every lumber camp site, bridge, tote road, corduroy way, and Barringer brakes left on slopes by the Santa Clara Lumber Company has piloted archeological studies and begun a manuscript underlining his findings. Frisky otters still belly-slide down slippery Cold River slopes. A variety of birds, fox, fisher, rabbits, marten, weasels, black bear, and deer still call Cold River home.

In October 2010, Bob Bates, Tim Roe, Bette and I combed the remains of Camp Seward. We had hoped to locate the large iron kettle and lid that Doc Latimer had submerged in a spring below camp. In it the campers would leave butter, eggs and other perishables for Noah's use. We also plan to return as soon as we can with a metal detector. We'll also explore the old routes the Latimer party followed uphill from Camp Seward. Each year a camp work crew cleared a long winding route called Seward Trail. It passed an old beaver pond on its way to a favorite deer watch at Broken Bridge creek.

Future plans include attempting to locate and trace those old routes and find Maude's Rock, a favorite boulder Maude Gregory enjoyed sitting on.

Rondeau had no way of knowing how far-reaching his real-life legend would be. Knowing so many people who have shared their memories of the hermit started me on a path that has chronicled one of the Adirondacks' most interesting characters.

I'm convinced all the good hermit stories have not already been told. Last year I met retired ranger Gib Manley. The spry 94-year-old relived the construction of the Calkins Brook lean-tos he originally built. Gib showed an equal interest in the efforts of Lean2Rescue. I related the October 2011 work of the volunteer group who renovated the timeworn log buildings. Gib ended his phone conversation with, "The next time we talk I'll have to tell you about my time at Shattuck Clearing in the '40s. Every time a group of us rangers got together with Lou Russell back there, somehow Rondeau caught wind of the gathering and showed up. He knew we'd always put a good feed on the table for him."

My next project will be *The Hermit and Us: Noah John Rondeau—Hermit-Mayor of Wigwam City, Population 1.* Through people who knew Noah you will come to know a man who shaped Adirondack folklore.

May 17, 2013. Mid-60s. Spring day of sunshine. Bold blue sky. Charming day. Wildflowers are in bloom. Birds swoop over the clearing. So charming we could sit all day enjoying nature's charms.

For fun—checked Noah's journals for the same day. The entries report he was often "transplanting pansies," enjoying the blooms of painted trilliums and performing housework. "I swept hermit Floors (gravel)." He sited "Myrtle Warblers and Gold Finches arrive" and "Last Snow Vanishes around Camp." Photograph by author

Bibliography

Books

Anderson, Jack. *Goodbye Mountain Man*, New Castle, PA.: Commercial Printing Company, Fourth Printing Under the Direction of Nick Wyshinski, 1989.

Angus, Christopher. *The Extraordinary Adirondack Journey of Clarence Petty.* Syracuse, New York: Syracuse University Press, 2002.

Arakelian, Mary. *Doc, Orra A. Phelps, M.D., Adirondack Naturalist and Mountaineer.* Utica, N.Y.: North Country Books, Inc., 2000.

DeSormo, Maitland. *Noah John Rondeau Adirondack Hermit.* Boonville, New York: The Willard Press, 1969.

Hudowalski, Grace L. *The Adirondack High Peaks and the Forty-Sixers.* Adirondack, New York: The Adirondack Forty-Sixers, 1970.

Mc Martin, Barbara. Discover the Adirondack High Peaks. North Country Books, Inc. Third edition, 2004.

O'Hern, William J. *Life With Noah: Stories and Adventures of Richard Smith with Noah John Rondeau*, Utica, New York: North Country Books, Inc., 1997.

-----. *Adirondack Wilderness Days of Noah John Rondeau*, Cleveland, New York: Forager Press, 2009.

Plum, Dorothy. *Adirondack Bibliography*, Gabriels, N.Y.: Adirondack Mountain Club, Inc., 1958.

Tefft, Tim (editor). *Of the Summits, of the Forests.* Morrisonville, New York: Adirondack Forty-Sixers, 1991.

Magazines

Creighton, Mary Malcolm. "God's Peace in the Mountains." *Guideposts*, No. 68, 1947.

Hudowalski, Grace L. "The Hermit of Cold River." *High Spots*: 1939.

Byrne, Peggy. "Noah John Rondeau." New York State *Conservationist*: October-November, 1972.

Dailey, E.J. "Fur-Bearers of the Adirondacks." *The Conservationist*: Volume IV; Number 12, December 1921.

-----. "*Life in Trappers Country.*" Harding's Magazine: Volume 48; Number 4, October 1928.

Miller, P. Schuyler. "Blowdown Aftermath." *Adirondac* magazine: July-August 1951.

Seager, Clayt. "The Hermit of Cold River Flow." New York State *Conservationist* magazine. 1947.

Smith, Richard J. "Roaming and Trapping." *Adirondack Life* magazine, April 1995.

Wolff, Phil. "Knowing Noah John." *Adirondack Life* magazine, May/June 2010.

Wood, Dick. "Cabin Life." *Fur News and Outdoor World*, January 1921.

-----. "The Cold River Trail. *Fur News and Outdoor World*, February 1921.

-----. "The Otter's Trail." *Fur News and Outdoor World*, March 1921.

-----. "Afoot in Deer Country." *Fur News and Outdoor World*, November 1921.

Journals, Manuscripts, and Scrapbooks

Gregory, Jay L. Log Book Cold River Trips. October 1934 to June 1939, owned by his granddaughter, Nancy Bliss Johnson.

Gregory, Jay L. Letters between Gregory and Noah J. Rondeau (1940 – 1948), formally owned by Nancy Bliss Johnson. Original letters now property of the Adirondack Museum, Blue Mountain Lake, NY.

Latimer, C.V. Sr. and Jr. Camp Seward Log Books 1931–1948, owned by Christopher Latimer.

Rondeau, Noah John. "Recollections of 60 Years" (unedited and unpublished version), owned by the Adirondack Museum, Blue Mountain Lake, NY.

Poems

Rondeau, Noah John. "Aerobatic Autumn Leaves," formally owned by Richard J. Smith now property of the Adirondack Museum, Blue Mountain Lake, NY.

-----. "Springtime Scramble," formally owned by Richard J. Smith now property of the Adirondack Museum, Blue Mountain Lake, NY. A duplicate copy is held at the North Elba-Lake Placid Historical Society.

-----. "To a Fox," formally owned by Richard J. Smith now property of the Adirondack Museum, Blue Mountain Lake, NY.

-----. "Information to September," formally owned by Richard J. Smith now property of the Adirondack Museum, Blue Mountain Lake, NY.

-----. Scrapbooks and personal photo albums, formally owned by Richard J. Smith now property of the Adirondack Museum, Blue Mountain Lake, NY.

Newspapers

Dittmar, Aldolph. "Cold River Hermit Honored by 46ers." *Troy-Record* newspaper, January 7, 1938.

Mooney, Charles L. "Round the Clock with Noah John Rondeau, Hermit of the Adirondack Wilds." Albany, N.Y.: *The Knickerbocker News*, September 11, 1946.

-----. "Noah Rondeau Bulletin." *Essex County Republican*, February 14, 1947.

Rondeau, Noah John. "Air Lift to Fame." February 12, 1947

-----. "Rondeau Arrives in New York for Show." February 15, 1947.

Sillman, Don. "Sportsmen's Show Forced to Jump Gun." New York *Herald Tribune*, February 16, 1947.

-----. "Rondeau Tells of His Experiences at Albany Exposition." *Adirondack Record-Elizabethtown-Post*, March 6, 1947.

-----. "Noah Rondeau Plans Attendance Buffalo Sportsmen's Show." *Essex County Republican*, March 14, 1947.

-----. "The Adirondack Hermit Travels Via Airplane." *Essex County Republican*, April 4, 1947.

-----. *North Creek News* February 17, 1950

-----. "No Other Hermit." *The Knickerbocker News*, October 6, 1950.

Marathon Independent February 1, 1951

-----. "Famed Hermit of Cold River Flow." *Adirondack Record-Elizabethtown-Post.* August 31,1967.

Correspondence

Anderson, Donald "Jack" to William J. O'Hern

Bates, Bob to William J. O'Hern

Carr, Harvey to William J. O'Hern

Burguiere, Oscar to Noah J, Rondeau

Burguiere, Oscar to Richard J. Smith

Burguiere, Oscar to Don Latimer

Cushman, Jean Burger to William J. O'Hern

De Sormo, Maitland C. to William J. O'Hern

Dittmar, Aldoph Dittmar to William J. O'Hern

Dittmer, Mary Colyer to William J. O'Hern

Donlon, H. P. Donlon to William J. O'Hern

Freeman, Roger D. to William J. O'Hern

Hasenjager, John to William J. O'Hern

Hickey, John to William J. O'Hern

Latimer, Chris E. to William J. O'Hern

Latimer, Donald to William J. O'Hern

Manley, Gilbert E. to William J. O'Hern

Menz, Helen Colyer to William J. O'Hern

Miller, Edward to William J. O'Hern

Miller, Erwin H. to William J. O'Hern

Reeves, Fredric C. to William J. O'Hern

Reid, Edwin A. to William J. O'Hern

Richardson, Shelby P. to William J. O'Hern

Russ, Charlie to William J. O'Hern

Russell, Earle Russell to William J. O'Hern

St. George, Dorian to William J. O'Hern

Studer, Fred R. to William J. O'Hern

WGY Schenectady Radio to William J. O'Hern

Webb, Eleanor and Monty to William J. O'Hern

Whiteman, Clarence and Stacia to William J. O'Hern

Wolff, Phillip G. to William J. O'Hern

Wollner, Paul Wollner to William J. O'Hern

Wiezel, R.G. Letter to NJR

Interviews

De Sormo, Maitland C. Interview by William J. O'Hern.

Dittmar, Aldoph Dittmar. Interview by William J. O'Hern

Dittmer, Mary Colyer. Interview by William J. O'Hern

C.V. Latimer, M.D. Interview by William J. O'Hern

Plumley, Jim. Interview by William J. O'Hern

Whiteman, Clarence. Interview by William J. O'Hern

Taped Interviews

Dittmar, Aldoph Dittmar. Interview by William J. O'Hern

Dittmer, Mary Colyer. Interview by William J. O'Hern

Dodge, Madeline. Interview by William J. O'Hern

Wolff, Philip G. Interview by Holly C. Wolff for William J. O'Hern

Acknowledgments

MY DEEPEST THANKS to everyone who assisted with this project. Many hours of conversation, writing and e-mailings, telephone conversations, searching family paper records and photographs came together as I researched the historical background portion of *Adirondack Wilds* with Bette's and my backpack to Cold River Hill to make this book a special memoir.

This book would not have been written without the interest, support, and full cooperation of many willing contributors. In this respect, I feel especially fortunate for the generous response of the large number of persons listed below who have provided unmediated access to private papers and permission to use detailed information about their lives and early days in and about the Seward Range of the Adirondack High Peaks, and in many instances, have likewise loaned their cherished pictures, most of which were very old and consequently greatly prized by their owners.

Grateful acknowledgment is made to Richard Smith for permission to print material from Noah John Rondeau's 1943, 1944, 1949, and 1950 journals, now property of the Adirondack Museum, Blue Mountain Lake, NY; and for permission to print material from Noah John Rondeau's scrapbooks and photo albums, now property of the Adirondack Museum, Blue Mountain Lake, NY; for permission to print material from Noah John Rondeau's poems: "Autumn," "Acrobatic Autumn Leaves," and "To a Fox," now property of the Adirondack Museum, Blue Mountain Lake, NY.

Grateful acknowledgment is made to the Adirondack Museum for permission to print material from Noah John Rondeau's papers (MS 75-3 and MS 09-32.8).

Grateful acknowledgment is made to the North Elba-Lake Placid Historical Society for permission to print material from Noah John Rondeau's 1960, 1961, 1962, and 1963 diaries.

For permission to reprint, *Noah John Rondeau, Hermit of Cold River*, by Adolph G. Ditmar, from the book, *The Adirondack High Peaks and The Forty-Sixers* (The Adirondack Forty-Sixers, 1970), grateful acknowledgement is made to The Adirondack Forty-Sixers.

I am indebted to my friend and editor, Mary L. Thomas for her invaluable support and constructive advice in making this book happen. She has been my invaluable second right hand from the onset of the manuscript's development.

Neal Burdick edited the final draft. His knowledge, insight and instincts were instrumental in reshaping the manuscript following several rewrites. His constructive comments and observations tightened and focused the story, suggesting that much jettisoned material might be perfect for a final Rondeau project.

The following businesses and people helped me in ways both great and small. To those who consented to be interviewed for this book, thanks for sharing your memories: *Adirondack Life* magazine; Adirondack Museum at Blue Mountain Lake; Donald "Jack" Anderson; Bob Bates; Harvey Carr; Oscar Burguiere; Maitland C. De Sormo; Adolph Dittmar; Mary Colyer Dittmer; Madeline Dodge; H. P. Donlon; Roger D. Freeman, M.D.; John Hasenjager; John Hickey; Jenny Rondeau Kelton; Chris E. Latimer; C.V. Latimer, Jr. M.D.; Donald Latimer; Helen Colyer Menz; Edward Miller; Erwin H. Miller; Jerry Pepper; Jeff Pescia; Fredric C. Reeves; Edwin A. Reid; Shelby P. Richardson; Chester Rock; Steve Rock, Burton Rondeau, Jenny Rondeau, Charlie Russ; Earle Russell; Dorian St. George; Judy Sorrell; Fred R. Studer; WGY Schenectady Radio; Eleanor and Monty Webb; Clarence and Stacia Whiteman; Cynthia and Holly C. Wolff, and Paul Wollner.

Finally, and most importantly, I thank my beloved wife, Bette M. (Kelsey) O'Hern, who put up with more days of trail life inconveniences than she might care to catalog, but whose interest in the Seward Range remains strong. Following our backpack trip we joined DEC and ADK's Adopt a Lean-to Program, becoming adopters of Calkins Brook #1 and #2 shelters a few miles from Cold River with a beautiful view of the Seward Range. Our annual spring and fall volunteer treks to the log shelters will keep us linked with the Cold River wild lands for years to come.

I have made every effort to acknowledge the assistance of everyone who helped; any omission is an unintentional oversight. —*William J. O'Hern*

Index

CURRENT TITLES

by William J. O'Hern

Spring Trout and Strawberry Pancakes:
Quirky Cures,Borrowed Tales, Camp Recipes
and the Adirondack Characters
Who Cooked Them Up, 2014

Adirondack Memories and Campfire Stories
Edited and with Biographical
and Historical Commentary
by William. J. O'Hern
In the Adirondacks, 2014

Adirondack Wilds: Exploring the
Haunts of Noah John Rondeau, 2014

The Hermit and Us: Our Adirondack
Adventures with Noah John Rondeau
In the Adirondacks, 2014

Adirondack Kaleidoscope
and North Country Characters
Edited and with Biographical
and Historical Commentary
by William. J. O'Hern
In the Adirondacks, 2013

Thomas C. O'Donnell's
Life in a North Woods Lumber Camp
Edited and with Biographical
and Historical Commentary
by William J. O'Hern
The Forager Press, LLC, 2012

Adirondack Adventures:
Bob Gillespie and Harvey Dunham
on French Louie's Trail
By Roy E. Reehil and William J. O'Hern
The Forager Press, LLC, 2012

Noah John Rondeau's Adirondack
Wilderness Days: A Year with the hermit
of Cold River Flow
The Forager Press, LLC, 2009

Under An Adirondack Influence:
The Life of A. L. Byron-Curtiss, 1871–1959
By Roy E. Reehil and William J. O'Hern
The Forager Press, LLC, 2008

Adirondack Stories of the Black River Country
North Country Books, Inc. 2003

Adirondack Characters
and Campfire Yarns:
Early Settlers and Their Traditions
The Forager Press, LLC, 2005
Adirondack Stories of the
Black River Country
North Country Books, Inc. 2003

Anyplace Wild in the Adirondacks
Self-published, 2000

Life with Noah: Stories and
Adventures of Richard Smith
with Noah J. Rondeau
North Country Books, Inc.
Second Paperback Printing 2013

UPCOMING RELEASES

by William J. O'Hern

At Our Adirondack Table:
Recipes and Stories from Mountain Camps

From Mountains to Foothills and
Campfire Tales: Gathered Memories
from New York's Adirondack-
North Country and Tug Hill Region

Adirondack Pastimes:
Camping and Sporting Adventures in the Cold
River Country with
Hermit Noah John Rondeau (1913–1950)

Remembering Adirondack Legend
Noah John Rondeau: Following a Hermit's
Footsteps Through His Final Years (1913–1967)

Gathered Memories and Fireside Stories
A Celebration of Past Adirondack-
North Country and Upstate New York Life
Compiled, edited and with Biographical
and Historical Commentary
by William J. O'Hern

Logging in the Adirondacks:
The Revolutionary Linn Tractor
and Lumber Camp Stories

The Informal History
of the Moose River Plains

available online at www.adkwilds.com